Interpersonal and Group Skills for Law Enforcement

Second Edition

Terri M. Geerinck
Sir Sandford Fleming College

C. Tracey McGruthers
Georgian College

PEARSON
Prentice
Hall

Toronto

To my husband Glenn Dusome, for his love and belief in me. And to my daughters Sarah and Gracie, who bring me great joy. — C. Tracey McGruthers

To Rod, my continued inspiration. And to Adelaide and Skyler, who make all things possible. — Terri M. Geerinck

Library and Archives Canada Cataloguing in Publication

Geerinck, Terri, 1958–

   Interpersonal and group skills for law enforcement / Terri M. Geerinck, C. Tracey McGruthers. — 2nd ed.

ISBN 0-13-174468-2

   1. Police training. 2. Interpersonal communication. 3. Interpersonal relations. 4. Group relations training. I. McGruthers, C. Tracey II. Title.

HV7936.P75G43 2007   363.2'3   C2006-902266-6

ISBN 0-13-174468-2

Editor-in-Chief, Vice-President of Sales: Kelly Shaw
Executive Acquisitions Editor: Ky Pruesse
Executive Marketing Manager: Judith Allen
Associate Editor: Rachel Stuckey
Production Editor: Richard di Santo
Copy Editor: Julie Fletcher
Proofreader: Martin Townsend
Production Coordinator: Sharlene Ross
Composition: Laserwords
Art Director: Julia Hall
Cover Images: Various images © Lindsey Maier Inc., www.lindseymaier.com; Brad Filman; and Photodisc

10 11 12 DPC 12 11 10

Printed and bound in Canada.

Contents

Preface vii

Part 1   **Interpersonal Communication** 1

Chapter 1   **Introduction to Interpersonal Communication** 2
  Learning Outcomes 2
  Introduction 2
  Why Study Interpersonal Communication and Group Dynamics? 3
  How This Book Can Help You 4
  The Communication Process 5
  Interpersonal Communication 7
  Strategies to Improve Your Interpersonal Communication Skills
     and Gain Communication Competence 10
  Summary 12
  Websites 13
  Journal and Discussion Questions 15
  Skills Practice 1-1 16
  Skills Practice 1-2 17

Chapter 2   **Self-Knowledge and Communication** 19
  Learning Outcomes 19
  Introduction 19
  The Changing Face of Police Work 20
  Communication and the Self 22
  Needs and Communication 26
  Improving Your Self-Concept and Increasing Self-Esteem 29
  Summary 31
  Websites 31
  Journal and Discussion Questions 32
  Skills Practice 2-1 33
  Skills Practice 2-2 34
  Skills Practice 2-3 36

Chapter 3   **Interpersonal Communication and Perception** 37
  Learning Outcomes 37
  Introduction 37
  The Perceptual Process 39
  Strategies To Improve Perception 49
  Summary 51
  Websites 51
  Journal and Discussion Questions 52
  Skills Practice 3-1 53
  Skills Practice 3-2 54
  Skills Practice 3-3 55

Chapter 4   **Nonverbal Communication** 57
  Learning Outcomes 57
  Introduction 57
  Six Functions of Nonverbal Communication 58
  Gender Differences in Nonverbal Communication 60
  Types of Nonverbal Communication 61
  Skills for Interpreting Nonverbal Communication 68
  Listening 70
  Summary 73
  Websites 74

Journal and Discussion Questions 75
Skills Practice 4-1 76
Skills Practice 4-2 78

Chapter 5   Verbal Communication 79
Learning Outcomes 79
Introduction 79
Words and Their Meanings: Characteristics of Words 80
Barriers To Effective Verbal Communication 83
Communication Climates: Defensive versus Supportive 86
Improving Communication: Listening and Responding 88
Summary 94
Websites 94
Journal and Discussion Questions 96
Skills Practice 5-1 98
Skills Practice 5-2 99

Chapter 6   Conflict Management and Problem-Solving Skills 101
Learning Outcomes 101
Intoduction 101
Defining Conflict: Is Conflict Good or Bad? 103
Causes of Conflict 104
Conflict Management Styles 106
Conflict Management Strategies 108
Problems versus Decisions 116
Overcoming Barriers to Effective Group Decision Making and Problem Solving 120
Crisis Management 122
Summary 125
Websites 126
Journal and Discussion Questions 128
Skills Practice 6-1 130

Chapter 7   Understanding and Managing Diversity 131
Learning Outcomes 131
Introduction 131
Understanding Culture 132
Dimensions of Cultural Differences 134
The Groups and Cultures of Canada 135
Barriers to Effective Intercultural Communication 139
Improving Intercultural Communication and Fostering Understanding 142
Diversity in Policing 145
Summary 146
Websites 147
Journal and Discussion Questions 148
Skills Practice 7-1 149

Part 2   The Dynamics of Groups and Teams 151
Chapter 8   Work Groups and Teams 152
Learning Outcomes 152
Introduction 152
What are Groups and Teams? 153
Why Do We Belong to Groups and Teams? 155
Interpersonal Attraction 156
Social Exchange Theory 158
The Stages of Team and Group Formation and Development 159
Influences within Groups and Teams: Conformity, Compliance, and Obedience 160
The Advantages and Disadvantages of Group or Team Work 161

Effective and Ineffective Groups and Teams   163
Designing Effective Teams   169
Summary   176
Websites   177
Journal and Discussion Questions   178
Skills Practice 8-1   180
Skills Practice 8-2   181
Skills Practice 8-3   182
Skills Practice 8-4   183

Chapter 9   Community Relationships and Leadership Skills   185
Learning Outcomes   185
Introduction   185
Why Building and Maintaining Relationships is Essential in Policing   186
How to Build and Maintain Effective Relationships   187
Leadership and Management   189
Theories of Leadership   189
Power   192
Leadership Styles   194
Developing Leadership Skills   195
Skills for Dealing With Superiors   200
Policing and Leadership in a Changing Environment   201
Summary   204
Websites   205
Journal and Discussion Questions   206
Skills Practice 9-1   208
Skills Practice 9-2   209

Chapter 10   Adapting to Change   211
Learning Outcomes   211
Introduction   211
What is Change?   212
The Change Process   215
Methods to Overcome Resistance to Change and Ease Transition   217
Changes Impacting Policing in Canada   221
Summary   227
Websites   228
Journal and Discussion Questions   229
Skills Practice 10-1   230
Skills Practice 10-2   231
Skills Practice 10-3   232

Glossary   235
References   239
Index   244

Preface

This text is designed for policing students taking courses on interpersonal relations and working in teams and groups. As frontline workers, officers encounter many different situations that challenge essential communication skills. Dealing with members of the public who may be in great turmoil–victims of crime, perpetrators, suspects, and members of the general public–demands a wide variety of skills. There are probably few other jobs that deal with such a cross section of the Canadian population. No less important, officers also have to work with each other as well as with a variety of other agencies and organizations, including the judicial and penal systems.

In response to these demands, most policing students will take at least one course in building effective communication skills and teamwork for dealing with others. For many, these courses are wrapped into one, such as Police Foundations Training. This text was written in response to the lack of material designed for policing students in the areas of interpersonal communication skills and teamwork skills, and puts these two areas together with an emphasis on application in law enforcement. A wide variety of sources are used in this text, including a large number from the fields of law and justice. These sources include research from psychology and social psychology, business applications, organizational behaviour, cultural diversity publications, interpersonal and team skills texts and publications, and a number of police publications from both Canada and the United States.

Although not police officers ourselves, both of us have been teaching in the area of law and justice for many years. With our combined backgrounds in social work, counselling, and within community organizations, we have worked with many officers over the years. For the most part, they are to be commended for their hard work and dedication. Considering the issues that have surfaced over the last decade, we do not foresee policing becoming an easier job, but rather a more difficult one. The officers who have visited our college classrooms over the last few years indentify these issues and reiterate what we have said to our students: communication is the key to building and sustaining relationships whether it be for a brief or a long-term encounter.

In policing, how you communicate and how others communicate to you may be the difference between walking away from an encounter and being carried away from it. Therefore, this text focuses not only on how you communicate, but how others respond to you. You can assess your current interpersonal communication and then study the chapters, paying special attention to your weaker areas. Some of the topics in the first part of the book include diversity, conflict, nonverbal communication, listening, perception, and verbal communication.

The second part of the text concentrates on group and team skills, with a focus on work teams and work groups. Some of these teams are primarily made up of law enforcement personnel, but there will also be other teams that you will encounter in community policing. Issues concerning leadership, problem solving and decision making, change, group make-up, and effective and ineffective teams are all discussed from a policing perspective.

We have attempted to make this book as practical as possible without losing the rich research and theoretical background of some of these concepts. Most chapters explore a topic, relate it to policing, and offer strategies and suggestions on how you can improve in that topic area. Throughout the text there are *Canadian Perspective* and *Law and Justice Perspective* feature boxes. The *Canadian Perspective* boxes allow you to examine current Canadian issues and assess the impact of these issues on you. The *Law and Justice Perspective* boxes give you the opportunity to see how these skills are actually applied in law enforcement, such as the use of a group problem-solving model by the RCMP and the Ontario Provincial Police. Many skills-based chapters also provide opportunities for skills practice, self-assessment, and other "try-it" activities that can be used as a self-study or learning tool, or can be used by small groups in the classroom. We firmly believe that these activities will help you improve your skills and help you be a better officer.

The personal and public demands on a police officer will continue to be difficult ones. With recent media attention surrounding ethics, diversity, use of force, and recent violent crimes, officers will need effective communication skills to deal with the public. As well, skills to work effectively within police organizations are critical, as services will continue to undergo rapid change to meet the demands of a continuously changing society.

We wish you all the best as you undertake your studies with this text. We hope that you continue to grow and to develop in order to become the best officer that you can be in the near future.

ACKNOWLEDGEMENTS

This book includes efforts from many people, and we wish to thank all who helped in the preparation of this manuscript. For their feedback on this edition, we would like to thank the following reviewers:

Tom Allen, Kwantlen University College

Leo de Jourdan, Canadore College

Ted Dionne, Durham College

Janne A. Holmgren, Mount Royal College

Margaret Joiner, Nova Scotia Community College

Dana Lennox, Algonquin Community College

Reg Liebel, Medicine Hat College

Sgt. Rick Parent, Justice Institute of British Columbia

D. Scharie Tavcer, Mount Royal College

First, I would like to thank my family for putting up with me while I worked. They gave me the time I needed. Thanks also to my friends who kept me going whenever I got stuck.

Second, I would like to thank my colleagues in the Law and Justice Department at Sir Sandford Fleming College who were invaluable with their information, support and thoughts. My colleagues in Interdisciplinary Studies were also of great help with their understanding and thoughts.

I would also like to thank my Police Foundations students who continue to teach me about what works and sometimes what doesn't work in Interpersonal and Group Dynamics courses. Many of you will make excellent police officers, and some of you already are.

A special note of thanks to Constable Geoff Stark of the Peterborough Lakefield Community Police Service who took the time to read and critique the first edition manuscript and provided invaluable input on being a police officer and on the kinds of issues that officers face. It is officers like Geoff and many others with whom I've spoken who point out the need for increased human relations skills in the complex work of community policing. Thanks also to Staff Sergeant Wayne Tucker of the Peterborough Lakefield Community Police Service and Senior Constable Brad Filman of the Ontario Provincial Police, Peterborough Detachment who provided photos for the first edition.

— *Terri M. Geerinck*

I would like to thank my family for their patience and encouragement while I worked. They understood the time commitment and energy required and cheered me on. Thanks also to my friends, whose support I am so grateful for.

I would also like to thank my colleagues in the Justice and Public Safety Institute at Georgian College who were also invaluable with their information, support and thoughts.

Thanks must also go to the Police Foundations and Law and Security students from my Interpersonal and Group Dynamics classes–they are the reason I worked on this book. Many of them have gone on to be excellent police officers. I wish them all success in their future endeavours. Special thanks go to Lindsey Maier for providing photos for this new edition, and to the officers and students featured in those photos.

— *Tracey McGruthers*

Finally, we would both like to recognize the many wonderful and dedicated people at Pearson Education Canada for their hard work on this edition. Thank you to Ky Pruesse for his support and excellent communication and special thanks to Rachel Stuckey for her support, guidance, and editing efforts, which helped make this project a success. There are many others behind the scenes at Pearson who deserve our thanks and admiration as well. Thank You!

Part 1

Interpersonal Communication

Chapter 1   Introduction to Interpersonal Communication   2

Chapter 2   Self-Knowledge and Communication   19

Chapter 3   Interpersonal Communication and Perception   37

Chapter 4   Nonverbal Communication   57

Chapter 5   Verbal Communication   79

Chapter 6   Conflict Management and Problem-Solving Skills   101

Chapter 7   Understanding and Managing Diversity   131

Introduction to Interpersonal Communication

After studying this chapter you should be able to:

- Describe the components of the communication process.
- Define interpersonal communication.
- Identify various levels of intimacy and self-disclosure using the Continuum of Interpersonal Communication.
- List the six principles of interpersonal communication.
- Identify reasons why knowledge of interpersonal skills and group dynamics is important for personal and career success.
- Identify strategies that will improve your ability to communicate more effectively.

INTRODUCTION

Stop! Police! Drop the knife!

I love you!

I can tell you're lying by the way you're fidgeting.

What do all of the above statements have in common? Though they arouse very different feelings, they are all examples of communication. More specifically, they are all verbal human communication into which you can probably read more than just verbal content. The first statement is **tactical communication**, whereby an officer orders an individual to put down a weapon. The second statement has a very different tone and is probably a declaration of affection. The third statement is a response to a statement that is perceived as untruthful. These three statements illustrate the complexity of communication. According to one researcher, while it may be easy and natural to communicate, it is difficult to communicate effectively (Puth, 1994). You may find it easy to say something to someone, but you cannot always be sure that the message will be understood as you intended. For successful interpersonal communication to occur, the meaning of the message must be shared accurately. The good news is that effective communication is a skill that can be learned and that will greatly enhance your effectiveness as a police officer.

Bike patrol offers many opportunities to communicate with the public.
Barrie City Police Services / © Lindsey Maier Inc., www.lindseymaier.com

This chapter introduces you to the topic of interpersonal communication, which will be explored in further detail (particularly in the next six chapters). In this chapter, we will examine interpersonal communication, define the communication process, explore the principles of communication, list the ways that this book will help you understand the complexities of interpersonal and group dynamics, and identify strategies that can improve your ability to communicate more effectively. Before you proceed with this chapter, assess your current level of interpersonal skills and knowledge with the questions in Skills Practice 1-1, found on p. 16.

WHY STUDY INTERPERSONAL COMMUNICATION AND GROUP DYNAMICS?

Students in law and justice programs often question why they should study interpersonal communication and group dynamics. Statements such as, "I've done fine so far; why should I learn new strategies and ideas?" or "It's just more psycho-babble" are not uncommon. Courses about law, investigative techniques, and police powers are often more appealing for law enforcement students. However, research has repeatedly noted the need for well-trained officers who can communicate effectively and manage in a diverse and changing society (More, 1985).

Many officers would agree that communication is the first and often most effective weapon in situations that might escalate. Crisis intervention can start at a verbal or non-verbal level. Effective communication at this stage may lead to solving the problem. Poor communication at the beginning of a crisis can lead to further escalation—and possible injury to the officer.

The amount of contact an officer has with others also illustrates the need for communication. This contact may be with the public (including victims and suspects), with other law enforcement and correctional officials, with legal representatives (including the Crown attorney and judges), or with the officer's own team members and partners. Diversity in Canada is also increasing (see Chapter 7), which means an increase in the diversity of the officer's contacts. Therefore, effective communication skills are critical because interpersonal communication is the key way to build, improve, and change any of these relationships. In addition, studying interpersonal and group dynamics will help you understand yourself, which is essential before you can help anyone else.

HOW THIS BOOK CAN HELP YOU

Increased Knowledge about Interpersonal Communication and Teamwork

Knowledge is the first step towards changing your current behaviour. This text includes both individual and team skills that will help you become more successful as you communicate and work with others on the job. Applying this knowledge to your interpersonal relationships can make them more satisfying and meaningful.

Increased Self-Knowledge

This text presents psychological information that will help you get to know yourself better, in order to become more aware of your strengths and identify personal challenges for self-improvement.

Better Awareness and Understanding of Diversity in Canada

Canada is becoming increasingly diverse. Being aware of this diversity and understanding the differences between people of different cultures, backgrounds, and lifestyles will reduce barriers to communication and enhance effective team and group work. Many conflicts are caused by cultural differences and different values. Increasing your knowledge of various cultures and learning effective communication techniques will reduce many of the conflicts that occur as a result of these differences. Continued immigration trends and the federal emphasis on multiculturalism in Canada will continue to be a challenge for law enforcement workers and officers, particularly in urban areas. In the chapter on diversity we will examine the nature of diversity in Canada and the differences among cultures and groups.

Knowledge about Team and Group Development

How do groups form? Why are some groups better than others? Answers to these and other questions will help you become a productive group or team member. Part of being a team member may mean leading the team. Changing demographics, economics, patterns of major crime and disorder, and new technology are just some of the challenges that a new police leader will face in the twenty-first century (Lunney, 1989).

New Strategies to Manage Conflict, Solve Problems, Make Decisions, and Manage Change

Research has pointed to effective strategies for handling conflict, solving problems, and making decisions that don't require tossing a coin, arguing, or using your best guess. As well, you need skills to help you understand and manage the numerous changes occurring in policing and in the nation.

THE COMMUNICATION PROCESS

To understand how communication occurs, look at the process involved in the communication of a message. See Figure 1-1 on p. 6 for a diagram of this process. Communication involves three major steps (Coffee et al., 1994). Be aware that each step is presented ideally here. In reality, each step can have several problems called **interference**, or noise, which is explained later in this chapter. The following example may help you understand the three communication steps. Assume that your teenage son wants to stay out at night until 11:30. His normal weekend curfew is 11:00.

Step One: Encoding

Encoding is a process of organizing ideas into a series of symbols that can be used to deliver the message. Examples of symbols include words and gestures. The words that we choose and the unintentional gestures we use can strongly influence the effectiveness of the communication. Your son says, "Can I stay out until 11:30 Friday night? There is a late basketball game on TV and I would like to go over to Eddy's house to watch it. His dad will drive me home after."

This is a different message from one in which your son says, "I never get to do anything, so I'm going to Eddy's Friday night to watch a basketball game. Are you going to let me or what?"

Step Two: Transmission

The message is transmitted using a medium such as face-to-face verbal and nonverbal communication, email, telephone, or paper. Face-to-face communication allows more nonverbal communication to take place through voice tone, volume, gestures, and facial expressions. If your son yells the second request at you with his arms crossed, you may perceive that something more is going on than a simple request for a change in curfew.

Step Three: Decoding

In the third step, decoding, the message's receiver interprets the message into meaningful information. The receiver attempts to understand what the sender is trying to convey. It is during this step that many communication problems occur. We can make many mistakes as we try to interpret a message. If your son yells his request, you may respond with "Why are you shouting at me?" or "What do you mean you never get to do anything?" An argument may start about other issues, such as parental control.

Decoding the message usually leads to some type of action or response by the receiver. If your son uses the first type of request, you may say, "Sure, that sounds fine. If Eddy's father can't bring you home, give me a call, and I'll come to get you." Your son would probably say this communication experience was successful.

Interference

Unfortunately, not all communication experiences are so successful. Interference—or noise—often distorts or blocks a message and leads to misinterpretation by the receiver. Yelling may be perceived as anger, but your son may not realize he is yelling because he has just finished listening to loud music, or maybe because he is excited about the basketball game. Even email and paper communication can have interference as we attempt to read between the lines. Have you ever received an email that was bossy or offensive?

Interference is usually divided into three main types (Devito, 1995). **Physical noise** is interference with the physical transmission of a message; for example, trying to listen to someone in a noisy restaurant. **Psychological noise** is interference that produces barriers in the decoding and processing of information, such as being distracted while trying to listen to someone. **Semantic noise** is interference that is created when the receiver does not decode the message in the way that is intended by the sender. A receiver who does not know the meaning of a word will have more difficulty decoding the message. Nonverbal communication has a great impact on this communication process, as we will see in Chapter 4.

Most communication between people is active and ongoing, with messages being sent back and forth at the same time, both verbally and nonverbally. At any point, problems can occur in the process. These problems may be caused by interference—and this interference can also be internal. Our thoughts, personalities, current physiological state, health, and other internal characteristics impact on the way we encode and decode messages. For example, have you ever found it hard to listen when you have a really bad cold? Other key sources of interference may be differences in culture, values, and beliefs. For instance, some cultures show respect by not maintaining eye contact while communicating, whereas other cultures may perceive lack of eye contact as being inattentive or rude.

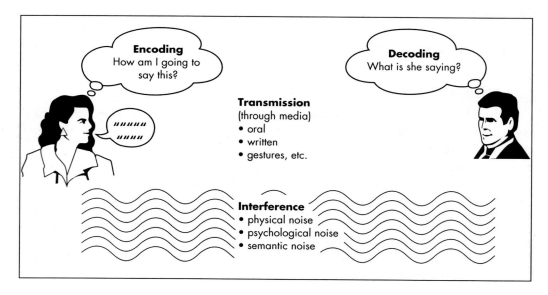

Figure 1-1   The Communication Process
Source: Based on models described by Robert E. Coffee, Curtis W. Cook, and Phillip L. Hunsaker (1994). *Management and Organizational Behaviour*. Burr Ridge, IL. Irwin, pp. 197-120; and Joseph A. Devito (1995). *The Interpersonal Communication Book*, 7th edition. United States: HarperCollins.

INTERPERSONAL COMMUNICATION

We have talked about the communication process, but what is interpersonal communication? Communication is an active and ongoing process through which an individual creates shared meanings by receiving information, thinking or acting upon that information, and sending information. **Interpersonal communication** occurs "when we interact simultaneously with another person and mutually influence each other usually for the purpose of managing relationships" (Beebe et al., 2004).

Let's examine this definition more closely. Interpersonal communication is a type of **human communication**. We make sense out of the world and share it with others by using our five basic senses: seeing, hearing, smelling, touching, and tasting. We then share our conclusions with others (Beebe et al., 2004). The depth of this sharing differs depending upon the situation and upon whether we treat the other person as a unique human being. Therefore, human communication occurs on a **communication continuum** (see Figure 1-2) ranging from impersonal to very intimate.

Impersonal communication and intimate communication are at opposite ends of the communication continuum. Impersonal communication occurs when we treat others as objects rather than as real people. If you say to a server, "Get me a coffee," you are likely communicating with his role rather than with the person. Ignoring someone who asks for change on the street is also impersonal communication. Moving along the continuum, communication becomes more personal and takes on more of the characteristics of interpersonal communication. If you frequent the same coffee shop day after day, you may get to know the server as a person, making communication more personal. Through continued contact, you may learn names, interests, and even some life experiences of this person. While the server may never become your friend, your relationship will have moved further away from the impersonal end of the continuum.

As a future police officer or other law enforcement worker, think of the kinds of dealings you may have with the public. Policing in a small town rather than a large urban centre may mean fewer impersonal relations. In a small town, you may see and manage the same people on a much more regular basis.

As we move along to more interpersonal communication, communication becomes more intimate and less formal and includes more personal and self-revealing content. By increasing or decreasing the amount of **self-disclosure**, we increase or decrease the level of intimacy. What happens when someone is too self-disclosing? Choosing a level of self-disclosure can be difficult, and we can become very uncomfortable when we feel someone is telling us more than we want to hear. Sometimes we also feel uncomfortable when the level of self-disclosure has not been reciprocated. Have you ever felt that you told someone too much? We try to choose the level of self-disclosure that we feel comfortable with, and choose whether we want to maintain a current level of **intimacy**, or increase or decrease it. As we get to know someone and feel closer, intimacy (Figure 1-2) tends to increase.

The second part of interpersonal communication is concerned with the simultaneous interaction between individuals that occurs when both people create meaning at the same time by reacting to both verbal and nonverbal communication. For instance, in the third example of communication at the beginning of this chapter, one person believes another is lying because of perceived "fidgeting."

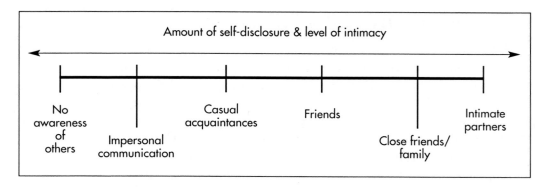

Figure 1-2   Continuum of Interpersonal Communication

Mutual influence is the third component that defines interpersonal communication. Mutual influence means that both parties are affected by the communication exchange. When one person accuses another of lying, both people are affected. The situation and the degree of intimacy between the two parties varies; having a stranger smile at you is very different from having your lover smile at you.

The last component of interpersonal communication is the way in which we use it to manage our relationships. It is through the process of interpersonal communication that relationships develop, are maintained, or are terminated. In the initial stages of a relationship, we do not self-disclose very much. As trust and intimacy increase, we self-disclose more information and increase our interactions. As we move along the continuum, conversations and behaviours become more intimate. Decreasing interaction and reducing intimacy "cools" a relationship and can result in its termination. In this way, the continuum can move both ways: from less intimate to intimate, and from intimate to less intimate. Police officers often have to reduce interpersonal communication with victims of crime who may reach out for physical comfort that may be inappropriate or seen as unprofessional conduct by the officer.

KEY LEARNING POINTS

Communication Misconceptions

- Effective communication is not a natural ability. Communication is a skill that can be developed by training and practice.

- More communication is not always better. Sometimes talking too much can be a mistake.

- No single person or event causes another person's reaction. We are responsible for the words we choose and our behaviour, but we are not responsible for the way others perceive and respond.

- Meanings are not in words. Saying something and communicating are not the same thing. Meanings are formed based on the relationship we have with the other person. Our relationship with that person determines how we feel towards them and hence perceive their communication.

PRINCIPLES OF INTERPERSONAL COMMUNICATION

Now that you have developed an understanding of interpersonal communication, we will move on to explore the six principles of interpersonal communication (summarized from Wood and Henry, 2002). An understanding of these principles will help you develop communications skills.

1. **We cannot avoid communicating.** As long as you are around others, you cannot help but communicate. No matter what you say (or don't say), people will attempt to interpret your behaviour. You may even be unaware that you are communicating; for example, you may not be aware that you are clenching your fists when you are angry, but someone else may observe this behaviour.

2. **Communication is irreversible.** What you say and do has an impact and cannot be undone. It becomes part of the interpersonal relationship and affects others. Responsible people understand that there are ethical choices involved in interpersonal communication. Studying this text will help you choose more carefully what you say and how you decide to say it.

3. **Meanings are constructed in interpersonal communication.** Each relationship is unique and the meanings of communication within that relationship are also unique. As relationships develop, meanings are assigned to the ongoing communication in the relationship. One friend may call you crazy and you both will laugh about it. However, being called crazy in another relationship may have a very different meaning and may be nothing to laugh about.

4. **Interpersonal communication is the most important way to develop and sustain relationships.** This is part of our definition of interpersonal communication. As well, communication allows us to define and re-define current and past relationships. Old boyfriends or girlfriends don't really mean as much to us as we thought they did—now that we have new loves in our lives. Communication also allows us to build futures in relationships. We can ask a potential friend to go bowling next week, and if the reply is positive the relationship has a future.

5. **Interpersonal communication is not a cure-all.** While good interpersonal communication skills are essential for working out problems in relationships, these skills will not solve every relationship problem. We can't control how others receive our communication. Also, not all people or cultures support the idea that "things should be talked out."

6. **Interpersonal communication skills can be learned.** We can all become better communicators by learning and practising the skills presented in this text and in related courses.

KEY LEARNING POINTS

Communication Competence

- Gain knowledge and practise skills.
- Be flexible and open-minded.
- Create a desire for change.
- Be other-oriented.
- Self-monitor your communication.
- Commit to communication competence.

STRATEGIES TO IMPROVE YOUR INTERPERSONAL COMMUNICATION SKILLS AND GAIN COMMUNICATION COMPETENCE

Communication competence is achieving your goals while ideally maintaining or enhancing the relationship in which communication occurs. To accomplish this you need to acquire certain skills. Suggested below is a six-part strategy that is expanded upon in the remainder of this book and is an adaptation of Beebe et al., 2004; and Wood and Henry, 2002.

Gain Knowledge and Practise These Skills

You are already increasing your knowledge about interpersonal communication by reading this textbook and taking this course. You can also gain knowledge through observing a role model who demonstrates effective interpersonal communication skills. People who are effective communicators know how communication works. They understand the principles, theories, rules, and strategies for more effective interpersonal communication.

Knowledge is the starting point. The old saying "practice makes perfect" applies to learning and using communication skills too. You can memorize the steps of a problem-solving model, learn the skills for effective listening, and learn about Japanese culture. Such knowledge will have little relevance (other than on an exam) if you do not apply this knowledge so that it becomes a useful skill. Keep in mind when learning these new skills that you may go through several stages. Initially, you may feel awkward. Many students who first learn the steps of active listening report that it feels unnatural to actually try it with another person. Many new skills feel strange when you first try them. As you keep overcoming the awkward stage, you will become consciously skilled. Use the text exercises to practise new skills so that they start to feel natural. You have probably had two decades or more to develop your current communication skills, so they will not change overnight for you. Developing a skill takes time, patience, and practice. After a while, you will perform these new skills without thinking about it and they will feel natural to you.

Be Flexible and Open-Minded

Every situation you encounter is unique. A person in crisis and a person who is wielding a knife will demand a different set of communication skills from you, the officer. The same set of skills will not work in all situations. Would you be able to quietly say to both people in the above example, "Now, now, calm down"? Effective communicators examine the situation, their goals, the people involved, the context, and other factors (sometimes very quickly) to establish a relationship at the appropriate level.

Create a Desire for Change

If you feel your skills are perfect or at least decent, you will have very little motivation to try and change those skills. In Chapter 2 we will briefly discuss changes in policing. This discussion may help you realize that changes in police services across the country demand a change in policing style and abilities. Without effective communication skills, your chances of being hired may be reduced. New testing in police foundations requires knowledge of psychology, and interpersonal and group dynamics. In general, employers are looking for workers who can demonstrate good interpersonal communication and teamwork skills. See the Canadian Perspective box on p. 11 for more details on employability skills.

CANADIAN PERSPECTIVE

Required Skills for Employees in Canada

What are essential skills for workers in Canada? The Conference Board of Canada has published an Employability Skills Profile based on information gathered from a survey of Canadian employers. The skills were classified into three main categories: academic skills, personal management skills, and teamwork skills. Here we will explore personal management and teamwork skills. Please note that all the requirements are not listed here. Instead, the ones specific to this type of course are highlighted.

Under personal management skills, Canadian employers cite the need for a person who has self-confidence and self-esteem; a positive attitude towards learning, growth, and personal health; the ability to set goals and priorities in work and personal life; and the ability to recognize and show respect for diversity and individual differences.

Under teamwork skills, Canadian employers cite the need for someone who can work within the culture of a group; plan and make decisions with others and support the outcomes of those decisions; cooperate to achieve group results; use a team approach when necessary; and take on effective team leadership when necessary.

These are just a few of the skills required by Canadian employers that will be reviewed in this text. While many of these are labelled as "soft skills," in a changing, competitive job market they are the critical employability skills that may land you the job.

Source: Adapted from Corporate Council on Education, a program of the Conference Board of Canada, "Employability Skills Profile: What Are Employers Looking For?" To view the entire document, visit the website at www.conferenceboard.ca/education/pdf/emskill.pdf.

Be Other-Oriented

In North American society, many of us are largely focused on ourselves: our own feelings, beliefs, problems, and ideas. Like the individual who self-discloses too much too soon, many people show little concern for the other person in a situation. Such self-focus interferes with effectively communicating with others. We may ignore the characteristics of the other person, listen poorly, or miss other vital clues that would enhance our ability to communicate effectively. When communicating with others, we need to adapt our messages to make them more easily understood. "Other-oriented communication suggests that we consider the needs, motives, desires and goals of our communication partners while still maintaining our own integrity" (Beebe et al., 2004). When we become other-oriented, we think not only about ourselves but also about the other person. For example, when talking with a young child, we adjust our words to the level of understanding of the child. If we are speaking to a new Canadian who has difficulty with English, we may simplify our vocabulary or speak more slowly and clearly.

Being other-oriented involves several skills, and according to at least one researcher (Argyle, 1983), these skills can be systematically learned and applied in human interaction. Several of these skills will be discussed further in this book. For instance, examining the development of self-concept and self-esteem, understanding perceptions and being able to develop accurate perceptions, and being able to adapt to others considerably different from you are just a few of the skills that will help you become other-oriented.

Two other skills that will help you become other-oriented are **decentring** and **empathizing** (Beebe et al., 2004). To decentre is to consciously shift the focus from your own thoughts to the other person's thoughts and feelings. If you are the police officer, what is the driver thinking when you flash your lights to signal her to pull over? What would your significant other think if you came home with your belly button pierced?

Empathy requires that you also think about *how* the other person is feeling (although the feelings and thoughts often occur simultaneously). Empathy is one of the most important aspects of communication competence. Empathy enables you to consider an issue from several angles and understand different points of view. Would your significant other feel happy with the new ring in your belly button—or think that maybe you have a serious emotional problem? When you stop a vehicle, is the driver feeling scared because the car is stolen, or angry at the inconvenience?

We try to figure out another person's thoughts or feelings based on our own experiences and knowledge. The more knowledge and experience you have, the better your educated guess. If you know that your significant other likes novel ideas and strives to be different, your belly button ring may be a success. But you can only gauge this probability based on your experience to date with this person. As an officer, you have no previous experience with the person in the vehicle, so you must rely on procedures (how to stop a vehicle) and your own knowledge from past experiences. Knowing that traffic stops can be very dangerous, you approach with caution and watch for any signs of unusual activity by the individual (such as reaching under the car seat as you approach). If the driver is angry because of the stop, you empathize with her, because no one likes to be detained or inconvenienced.

Becoming other-oriented helps you to become a better communicator as you strive to think and feel what the other person is thinking and feeling. With this knowledge, you can become more tolerant and understanding of another person's perspective, which is particularly useful in times of conflict or misunderstanding. Being other-oriented does not assume that you agree with the other person; only that you understand that person's feelings.

Self-Monitor

When we self-monitor we observe our own behaviour and use that observation to change our behaviour. If you notice, for instance, that one communication technique is not successful in a particular situation, you can change to another technique to accomplish your goal.

Make a Commitment

People who seem to care about relationships communicate better than those who don't. Change is difficult and takes hard work. Commit to the communication process. Be open to new ideas, be willing to listen without rushing someone, and have a desire to understand.

SUMMARY

In this chapter we introduced and explored interpersonal communication. The communication process is a three-step process of encoding, transmitting, and decoding information. This process is not always accurate because of interference or noise that can distort communication and lead to misunderstandings between the sender and the receiver. We defined interpersonal communication as interacting and mutually influencing each other in order to manage a relationship. This interpersonal communication takes place along a continuum that varies in the level of self-disclosure and intimacy. On one side of the continuum, communication is impersonal, and at the other extreme, communication is intimate, with a high degree of self-disclosure.

Six principles of interpersonal communication introduced you to possible ways of improving your interpersonal communication skills and explained why you should study and improve your skills. Finally, this chapter outlined a six-part strategy to improve skills that will be explored and elaborated upon in future chapters.

WEBSITES

www.selfgrowth.com/index.html
A site devoted to personal growth, self-improvement, self-help, and personal power. Although this is a commercial site, you can get a free self-improvement newsletter.

www.conferenceboard.ca
This is the site for the Conference Board of Canada, the foremost independent, not-for-profit applied research organization in Canada.

www.bccf.bc.ca/improving_communication.htm
The British Columbia Council for Families skill card on improving communication.

www.books4selfhelp.com
A guide to self-help books.

www.jobsetc.ca/toolbox/checklists/employability.jsp?lang=e
Rate your own employability skills at this Service Canada training and careers site.

www.labourmarketinformation.ca/standard.asp?ppid=119&lcode=E&prov=&sga id=&occ=&search_key=1&pre_sel_criteria=0
Service Canada site on job and skill requirements for Canadian police officers.

www.hrsdc.gc.ca/en/home.shtml
The Human Resources and Skills Development Canada site on essential skills for work, learning, and life.

JOURNAL AND DISCUSSION QUESTIONS

1. Do you think that all law enforcement workers should have extensive training in interpersonal and team skills? Why or why not?

2. At a presentation on interpersonal communication, the presenter, a police constable with 16 years of training, stated, "Good interpersonal skills are your best weapon." Do you agree or disagree with this statement? Support your answer.

3. Review your own interpersonal skills. What are your strengths? What are your weaknesses? How will this book be useful for your own needs?

SKILLS PRACTICE 1-1
Interpersonal Skills Assessment

For each of the following statements, answer True if you think the statement is true or mostly true, and answer False if you think the statement is false or mostly false.

_____ 1. Nonverbal communication is the greatest source of information about another person.

_____ 2. Active listening should only be used in certain situations.

_____ 3. Stereotypes are the same as prototypes.

_____ 4. Various vocal cues make up paralanguage.

_____ 5. Empathy is different from sympathy.

_____ 6. Learning how to speak correctly is the most essential communication skill.

_____ 7. Interpreting nonverbal communication is easy once you learn how to do it.

_____ 8. One of the problems of rigid thinking is that it leads to static evaluation.

_____ 9. Conflict should be avoided.

_____ 10. Ethnocentrism reduces prejudice and discrimination.

_____ 11. Canada is still a largely masculine culture.

_____ 12. Assertive people aggressively pursue their rights.

_____ 13. "I" language should be used to get what you want from others.

_____ 14. During a crisis, people often want less personal space.

_____ 15. Physical techniques should be used as a last resort in managing a crisis.

ANSWER KEY

Give yourself one point if you answered True for questions 1, 2, 4, 5, 8, 11, and 15.

Give yourself one point if you answered False for the rest of the questions: 3, 6, 7, 9, 10, 12, 13, and 14.

Interpretation: 0-5—This part of the text will help you learn the skills essential to improving your current interpersonal skills level.

6-10—You have a moderate level of interpersonal skill, and this part of the text will fill in some of the gaps in your skill level.

11-15—You have a good level of skill. You will be a great asset in class discussions and activities. Pay special attention to the chapters where you feel you need some improvement.

SKILLS PRACTICE 1-2

Self-Disclosure: Applying the Continuum of Interpersonal Communication

For each of the following statements, discuss whether the level of self-disclosure was too intimate, not intimate enough, or appropriate. Support your answers. This is a good in-class activity about self-disclosure and intimacy. For added interest, formulate a reply to this person. Did your reply increase, decrease, or maintain the current level of self-disclosure?

1. This is your second class in Interpersonal and Group Dynamics. While on a class break, another student holding a cup of coffee approaches you and sits beside you. You talked very briefly in the last class about the weather and the large amount of work in this course. She says, "I really don't like night courses like this. I always worry about leaving my kids with Jim. I'm afraid he might start drinking around them or start hitting them again. Do you have any kids?"

---

2. You have been dating someone for six months and feel that this is a very serious relationship. It is this person's birthday and you want to announce your love. You have already purchased a gold ID bracelet, and have had "I love you" engraved on the back, with your name. You have made a reservation at a quiet and intimate restaurant, and over dessert you present your gift and say, "Happy Birthday! I have something very special to tell you!" Your friend opens up the gift, reads the back, and

says, "This is great! Thank you!" Your friend puts the bracelet back in the box and sits back with a cup of coffee and says, "What should we do now?"

_____

_____

_____

_____

_____

_____

_____

_____

_____

_____

_____

3. You are having a really bad day. First, your car would not start and you had to buy a new battery for it. When you arrived home, you noticed the cat had used your bed instead of the litter box (again), and you received a very large credit card bill. After playing baseball that night, you're out with a friend and you say, "I have had one of those days! Between the cat, the car, and the bills, I could just explode!" Your friend replies, "That cat using your bed again? I know what you mean! Sometimes, you wonder why you ever bothered to get out of bed!"

_____

_____

_____

_____

_____

_____

_____

_____

_____

_____

Chapter 2

Self-Knowledge and Communication

After studying this chapter you should be able to:

- Outline contemporary policing.
- Define self-concept, self-esteem, and self-presentation and discuss how each relates to communication.
- Apply Maslow's Hierarchy of Needs to communication.
- Explain diversity and managing technology as human needs.
- Describe five strategies to improve self-concept and self-esteem.

INTRODUCTION

Casey is a new police officer in a large metropolitan area. She was excited about starting work and looking forward to a great career protecting people from criminals. After two weeks on the job, she is feeling let down. She has not apprehended a single criminal or done anything that she considers to be real police work. There are reports to be filled out, other deskwork to do, and most of her contact with the public seems more like social work. To add insult to injury, during day shifts she is now being placed temporarily on school detail, which involves going to community schools to talk about drugs. Her staff sergeant says her youth and great sense of humour are ideal for the school program. Her self-esteem is plummeting, and she is beginning to question her career choice.

What Casey is experiencing is not uncommon in any kind of work. How we perceive a job and what the job actually entails may not be the same. Most of us who get the chance to choose our careers experience disappointments, and these disappointments can affect our self-concept and lower our self-esteem as we begin to doubt our choice. As individuals, we act and react differently to changes in our lives. Since no two people are alike, we have different needs, goals, and ideas about how to communicate and work with others.

Knowing yourself is a vital part of being an effective communicator. Without self-knowledge, you have little awareness of your strengths and limitations. If Casey wants to learn more about her career choice and to be more effective on the job, she will have

Police officers take on many roles in their daily work, including the role of educator.
Mnjikining Police Service / © Lindsey Maier Inc., www.lindseymaier.com

to learn more about herself. She will have to examine policing and how this profession is changing, learn how to get along with others, and communicate with others in a diverse community.

This chapter will briefly examine the changing nature of police work. Then, in order to begin the process of self-knowledge, we will discuss and examine the "self" and its three components (self-concept, self-esteem, and self-presentation) in relation to interpersonal communication.

When we express the things that we want or need, we communicate our needs to others. We will examine how needs influence interpersonal communication. Finally, we will discuss strategies to improve our self-concept and self-esteem.

THE CHANGING FACE OF POLICE WORK

Globalization had a significant impact on our social, economic, and political systems, which in turn has affected the direction of police services and the role of the police officer. The role of the police officer has become complex in today's society. A police officer fills roles other than "crime fighter," including social worker, medic, psychologist, report-taker, and teacher (Dantzker and Mitchell, 1998). Within community policing, additional roles include public and community relations.

A **role** can be defined in two ways: as a position or a place that you hold in society, or as a set of attitudes and beliefs attributed to a position held in a social structure. Often, these definitions may conflict with each other. For example, as an officer, you may be called to a convenience store where the owner has apprehended a "thief." When you get there, you find that the thief is a 10-year-old boy who has stolen a loaf of bread and a jar of peanut butter. It is obvious to you that the child is starving and most likely homeless. What do you do? See the Law and Justice Perspective box for more on the conflicting nature of police work.

Crime Fighter, Public Relations Worker, or Social Worker: Are Police Officer Roles Changing?

The public, perhaps influenced by the media, still perceive police officers as crime fighters who are there to prevent and control criminal behaviour. Numerous studies have found that most calls for service are unrelated to criminal activities (Dantzker and Mitchell, 1998). Calls to quiet a noisy party, remove bothersome animals, deal with an unruly teenager, remove someone who has been drinking from a home, and other domestic calls are rarely criminal in nature. Many community agencies, such as churches or other community support systems that used to deal with such social issues, are not used as often today. With lack of funding, school systems and public counselling services have cut back on their services, often leaving individuals little choice but to call the police. Every day there are new stories about police officers playing social service roles, for example, responding to a call about abandoned children left to fend for themselves in an apartment.

Many members of the public, including police officers themselves, are reluctant to shed the crime fighter image. Is "crime fighter" part of an officer's self-concept? Has society assigned this role, and is it now reluctant to see the role change to a more complex one involving the public relations and social worker role? As future law enforcement workers, you may need to ask yourself these questions as you pursue your career.

Social changes have required police services to undergo many changes, including merging and centralizing while still trying to maintain contact with the local community. Across Canada, the term **community policing** has taken a firm hold as efforts have been made to restructure services in consultation with communities. Police services use the label "community policing" to address what services should be offered, what current community problems need attention, and how these services should be implemented for maximum effectiveness. Community policing differs in many ways from traditional reactive policing, and requires different skills. In community or "contemporary policing," the community and police jointly identify issues and together resolve these issues to mutual satisfaction.

Traditionally, emergency calls and other complaints were the foundation for service, and policing was more reactive. Today, while policing is still reactive, more proactive and preventative crime measures are being undertaken by a joint force of police and community stakeholders (OPP, 2005). Like many police services, the Royal Canadian Mounted Police have reflected commitment to the community in their core values statement.

LAW AND JUSTICE PERSPECTIVE (*Continued*)

Core Values of the Royal Canadian Mounted Police

The Royal Canadian Mounted Police are committed to our communities through:

- Unbiased and respectful treatment of all people
- Accountability
- Mutual problem solving
- Cultural sensitivity
- Enhancement of public safety
- Partnerships and consultation
- Open and honest communication
- Effective and efficient use of resources
- Quality and timely service

Source: Adapted from RCMP mission, vision, and values, at www.rcmp-grc.gc.ca/html/vision_e.htm. Retrieved December 28, 2005.

The shift to community policing and community relations programs impacts and expands the role of the police officer and demands additional skills. With increasing emphasis on the community, and on building and maintaining relationships, police officers must have excellent communication skills, teamwork skills, and the ability to work with a wide variety of people from the community. Police–community relations programs, which promote community involvement and make the police more visible, accessible, and accountable to community members, are becoming popular across Canada.

The first step to becoming an effective communicator in such complex work is to discover who you are. Your "self" affects your communication style, your perception of a situation, and how well you work on a team.

Two other steps are also important for gaining self-knowledge. First, you must examine your needs. Your needs determine your behaviour—or at least how you would like to behave—and many of your needs are met through interpersonal communication. Second, you must appreciate the needs of others who may be very different from you. Managing yourself and communicating effectively in a diverse society is essential for personal and career success. In addition to communicating effectively in a diverse society, the ability to master different technologies is critical in today's information age.

COMMUNICATION AND THE SELF

Your "self" consists of three components—**self-concept**, **self-esteem** and **self-presentation**—which interact and form the basis of the self. How you communicate is based on your perception of who you are as a person and how you view your profession. Be aware that all three components interact with each other to form your "self."

Self-Concept

Your self-concept comprises who you think you are and all your thoughts about yourself (Philipchalk, 1995), including your race, culture, gender, family roles, social roles, and career. A positive self-concept leads to high self-confidence. For instance, if Casey has a positive self-concept, she may think that being on school detail is a good starting point to demonstrate her communication skills with youth. If she talks to other officers she may soon realize that working with schools allows more day-shift opportunities, which will allow her to spend more time with family and friends after hours. She will probably understand that having good reports make their way back to her superiors will lead to better assignments in the future. On the other hand, a more negative self-concept may lead her to self-doubt. She may think that she doesn't really have what it takes to be a good officer and that school detail is all she is good for on the service.

Our self-concept arises through interaction and communication with others. Early in life, parents and other primary caregivers have the heaviest influence on our self-concept, and **reflected appraisal** from others forms a basis for much of our self-concept. Reflected appraisal is your view of yourself based on the assessment of others (Philipchalk, 1995). If Casey's parents let her know that they viewed her as smart and capable, then she would start to view herself that way, and this would be reflected in her behaviour. Similarly, if others treated her this way (such as teachers, other relatives, friends), she would **internalize** these beliefs as part of her self-concept. Thus, **feedback**—information that you receive from others about yourself—has a great deal of influence on how you view yourself. When Casey was young, her parents may have praised her for trying hard when she was learning to ride a bike and told her how smart she was to learn the skill so quickly. This early feedback increased her concept of herself as being capable, and boosted her self-confidence. This kind of feedback has the most influence, although it does not preclude a single experience from having a major impact. Some single experiences, such as a traumatic event, can have a major impact on self-concept.

While reflected appraisal is one way of discovering who we are, **social comparison** arises as we notice differences between ourselves and others (Philipchalk, 1995). Through social comparison, we tend to describe ourselves in terms of how we differ from others, by observing the behaviour of others and comparing it to our own abilities, characteristics, and behaviours. This process also provides insight into ourselves.

And finally, our self-concept increases in complexity as we get older and more mature, and we start to recognize more complex social and psychological qualities (Hart and Damon, 1986). While many people have a positive self-concept and through these processes have come to know and like themselves, others have negative self-concepts and beliefs about who they are.

Many people suffer from shyness and social phobias that debilitate them in social situations. In a North American culture that values physical beauty, many people feel they are ugly, too fat, or that their teeth are not white enough. While this text does not deal with these problems, we should all be aware that everyone has problems with maintaining a positive self-concept and feeling good about who they are. At the end of this chapter, some strategies for improving self-concept may help you to feel better about yourself.

The Johari Window and Self-Concept

Another way of gaining insight into who you are is to use the Johari Window model of self-disclosure, which is named after its creators, Joe Luft and Harry Ingham (Beebe et al., 2004). As Figure 2-1 shows, the Johari Window model has four sections that represent your self. These four sections make up the window that helps you understand how you learn and gather information about yourself. The first section is the "open" area. It contains information about you that is known to you and to others. The more you self-disclose, the larger this area will be. Information in this area includes things like your age, height, and occupation.

The second area is called the "blind" area, and it contains information about you that is known by others but which you do not know. For example you may see yourself as a good listener while others see you as someone who listens poorly. When you learn how others see you and accurately get to know yourself, this window becomes smaller.

The third section is the "hidden" area. This section contains information about you that you are aware of, but that others don't know about you, including thoughts or actions you choose to keep private.

The fourth section is the "unknown" area, and it contains information about you that is unknown to you and to others. This information includes things you have not experienced or developed yet. You may not know, for example, what kind of police officer you will make until you actually have experience performing that job.

A vital part of being an effective communicator requires knowing who you are, including having an awareness of your strengths and limitations. You can use the Johari Window model to gain valuable insight for building your self-knowledge. Specifically, you can do this by being open to new ideas and broadening your life experience. You can ask those close to you for their perception of you and then reflect on that information.

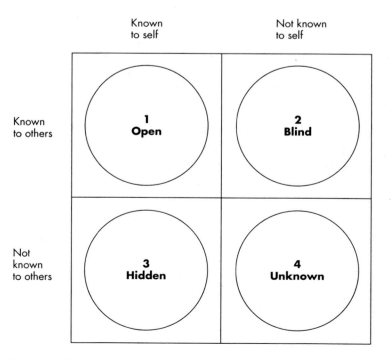

Figure 2-1   The Johari Window

By broadening your life experience and trying new things, you can identify qualities, talents, and strengths in yourself.

Self-Esteem

The second component of the self is self-esteem—how you feel about who you are (Philipchalk, 1995). People with positive self-esteem feel good about themselves and feel that they are worthwhile (Rinke, 1988). Feeling worthwhile helps to build a positive self-concept, and people with high self-esteem have a more positive outlook on life. If Casey has high self-esteem, she will remain confident about her career choice and give herself and the job more time before she makes any major decisions.

Think of someone you know who has high self-esteem. How does that person communicate self-esteem? With a more positive outlook or positive attitudes? Does he appear more confident in dealing with others? Now think of someone who you feel has low self-esteem. How does that person communicate a lack of self-esteem?

While we cannot see attitudes or outlook, they become apparent in our communication with others and in how we present ourselves to others.

Self-Presentation

Self-presentation is the behavioural expression of who we are—what we feel and think about ourselves (Philipchalk, 1995). It is the impression that we consciously create and display to others, and includes how we dress, the words we choose, the body language we use, and other behaviours. In police and other security work, the uniform becomes part of the self-presentation to which other people will respond. Some people present themselves assertively and with confidence, while others show less confidence in their self-presentation. At least one researcher suggests that we present ourselves in ways to verify our self-concept (Swann, 1992). We also engage in **strategic self-presentation** by presenting ourselves in a way that achieves a specific goal or goals in a relationship (Philipchalk, 1995).

You may present yourself in a certain way in order to get others to like you. You may use flattery, compliments, and favours, or say the right things and demonstrate interest so that others will evaluate you positively and like you. You may use self-promotion to impress others, and present yourself in ways to gain sympathy or help. You might complain to your roommate that you are not good at finding research material for a paper, hoping that she will feel sorry for you and maybe find the material for you.

Another goal of self-presentation may be intimidation of others. Police officers who use fear and other tactics to make people afraid often present themselves by standing in intimidating positions or by invading another person's personal space.

While this kind of behaviour may seem phoney and contrived, we often use self-presentation to achieve a variety of goals—from landing a job to getting a date. However, we are not always conscious of how we present ourselves or look to others. The way in which we manipulate our self-presentation and adjust to a wide variety of situations varies. Think about how you currently present yourself. What do you consciously do in order to present the image of interested student, caring friend, and confident worker? As you learn more about interpersonal communication skills, you will be able to improve how you present yourself.

Figure 2-2   The Three Components of the Self

Figure 2-2 presents these three components of self. Who you think you are (self-concept), how you feel about those thoughts (self-esteem), and how you present yourself (self-presentation) all impact greatly on how you communicate with others (interpersonal communication).

NEEDS AND COMMUNICATION

Our needs are another aspect of who we are that affects our communication. As we interact with others, we communicate our needs and goals; in fact, meeting needs is one of the main reasons we interact with others (Wood and Henry, 2002). If Casey needs reassurance that her career choice is the right one, she may ask a friend to give her feedback. Her friend may say, "Hey, you always wanted to be a police officer. And you'll make a great one!"

Abraham Maslow (1954) described human needs as a hierarchy (Figure 2-3) with lower-order needs that must be met before the next levels of needs, which are more abstract and less basic, can be met. While Maslow's theory has not always been supported (Williams and Page, 1989), many other theories also stress that humans (and other animals) seek to meet various needs at various levels. While Maslow's theory is sequential (i.e., one level of needs must be met before the next level can be met), other ideas and theories are multi-dimensional, and suggest that various levels and types of needs can be active at the same time (Greenberg and Baron, 1993). For example, if you are hungry while studying hard for an exam, a physiological need (hunger) and an esteem need (the need to achieve) are operating simultaneously. Regardless of which needs theory is correct, we all communicate for assistance in meeting various needs. We will use Maslow's theory to illustrate the use of communication to fulfill needs in our everyday lives.

Physical Needs

At the bottom of the needs pyramid are *physiological* needs, which include our basic need for food, water, and air. Babies alert their caregivers by crying—a basic form of

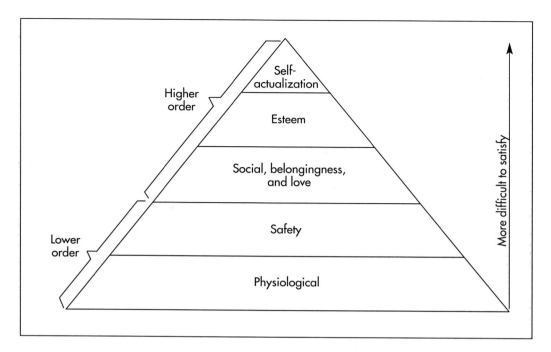

Figure 2-3 Maslow's Hierarchy of Needs

communication. As we mature, we still communicate to fill these basic needs, by going to the doctor when we feel unwell or by having someone fix our furnace so that we can stay warm. We make requests, ask questions, and solve problems even at this most basic level. Can you think of an example of how you communicate to meet a physical need?

Safety Needs

The second level, the need for *safety*, is also often met through communication with others. Safety needs include things like a safe place to live and freedom from harm. There are many ways to communicate safety needs. For example, someone who has been the victim of a break-in at home, and whose safety has been threatened, may no longer feel like home is the safe haven it once was. Acting on the advice of an officer or other security personnel, the individual may install a security system in order to feel safe at home. When safety needs are not being met, it is very difficult to focus on higher needs.

Belonging Needs

The third level of need is *belonging*. This is a social need to work, play, and live with others. Good relationships with others are essential for happiness, well-being, and health. Several studies have pointed out that personal happiness and good relationships keep us healthier and happier (Hojat, 1982; Litwin, 1996). If Casey can develop good and supportive relationships on the job, she will most likely be happier and more positive about being a police officer. She will develop a spirit of community and trust with her co-workers and may make several friends in the service.

Self-Esteem Needs

Self-esteem needs comprise the fourth level of needs, and relate to being valued and respected by those around us. These needs also have a great deal to do with liking and respecting ourselves. As stated earlier, much of our self-esteem relies on feedback from others. This feedback continues throughout our lives as we encounter others personally and professionally. It is through the process of interpersonal communication that we find our value and self-respect. As Casey meets new co-workers, their feedback will be important to her development as a police officer. This feedback may help or hinder her as she struggles in a new career. The way in which we give feedback to others on their performance and behaviour is important. We must learn effective feedback skills in order to critique the behaviour and performance of others in ways that help them change (see Chapter 9, Skills Practice 9-2, for information on giving feedback). Constructive feedback is preferable to creating a defensive and nonsupportive climate that hinders change.

Self-Actualization Needs

According to Maslow's hierarchy, *self-actualization* is the highest and most difficult level of needs to achieve. This level is about self-fulfillment, attainment of true harmony, and realization of our unique potential. Communication helps us meet this need by fostering growth and self-expression, and by challenging our perceptions. It is often through our experiences with others that we gain insight into ourselves. Others may see hidden talents and strengths of which we are unaware and point these out to us. A co-worker may notice how good Casey is at calming down victims or perpetrators and may see this as a strength. Casey might have been unaware of this unique skill and might have missed a chance to become involved in victim services later in her career. As we grow and trust in a relationship, we may also feel confident enough to share our dreams and goals with someone. Obviously, such communication requires support, empathy, and a nondefensive climate.

Living in a Diverse Society

Julia Wood (Wood and Henry, 2002) adds a sixth level of needs. This sixth level relies on the skills and abilities necessary to live effectively in a very diverse society. Through communication and experiences with others, we can learn about cultures, lifestyles, and philosophies that are different from our own. Casey will deal with a broad range of people as an officer, and she will need to develop skills, including communication skills, to manage people with such diverse backgrounds. To meet the needs at this level, you must learn to respect differences, including race, ethnicity, religion, sexual orientation, health practices, and so forth. Good communication skills will help you to deal with a diverse world.

For example, as a Canadian of Dutch background, Casey has learned to look at others when they speak to her. Through contact with the Asian community, however, she will learn that looking at someone in authority is disrespectful to some people. Good communication skills will help us live effectively in a diverse world. Chapter 7 explores in greater detail understanding and managing diversity in policing.

Mastering Technology in a Diverse Society

Our fast-paced and changing society requires that we have additional interpersonal skills to manage and use the rapidly changing technologies that are available to us, including the internet, and mass media and telecommunications. Technologies used in police management and operations help police with prevention, identification, investigation, management, and protection of police officers. In order to manage in this technological era, you must develop a wide array of skills to cope with advances. Casey will have to deal effectively with email, the internet, and computers. As with all new technologies, there are new terms to learn, new skills to master, and adjustments to be made in the work environment. Effectively managing stress in response to information overload and enhancements in technology is an important interpersonal skill to develop and will be addressed further in Chapter 10.

Technological advancements impact policing in other ways too. The internet has created a new wave of crime opportunities that require specialized police investigation and intervention.

IMPROVING YOUR SELF-CONCEPT AND INCREASING SELF-ESTEEM

We have looked at self-concept, self-esteem, self-presentation, and needs. How can this information help you improve your self-concept and self-esteem? Self-presentation is behaving in a way that presents who you believe you are. You also express your needs as part of who you are. If you feel you need more friends (i.e., a sense of belonging), you will need to come up with a strategy to make new friends. To do this requires some self-confidence, an understanding of yourself, and interpersonal communication skills. While you may feel good about yourself, like most people, you may have problem areas that need addressing now or in the near future. For example, you may be shy, lonely, prone to anger, or just wanting to learn more about who you are. Armed with a good self-concept and positive self-esteem, your interpersonal needs are more likely to be met in your career and personal life.

Gain Knowledge to Assist with Personal Change

With information from this chapter and other knowledge about the "self," you will be equipped to make changes. Self-assessments and self-tests from a variety of sources will help pinpoint problem areas. If you are shy, check out the shyness weblink at the end of this chapter. The internet is also a broad source of information on personal growth, health, and wellness.

Make a Firm Commitment to Change

Do you make New Year's resolutions only to break them by the second week in January? We tend to be creatures of habit, and our "self" resists change. Change only happens with firm commitment. Be determined to achieve the result you desire.

Set Realistic and Specific Goals

One of the major reasons people fail in their attempts to change is that their goals are unrealistic and unclear. If you are shy, setting a goal of meeting 20 new people soon is not only unrealistic but also unclear. How soon is soon? You may be setting yourself up for failure with unrealistic expectations. Write down your goals and revisit them regularly.

One important goal for changing your self-concept is to first accept who you are and be aware of your strengths as well as your weaknesses. What are some attributes that will make you a good police officer? Once you have those listed, think of one area of your self-concept that needs to be changed or improved. Start with a small goal that is realistic and that can be accomplished in a short span of time. For example, if one of your professors has given you feedback that during an oral presentation you kept your hands in your pockets, shuffled from foot to foot, and appeared very unprofessional, you may decide to change this nervous behaviour for the next presentation. You might ask friends and family to remind you to take your hands out of your pockets, and you might also practise 20 minutes a week, speaking in front of a mirror and maintaining a more professional pose. Accomplishing this one realistic goal will give you the self-confidence to set more difficult and long-term goals.

Solicit Support for Change

As the last example illustrated, you also need support for change. Trusted friends and family who are willing to offer feedback, ideas, and support will help you on your road to personal change. Unfortunately, not everyone will be pleased when you try to change. You may have to consciously choose people who can assist you or at least support you in your attempts. If you are trying to exercise more frequently in order to pass a fitness test, you may want to associate with people who have the same goal. Some individuals will actually try to sabotage your efforts for change—for example, the loved one who comes home with a cake when you are trying to change your eating habits.

Don't Get Easily Discouraged

Trying to make major changes in personal characteristics, behaviours, or other parts of your self-concept is an onerous task. Changing your self-concept is difficult because it requires constant effort—and it appears that the "self" resists change (Wood and Henry, 2002). We like consistency and tend to want to hold onto our self-image, even if it is a negative one. Change can be frightening, since we are never sure what its outcome may be or whether we will like that outcome.

While it is true that others may try to prevent us from changing, we are often our own worst enemy. We engage in **self-sabotage** or negative self-talk, or in other behaviours that interrupt our efforts to change. Don't let small setbacks stop your efforts. For example, say you have decided that you need to better manage your aggression while driving, as a way to better control your temper. You have three excellent trips and are calm through three traffic jams, where you were cut off several times. On your fourth trip, however, you curse and give an obscene nonverbal cue to another driver. Rather than telling yourself that you have failed, engage in positive self-talk and realize that 75 percent of the time, you have controlled your temper. Encourage rather than discourage yourself.

KEY LEARNING POINTS

Improving Your Self-Concept and Self-Esteem

- Gain knowledge to assist with personal change.
- Make a firm commitment to change.
- Set realistic and specific goals.
- Solicit support for change.
- Don't get easily discouraged.

SUMMARY

In this chapter we started to explore the self. To aid perspective, an overview of changes in policing was introduced that will continue to be explored in future chapters. We examined the "self" as a being that evolves and changes over our lives and that consists of three components: self-concept, self-esteem, and self-presentation. Through communication with others (including reflected appraisal), and by comparing ourselves with others, we discover and define who we are. Discovering who we are and having an awareness of our strengths and limitations is critical before we can effectively communicate to help others.

We communicate our needs as part of who we are. Meeting these needs helps us to grow and develop into the people we want to be in the future. Two additional areas of needs and opportunities for change were discussed: managing in the increasing diversity of our country, and coping with new technologies. Finally, we examined some strategies that will help us change our "self" if we so desire.

WEBSITES

http://ww2.heartandstroke.ca/Page.asp?PageID=24
This is the Heart and Stroke Foundation of Canada site, which provides a free newsletter and information on stress and quitting smoking.

www.shyness.com
This website is devoted to the problems of shyness and social phobia.

www.depression.com
This website offers a wealth of information on depression.

www.mindbodysoul.com
This site is devoted to the wellness of the entire person.

www.cmha.ca/bins/index.asp
The Canadian Mental Health Association offers a test for your knowledge of mind and body fitness, tips for mental health, and a newsletter.

future.sri.com/VALS/ovalshome.html
This site offers a values and lifestyles test that will categorize your personality type. Although designed for consumer information, it is an interesting test.

JOURNAL AND DISCUSSION QUESTIONS

1. Many people have a negative self-concept and poor self-esteem. What do you think are the major causes of these negative views of self? What can be done in the early developmental years to improve the self-concept and self-esteem of young children?

_____

_____

_____

_____

_____

_____

2. The new focus on community policing, emphasis on managing diversity, and increased formalized training will continue to influence how police business is carried out. What are some changes that you have witnessed in policing? What do you see as future trends in policing? Do you view these changes as positive or negative? Why?

_____

_____

_____

_____

_____

_____

3. Eating disorders such as anorexia nervosa and bulimia have been linked to distorted self-image. Those suffering from anorexia starve themselves in order to attain the perfect body, and those suffering from bulimia engage in a cycle of binge eating and purging. What do you see as some of the causes of these disorders?

_____

_____

_____

_____

_____

SKILLS PRACTICE 2-1

An Activity Using Reflected Appraisal: Who Has Been Significant in Your Life?

Take a piece of paper and make three columns. Label the first column: SIGNIFICANT OTHERS IN MY LIFE. Label the second column: WHAT THEY TOLD ME ABOUT ME. Label the third column: HOW IT AFFECTED ME. (See example below.)

One person may have told you several things about yourself that had a major impact. On the other hand, some people may have given you feedback that had little or no effect. You may be surprised by how many others have influenced you during your life.

SIGNIFICANT OTHERS	WHAT THEY TOLD ME ABOUT ME	HOW IT AFFECTED ME
Mother	*told me I was smart*	*I persist at projects*
Baseball coach	*said I was good hitter*	*I still love baseball*

SKILLS PRACTICE 2-2
Improving Your Self-Concept

1. Think about your self-concept. What is one area you would like to change or develop in yourself? Write down this goal. Why do you want to reach this goal?

_____

_____

_____

_____

_____

_____

_____

2. Identify what you need to have in place in order to achieve this goal. Do you need to gain skills or knowledge in a certain area? Are there relationships that need to be developed or abandoned to achieve this goal? Do you need to change your attitude or belief about something first?

_____

_____

_____

_____

_____

_____

_____

_____

_____

_____

_____

_____

3. Reflect on a time when you achieved a goal or when your self-esteem was enhanced. Describe how you felt and write out what your method for success was. Now imagine yourself achieving a new goal and how it will feel. How can you transfer your method for success, or parts of it, to assist you in reaching your goal? Write out how you will reach your goal.

_____

_____

_____

_____

_____

_____

_____

_____

_____

_____

_____

_____

_____

4. Take action. Keep a daily reflection journal for one month. Write about the positive progress you are making towards your goal and how it is shaping how you feel about yourself. Remember not to judge yourself, but instead look for progress in your change.

_____

_____

_____

_____

_____

_____

_____

_____

_____

_____

_____

_____

_____

SKILLS PRACTICE 2-3
My Values Statement

Just as organizations have value statements (see RCMP core values, p. 22), we should reflect on our own values. Doing so will help us identify what motivates us and shapes our communication with others. Values are those standards or qualities that we determine to be important and that guide our behaviour. List your own values. Add any new values you want to strive for. Some examples are respect, honesty, compassion, integrity, commitment to excellence, and professionalism. Write your own definition beside each value.

My Values

Value   Definition

_____

_____

_____

_____

_____

_____

_____

_____

_____

_____

New Values

Value   Definition

_____

_____

_____

_____

_____

_____

_____

_____

_____

Chapter 3

Interpersonal Communication and Perception

LEARNING OUTCOMES

After studying this chapter you should be able to:

- Define perception and interpersonal perception.
- List and explain the three stages of perception.
- Explain the impact of perception on interpersonal communication.
- Explain attribution theory.
- Describe errors, barriers, and biases in interpersonal perception and attribution.
- Identify additional factors that influence perception.
- Identify and give an example of five strategies to improve interpersonal perception.

INTRODUCTION

Pat, a police officer with a provincial service, is at the scene of a car accident. No one has been hurt, and there are two witnesses to the accident. One, a woman, was walking north with her dog, up the side of the highway facing the intersection where the accident occurred about an hour earlier. A second witness was driving behind the southbound vehicle and just narrowly missed being in the accident himself. The accident happened when one driver was attempting a left turn from a side road onto the two-lane highway and hit a car travelling south. Pat has separated the two drivers who have already had one heated exchange.

Pat is interviewing the southbound driver first. Immediately, this driver states, "I was just driving down to a friend's house for a visit when she comes right out of the road and hits me! Lousy woman driver! I'm a real careful driver, unlike that nut. I hope you take her licence!"

During the second interview, a female driver says, "He had his left turn signal on, and he was driving slowly. He was going to turn. He slowed right down, braked, and then for some reason he didn't turn. He was going slow enough that if he had braked more, he would have missed me. He's so old; he shouldn't be allowed to drive anymore! When I was talking to him, I had to yell at him just so I could be heard. These old people and their great big cars. Just look at my little beauty over there, wrecked!"

Pat then interviews the witness who was in the car following the elderly gentleman. He states, "I don't know if he had his blinker on. The sun was in my eyes. I can tell you

The officer and the person in the vehicle will have differing perceptions of each other.
Barrie City Police Service / © Lindsey Maier Inc., www.lindseymaier.com

that he was driving really slowly. I had to keep putting my brakes on so that I wouldn't rear-end him myself. He was slow-poking all the way down the highway. I don't think the old geezer knew where he was going."

The other witness states, "I thought everybody was driving too fast. The gentleman was being tailgated by that young creep there, for one thing! That would be enough to make anybody panic. If you ask me, it was his fault. The old guy did have his blinker on, but I think he was afraid to turn in case he got hit from behind. I know he was slowing down to turn, but he couldn't with that young college punk behind him. If I were you, first thing I'd do is take *his* driver's licence away!"

Obviously, Pat will have to ask many more questions in order to try to find the "truth" about what really happened here. The female driver did pull out into oncoming traffic, and this is a violation of the law. What is not known is whether the other driver's blinker was on. Was the young driver tailgating? Is it all right to pull out into traffic if the oncoming car's blinker is on and you feel the other driver is going to slow down?

All the witnesses have different stories. Are they lying? Maybe, maybe not. Each person has a different viewpoint or **perception** of the accident. These viewpoints come from differing personal perspectives of the sequence of events. For instance, what is "driving too slowly"? For some, adhering to the legal speed limit is driving too slowly. How often have you been passed by a speeding driver when you were already travelling 10 kilometres over the speed limit? How fast does a car appear to be going as it travels towards you, away from you, or past you? Also, the witnesses appear to have distorted perceptions about each other—young creep, lousy woman driver, and old geezer.

These differing perceptions will affect the interpersonal communication among these people. How will the young driver treat the older driver whom he believes is too old to drive? How do we view people we perceive as "tailgaters" and inconsiderate drivers?

As an officer, you must try to find the truth—not always an easy task. How accurate is eyewitness testimony? How accurate are your perceptions during a car accident? Does your personality affect this accuracy?

This chapter introduces the process of perception, with particular attention given to interpersonal perception and its impact on interpersonal communication. We will define perception and interpersonal perception, and examine the three parts of the perception process. Then we will pay particular attention to the processes we use in perceiving others, and discuss errors in interpersonal perception. Finally, we will explore five strategies to improve interpersonal perception in order to prevent misunderstandings.

THE PERCEPTUAL PROCESS

Perception is a process of selecting, organizing, and interpreting the information our five senses continually bombard us with (Figure 3-1). Stop reading this page for a moment and sit back and attend to as many stimuli as possible. If you are sitting in your campus library, what are you experiencing? Can you *hear* others talking, *hear* pages being turned by someone nearby, *smell* anything? What do you *see?* What does the text *feel* like? Obviously, if you paid attention to all of these stimuli, you would never complete this chapter. Our capacity for selective attention allows us to focus on some stimuli and not others.

Interpersonal perception is very similar. Through interpersonal perception we decide who a person is and interpret or give meaning to that person's actions by analyzing and reaching conclusions from incoming stimuli. We make judgments about characteristics, and like detectives, make inferences from our observations. If someone is driving too closely behind us, we label that person a tailgater, and may infer that he is rude, inconsiderate, or maybe just late for an appointment.

There are three stages in perception and in interpersonal perception: selecting, organizing, and interpreting. For purposes of study, these processes will be discussed as separate categories, but in reality, they often act together or in different order as we try to make sense out of the world.

Selecting

Selection is the first stage of the perceptual process. During this stage we select the pieces of information to which we are going to pay attention, as we cannot pay attention to everything going on around us. Our own needs, expectations, and motives affect what we see and don't see. We tend to notice things that are intense, repetitious, and attention-grabbing. Two strategies that help us select information are *categorization* and *simplification* (adapted and expanded from Beebe et al., 2004).

We use categorization to reduce the number of stimuli that demand our attention, and we do it in several ways. One way is to place stimuli in categories by **proximity**, or nearness (Baron, Earhard, and Ozier, 1995). If you see three people standing close together prior to class, you may perceive them as friends. **Similarity** is another grouping

Stage 1		Stage 2		Stage 3
SELECTION	→	ORGANIZATION	→	INTERPRETATION

Figure 3-1   Stages of the Perceptual Process

used for categorization. We tend to perceive similar items as part of a group, and these similar items share similar characteristics. Classifying all women as incompetent drivers is using the rule of similarity.

Simplification is the most overriding principle of selection. Categorizing is, in many ways, also an attempt to simplify and reduce the amount of incoming stimuli. When we simplify, we filter out information that we feel is irrelevant or unimportant. Unfortunately, we may filter out important information as well. Was the sun in the young driver's eyes, or was he simply not paying attention? When we simplify, we ignore and distort information and selectively attend to what we feel is important. In an accident, each person has a different idea about what is important (e.g., was the blinker off or on?) and how close one car was to another, and may distort the speed of the vehicles (though not intentionally).

Organizing

Once we have selected the information or stimuli, we need to organize it in some way to make it meaningful to us. We can do this using several strategies. One is to organize information into patterns that are convenient and understandable. These patterns allow for efficient storage of the information in our memory. (Stars are organized into constellations, and cities are organized into streets.) We also apply patterns in our interactions with other people, organizing stimuli into prototypes, stereotypes, scripts, and constructs.

Prototypes are knowledge structures that represent the best or clearest example of some category. For example, what comes to mind when you think of the word "grandmother"? You may envision someone with grey hair and wrinkles, who wears sensible shoes and bakes wonderful goodies. Few of us conjure up the image of a woman on a motorbike—though there are grandmothers who drive motorbikes. You probably have prototypes for a wide variety of categories, such as a good teacher, a true friend, and the ideal police officer.

Once you have placed someone into a prototype, you may automatically attribute qualities and characteristics to that person and communicate based on those attributes. If you have heard that someone is a good teacher and you pay more attention to what that person has to say, you have already made a positive evaluation without meeting that person. You may assume that this teacher cares about students, marks papers fairly, and takes time to listen to students' problems.

Obviously, using prototypes is efficient, but it can create problems. It may lead to rigid and inaccurate thinking and treating others in stereotypical ways.

Stereotypes differ from prototypes and are based on over-generalized characteristics that predict the behaviour of a person in a specific category. Stereotyping all elderly drivers as old geezers, all women as lousy drivers, and all young drivers as punks neglects the individual differences of these people. Stereotypes are often formed without any interaction with a member from that group. Not all stereotypes are negative, but many can lead to prejudice and discrimination, as in the case of racial profiling. Racial profiling, which is explained further in the Law and Justice Perspective box on p. 42, is based on stereotypical assumptions.

Scripts are a sequence of activities that we expect to encounter in our interaction with others. These scripts are guides that define what we should say and do in specific situations. As in a play, scripts simplify daily interactions, and guide and organize the sequence of activities. Each character knows what the other character is supposed to say and do. For example, you have a script that you use when you come to see a teacher during her office hours. If the door is closed, you knock and wait until the teacher says "Come in." You then open the door and continue the conversation. What if the teacher yelled, "Go away"? Such a response does not follow the usual script and would leave most of us bewildered.

There are scripts that govern dating, going out with friends, greeting casual acquaintances, and other daily situations. Problems in communication may result when someone does not follow a script. What happens and how do we feel when the lines are not followed in the "play," as when the teacher yelled at you to go away? Try Skills Practice 3-1 on p. 53 to test your knowledge of some of these social scripts.

Another way that we organize our perceptions of others is by creating a set of specific qualities or **constructs**. Constructs are a set of qualities that are polarized, or opposites of each other, such as good and bad, cold and warm. **Personal constructs** are specific qualities by which we categorize people into one of two groups of polar opposites: friendly or unfriendly, intelligent or unintelligent, extrovert or introvert, funny or serious, and so on.

Cognitive complexity refers to your ability to develop a wide and varied set of personal constructs. People with high cognitive complexity are more flexible in their interpretation of complicated information, may have more constructs, and are better able to integrate new information into their constructs. People with lower cognitive complexity have difficulty understanding information that does not fit easily into a previous construct (Wood and Henry, 2002). The more information you have about someone and the more cognitively complex you are, the better you are able to interpret that person's messages and behaviour.

Closure fills in missing pieces or gaps of incoming information. When we have an incomplete picture of another person, we fill in the gaps based on information that we currently have available. We may do this based upon how a person is dressed, how that person speaks, her age, or any other relevant information. An unkempt individual who shows up for a sales job interview will probably arouse many other ideas.

KEY LEARNING POINTS

We organize stimuli into:

- Prototypes—knowledge structures that represent the best or clearest example of some category
- Stereotypes—based on over-generalized characteristics that predict the behaviour of the person in a specific category
- Scripts—sequences of activities that we expect in our interaction with others
- Constructs—sets of qualities that are polarized, or opposites of each other

Interpreting

The third stage of perception is interpreting. Once we have selected and organized the stimuli, we are ready to give the information meaning. Interpreting is a subjective process. Based on how we were raised, and on past experiences and knowledge, we now attribute meaning to the experience or stimuli and create unique meanings and interpretations that will help us explain why things happen and people act the way they do. We apply impression formation, implicit personality theory, and attribution theory to help us interpret our perceptions.

If the elderly man in our example appears confused and disoriented and cannot remember if his blinker was off or on or which friend he was going to visit, Pat may use more discretion deciding whether he will charge the other driver with an offence. Pat may have experience with elderly drivers who have lost their way or who have become disoriented due to illness. Past experience will influence how Pat interprets this case. It is important to mention that, because the process of interpretation is subjective, we can make errors when we attribute meaning to an experience or stimuli. Errors and bias are discussed further in this chapter.

LAW AND JUSTICE PERSPECTIVE

What is Racial Profiling?

Racial profiling is a regular topic in the Canadian media. We have all heard stories about some member of a minority ethnic group who has been singled out at a border crossing or pulled over by police for no apparent reason. According to a May 26, 2005, CBC News Online article on racial profiling, "Anecdotal evidence and many surveys in ethnic communities have revealed a deeply held perception that members of some racial groups are singled out for special attention from authorities."

Racial profiling is a form of racial stereotyping. "As racial stereotyping and discrimination exist in society, it also exists in institutions such as law enforcement agencies, the education system, the criminal justice system, etc., which are a microcosm of broader society" (Ontario Human Rights Commission, December 29, 2005).

Racial profiling is defined by the Ontario Human Rights Commission (December 29, 2005) as "any action undertaken for reasons of safety, security or public protection, that relies on stereotypes about race, colour, ethnicity, ancestry, religion or place of origin, or a combination of these, rather than on reasonable suspicion, to single out an individual for greater scrutiny or different treatment." Stereotyping becomes a particular concern when people act on their stereotypical views in a way that affects others—leading to profiling.

Sources: "Racial profiling," May 26, 2005, CBC News Online article retrieved December 29, 2005, from www.cbc.ca/news/background/racial_profiling/.

"What is racial profiling?" and "The existence of racial profiling," December 29, 2005, Ontario Human Rights Commission, retrieved December 29, 2005, from www.ohrc.on.ca/english/consultations/racial-profiling-report-fact1.shtml.

Impression Formation

As we interact and communicate with others, we form an overall impression of their personalities. We gather information to attribute specific characteristics, and based on these characteristics, assign other characteristics that fit with that impression. This is known as **impression formation**. However, research has indicated that not all characteristics are given the same weight, and that once we have identified some characteristics, we fill in the blanks with our own ideas about individuals' other characteristics (Alcock, Carment, and Sadava, 2005). Classic experiments have demonstrated that we assign some characteristics or traits more importance than others (Asch, 1946; Kelley, 1950). These more heavily weighted traits are referred to as **central traits** because they appear to be related to a wide range of other traits. Traits that do not have these wide relationships are referred to as **peripheral traits**. In Kelley's experiment (1950), the central traits of "warm" and "cold" were varied and assigned to a guest lecturer (who, in reality, was part of the experiment). The "cold" lecturer was rated as more unsociable, unpopular, and humourless, compared to the "warm" lecturer. In reality, the lectures and the lecturer were identical. The difference was that during one introduction he was described as "cold" and in the other introduction he was described as "warm." We fill in the blanks—also part of implicit personality theory.

Implicit Personality Theory

Implicit personality theory overlaps with impression formation. With impression formation, we derive an overall impression of a person. Using implicit personality theory, we assign a pattern of characteristics to a person. As with the processes of closure and impression formation discussed earlier, we fill in the blanks from our past experiences and knowledge. Using the example of the lecturer, think about what other characteristics a "warm" person has. Is he happy, friendly, outgoing, honest, caring, annoying, or nosey? Chances are, you would not assign the last two characteristics, as they do not fit the personality of a "warm" person.

Assigning characteristics leads to the **halo effect** (Beebe et al., 2004). If we like someone and have formed a positive impression, this impression leads to assigning other positive characteristics. We all know this from training to conduct a successful interview. We present ourselves in the best way possible so that we make a good first impression. Once we have demonstrated a few positive traits and abilities, we hope that these traits spill over into the assignment of other positive traits that eventually land us the job.

The opposite of the halo effect is the **horn effect**. If we attribute negative characteristics to an individual and decide we do not like that person, we will then assign other negative traits to the individual. If the elderly driver hates women drivers, he will probably not describe the woman in the accident in glowing terms.

Attribution Theory

Attribution is the process by which we attempt to identify the causes of another person's behaviour (as well as our own behaviour), and it is central in interpersonal perception (Feldman, 1998). As we interact with others, we try to figure out who they are—their personal qualities and characteristics, their likes and dislikes, their attitudes and ideas about significant events, their beliefs and values. Psychologists and researchers have come up with several models to help us understand attribution.

One model by Kelley (1972) is concerned with identifying the cause of behaviour in social interaction. Three variables—distinctiveness, consensus, and consistency—are examined to arrive at a cause of behaviour. We will not go into great detail with this theory, but will point out a few important details that have direct bearing on interpersonal communication and perception.

First, we may look at the actor (the person performing the behaviour of interest) and examine whether this behaviour is unusual or *distinctive* for this individual. For instance, if the elderly driver in our example has a history of excellent driving and this is his first questionable involvement in an accident (high distinctiveness), Pat may attribute his slow driving to an external cause (fear of a young driver following too closely). If the witnesses agree, or have a high **consensus**, that the young driver was tailgating, Pat would have more evidence that the elderly driver was afraid of the tailgating, which caused him not to turn. *Consistency* refers to an individual reacting to a person the same way over time. For our example, Pat may not have any consistent data from witnesses. Pat may be able to ask the elderly driver if he had been tailgated before and how he reacted in the past to such an experience, but doing so may not shed light on this situation.

A second model is Weiner's theory of achievement attributions (1974, 1980). Weiner was concerned with the way we label our social experiences as either successes or failures, and suggested a three-step process (Alcock, Carment and Sadava, 2005). First, we look at the success or failure according to the dimensions of *internal* factors (caused by something inside of the person) or *external* factors (caused by something in the situation). Secondly, we decide if this cause is *stable* (occurs over and over again) or *unstable* (a one-time event). Thirdly, we determine whether the occurrence was under the *control* of or caused by the person who succeeded or failed. According to this theory, for example, if Pat finds out the young driver has a record of dangerous driving, several accidents, and a history of road rage, the young driver's behaviour (tailgating) is internal, stable, and under his own control. We might conclude that he is a dangerous driver who fails to control his behaviour—and was the cause of the accident.

Weiner's theory has some interesting applications to behaviours that we decide are or are not the fault of an individual—for example, alcohol addiction. If we view alcoholism as a disease, we may feel that a woman who suffers from it is not at fault and cannot help herself (internal, stable, out of individual control). We may treat her very differently, however, if we believe this behaviour is her own fault (internal, stable, within individual control). If we feel the latter is true, we may feel that she is weak and that she could, with a little effort, control this addiction. Other behaviours can be examined using this idea of fault or blame, including depression or other mental illnesses, and other addictions such as smoking cigarettes. Are smokers just weak-minded people who fail to control their own behaviour or do they suffer from a physical addiction that they cannot control? To what would you attribute this behaviour?

Errors and Biases in Perception and Attribution

Now that we have explored how the processes of perception, interpersonal perception, and attribution occur, we can identify the errors and barriers that interfere with accurate interpersonal perception of others. It is important to understand that attribution is not an infallible process because we do make errors and may be biased in our interpretation of events. We will first examine errors and barriers in perception, and then errors in attribution.

Errors in Selecting

One common error in selecting is that *we pay attention to what is obvious and ignore other details.* Information that is easy to pay attention to (remember selective attention) is given more weight than information that is difficult to access or understand. For example, appearance is easy to select for attention. If we see someone dressed a certain way, we arrive at conclusions and organize and interpret with this small amount of information. We use age, gender, affiliation with certain organizations, career choice, and recreational activities to make guesses about what a person is like. For example, if you learn that your new classmate is a police officer, you might make some attributions about his personality, depending upon what you think about police officers.

Part of selection is simplification, but *over-simplification* leads to errors in perception. Simple information makes conclusions easier. Even though behaviours are complex and people may behave a certain way for a multitude of reasons, we prefer simple explanations. As a police officer, you do not want the details of a crime suspect's family life and hardships; you want to know whether she is guilty.

Errors in Organizing

Stereotyping also occurs as we *organize* information into discreet categories such as good and bad, nice and not-so-nice, or other polarized groupings. Organizing information into categories also leads to imposing consistency on another person's behaviours. Once a person has responded in a certain way to something, we expect this behaviour to repeat itself. If you thank someone profusely for a birthday gift you do not like, such as a specific type of candy, don't be surprised to see it presented to you again and again for every birthday or special occasion.

We also select and organize information that fits our *prototypes* and *other preconceived notions.* If you think that police officers use excessive force too often, you may notice newspaper articles that illustrate this idea—and fail to notice articles of police heroism and acts of kindness. Sometimes we select information that fits with our preconceived notions, and ignore or dismiss information that does not fit with those ideas.

Stereotyping and categorizing also lead to poor perception. Labelling people and putting them into categories ignores individual differences, leading to the assumption that all people in this category act the same way, which in turn leads to over-generalizing and assuming similarities that are not really there. If you introduced yourself as a police officer to someone who said, "Oh, so you're one of those guys who like to beat up on the public," how would you feel?

First impressions do matter and often lead us to categorize an individual's behaviour so that it will fit with our early impressions of that individual. (Later we will discuss behaviour in the context of early impressions.) If a new employee is late the first day of work, we may fit that employee's later behaviour into the early impression that he does not care about work. What if the next week the employee accidentally breaks something at work? And what if the week after that the employee has to leave work early for a medical appointment? We tend to cling to first impressions, so it is important to monitor this and keep an open mind.

Errors in Interpreting and Attribution

When we make attributions, we are interpreting behaviour and deciding whether a person is behaving in a certain way due to internal dispositions or is responding to the external situation. Making attributions as a way to interpret information also has a number of problems and barriers. There is a great deal of information on different attribution errors, and each one has been dealt with separately.

The Fundamental Attribution Error When explaining another person's behaviour, we tend to overestimate a person's dispositional attributions and underestimate the situational attributions. This **fundamental attribution error** leads us to assign more internal causes, such as the personality characteristics of the individual, to behaviour. If a car is following us too closely, we may assign to the driver characteristics such as rude, inconsiderate, and irrational. We may ignore possible situational causes, not considering that perhaps the person is rushing to the hospital after hearing unpleasant news about a loved one. For more information on "road rage" see the Canadian Perspective feature that follows.

CANADIAN PERSPECTIVE

"Road Rage"—Misplaced Anger?

Open up any paper in Canada or any other country and you will find articles about aggressive and dangerous driving. "Road rage" (a term coined in the United States) appears to be increasing everywhere. Recent newspaper and magazine articles about road rage describe stabbings (Brampton, week of December 24, 2005), and dangerous tailgating by an off-duty police officer (Cobourg, week of January 11, 1999). According to the National Traffic Safety Administration in the United States, approximately 66 percent of traffic fatalities are caused by aggressive driving behaviour. It appears that aggressive driving is on the upswing (State Farm Insurance).

An article by the Automobile Association Driver Education Foundation (AADEF) of New Zealand explains that one of the causes of road rage is the erroneous perception that another person is driving aggressively. We may feel or perceive that another driver is invading the personal space of which our car is an extension—the bubble that we keep around us to mark our territory. Since the territory expands to the space around our vehicle, we may feel anger if another vehicle cuts in, and this may lead to a defensive response such as flashing our lights, tailgating (invading the other's space), following or chasing the car, or even more aggressive behaviour. According to the AADEF article, the driver's mood also plays a part, and the driver may displace her mood onto the event.

A survey reported in this article states that 90 percent of polled motorists had experienced road rage incidents, and 60 percent admitted to losing their temper behind the wheel (Joint, AADEF).

It appears then that road rage may be the result of a misperception or a misattribution by one driver of the other driver's motives. We label the offending driver as inconsiderate or dangerous, and we respond in some manner to indicate our opinion of his behaviour. We may also displace our bad moods onto often-innocent drivers. For example, the so-called offenders are sometimes not even aware of the behaviour that precipitated the attack. Two other factors seem to be important: there are more drivers on the road, and they spend more time—well over 40 hours a year in large cities—in traffic jams. Bad moods, flaring tempers, long and irritating waits, invasion of territory, and misunderstood intentions all seem to be factors in this aggression.

If you think you might be guilty of road rage, you can take an excellent survey found on the internet (see source below). Do you race with other drivers? Do you curse at other drivers? Do you brake suddenly to punish a tailgater? If you responded "Yes" to any of these questions, you may want to take the full test. And if you identify yourself as a potential "road rager," visit other weblinks to learn how to manage this stress.

Some simple tips are:

- Do not take poor driving incidents personally. The other driver may be unaware of what she did.

- Don't misattribute the situation or characteristics of the other driver.

- Stay calm in traffic jams and slow-moving traffic. Play relaxing music.

- Practise stress management techniques such as deep breathing.

All of these strategies will help to get you where you are going safely.

Sources: Adapted from Peel Regional Police Service media releases media archives, www.micro.newswire.ca/release.cgi?rkey=1312243791&view=62804-2&Start=160, and www.micro.newswire.ca/62804-2.html?Start=160. Retrieved December 28, 2005.

"Road rage on the rise," December 29, 2005, www.esurance.com/safe_auto_insurance/roadrage.asp).

"Are you an aggressive driver?" Road Rage Test, based on a driver stress test by Dr. John Larson, Institute for Stress Medicine, Norwalk, CT, 1998.

Matthew Joint, MSc, BSc, MCIT. *Road Rage*, The Automobile Association Driver Education Foundation, January 21, 1999. www.aadef.co.nz/roadrage.htm.

Actor-Versus-Observer Bias While we tend to believe the behaviour of others is caused by personality (internal), we tend to believe our own behaviour is caused by situational factors (external). This tendency is referred to as **actor-versus-observer bias**. Not only do we try to figure out why others behave the way they do, we also try to figure out why we behave in certain ways. While we use the fundamental attribution error for others and *overestimate* personal characteristics in their behaviour, we *underestimate* personal characteristics in our own behaviour. For example, if a classmate fails the next test in this course, you may attribute it to his lack of ability or motivation (internal causes). If you fail the test, you may attribute it to the unfair and hard marking of the teacher, the number of hours you have had to work recently, or to other external causes. Very rarely do we say, "Yes, I failed the test because I have a low IQ." In a car accident, we may want to blame other drivers rather than our poor driving skills. The actor-versus-observer bias may function to help us preserve our self-esteem, making it easier to identify situational (external) causes rather than our own lack of caring or selfishness (internal).

Self-Serving Bias The **self-serving bias** is a bias in self-attributions that may also help us maintain self-esteem. Using the self-serving bias we attribute success to our internal dispositions or traits and attribute failure to external factors—the weather, bad luck, or another person's characteristics—beyond our personal control. We have a tendency to judge ourselves in the most generous terms possible. For the young driver, the self-serving bias may preserve his self-esteem, making it easier for him to blame the elderly driver for driving too slowly, instead of acknowledging that he, the young driver, was knowingly tailgating.

Self-Handicapping Strategy The **self-handicapping strategy** is similar to the self-serving bias except that we set up possible external reasons for failure *prior* to the situation. If you are fearful that you may fail a test, you may tell classmates prior to the test that your boss is making you work too many hours and you couldn't find enough time to prepare. If you do fail, you have already stated the reason. On the other hand, if you pass, you can use the self-serving bias and explain the pass as a result of your great intelligence. In another example of self-handicapping, athletes will often complain about track or field conditions prior to competition.

The problem with overusing these attribution biases is that we may unduly inflate our abilities or ignore personal responsibility when we do poorly (Wood and Henry, 2002).

The Ultimate Attribution Error The **ultimate attribution error** is a combination of biases that we use to interpret the behaviour of people we like or dislike (Philipchalk, 1995). When we like someone, we believe his positive behaviour is dispositional (internal) and that his negative behaviour is caused by the situation (external). For example, your good friend has just been caught shoplifting—how do you explain this behaviour when he has never done this before? You might explain that he is having a difficult time at home (situational), stress at school (situational), or that he did it on a dare (situational). But what if someone you really dislike has been caught shoplifting? Then, according to the ultimate attribution error, you might explain her negative behaviour as dispositional and see her positive behaviour as just a response to the situation and not part of her internal disposition or character. She did it because she's sneaky (dispositional), crazy enough to think she could get away with it (dispositional), or stupid (dispositional).

In other words, we make attributions that fit how we feel about the other person, or in the case of stereotyping, how we feel about the membership group. Making attributions about others is similar to the self-serving bias with which we view our own behaviour.

Factors That Influence Our Perceptions

Some factors that influence our perceptions are discussed below, including our emotions and physiological state, the culture we were raised in, our social roles, gender, and self-concept. Each has an effect on our perceptions and shapes how we think about the world around us.

Our Emotions and Physiological State

Our emotions and physiological state influence our perceptions (DeVito, Shimoni, and Clark, 2005), as do our senses, age, health, fatigue, hunger, and biological cycles. As unique individuals, each of us experiences our five senses differently. Some of us like strong perfumes that others find intolerable. As we age, our ability to perceive life and people gets better and our health influences whether we perceive the world around us positively or negatively. When we are tired, we will perceive experiences differently and usually more negatively than we will when we are well rested. The same holds true when we have not eaten.

Our biological cycles influence our perception, and each of us has a daily cycle that puts our hormones at different levels. Think about how this applies to you. Do you prefer loud or quiet music? Are you a morning or night person? Our physiological state impacts our perceptions.

Culture

Every culture has its own way of looking at the world, and our own values, beliefs, and assumptions are shaped by the culture we are socialized in. This view of the world guides how we think, feel, act, and perceive the world around us.

Social Roles and Gender Differences

Social roles influence our self-concept and shape our perceptions. Social roles include, but are not limited to, gender roles and occupational roles. Men and women are socialized to view themselves and others differently. Likewise, because of occupational training that shaped her perceptions, a police officer may perceive an accident scene differently from a person involved in the accident.

Self-Concept

Our self-concept, personality, and self-esteem influence our interpersonal perceptions. A person with high self-esteem who feels good about himself will tend to think well of others, whereas someone with low self-esteem is likely to have a poor opinion of others (Lahey et al., 2005). Our self-concept may not only lead us to an inaccurate view of others, but also an inaccurate view (positive or negative) of ourselves.

How we think about situations and people, as well as our personal knowledge of others, affects how we select, organize, and interpret experiences. Our emotions may also affect how we explain our and other people's behaviour (as explained by attribution theory), which in turn shapes how we feel about people, other situations, or ourselves.

STRATEGIES TO IMPROVE PERCEPTION

So now that you are aware of all the errors you make in interpersonal perception, how do you go about improving your skills to make better and more accurate perceptions? Five strategies are suggested here to help you improve your skills.

Increase Your Knowledge of Perception and Attribution

Reading and understanding the material in this chapter will help you increase your knowledge of the processes of perception and attribution. Find out how others perceive you so that you can use these processes to pinpoint areas where you may need improvement.

Go Beyond First Impressions and Find the Truth

Don't rely on first impressions. Pay closer attention to people so that you notice things you didn't see with that first impression or meeting. Remember that people may be presenting themselves strategically—and this may not be an accurate representation of who they really are.

Engage in Perception Checking to Prevent Misunderstandings and Avoid Errors and Bias

Seek out more information about other people. Describe their observable behaviour as objectively as possible. Try to think of possible reasons for the person's behaviour. Check out body language, pay more attention to tone of voice, and don't ignore the small things. If you are unclear about a particular behaviour and what it means, ask about it in an appropriate way. If you are honestly seeking clarification or confirmation, most people will not react with anger. For example, if you are talking to someone and he does not appear (to you) to be listening, you may feel angry and hurt. You may want to say, "It appears that you are not listening to me. Is something wrong?" The answer may be, "I'm sorry. I'm trying to listen, but I have this awful headache."

Be Aware of Your Own Biases and Distortions

Assumptions about the behaviour of another person are almost made unconsciously. Often, we are not aware of our own biases when interacting with others. For example, if you have been raised in a culture that promotes eye contact when speaking, you may form a negative impression of someone who does not look you in the eye when speaking to you. But other cultures define eye contact as rude—and some people are just shy or withdrawn. Question and examine the assumptions you make about how other people behave. What are some stereotypes that you hold? How have you been interpreting the behaviour of someone you do not like? Are you making excuses for someone you do like?

Complete Skills Practice 3-2 on p. 54 to identify some of your own biases. Being aware of them will help you to correct them.

Become Other-Oriented by Using Empathy

To really understand someone, we have to change our own focus and try to understand "where others are coming from, to get inside their head, to see things from their perspective" (Beebe et al., 2004). Developing empathy allows us to see things from another person's perspective, to emotionally experience the world from another individual's point of view, and to show genuine concern and care for another's welfare. You do not have to agree with someone in order to empathize. Ask yourself how she is, what she is thinking, and what you need to learn to help you make an accurate analysis. Empathy is different from sympathy, and you can empathize with someone without sympathizing. Sympathy is feeling compassion for another's situation and accepting as valid the reasons for another's pain.

KEY LEARNING POINTS

Strategies to Improve Perception

- Increase your knowledge of perception and attribution.
- Go beyond first impressions and find the truth.
- Engage in perception checking to prevent misunderstandings and avoid errors and bias.
- Be aware of your own biases and distortions.
- Become other-oriented by using empathy.

SUMMARY

In this chapter we outlined the process of perception and applied it to interpersonal perception. The perceptual process includes selecting, organizing, and interpreting information or stimuli. Attribution theory was examined as a way of interpreting the behaviour of others as well as our own. Because the process of interpretation is subjective, we may make errors when we attribute meaning to an experience or stimuli.

Having discussed interpersonal perception and attribution, it is easy to see the number of barriers and problems that make perception and attribution an unscientific way of getting to know others. Perceptual barriers and attribution errors may give us false impressions about what another person is really like and may discourage us from further attempts at interpersonal communication. When we conclude that we do not like someone based on an inaccurate analysis, there will be few attempts for further communication, and any communication that does happen will be distorted by erroneous assumptions and beliefs. Additional factors, such as our physiological state, cultural and gender differences, social roles, and self-concept, influence our perception as well.

The chapter ended with a review of five strategies that will help us perceive and attribute more accurately. By applying these strategies, we can base our interaction with others more on who they really are than on an inaccurate and distorted picture of who we think they are or would like them to be.

WEBSITES

www.opp.ca
This is the home page for the Ontario Provincial Police. From this site, access is available to the *How Do We Do It* manual.

www.macleans.ca
This is the site for *Maclean's* weekly magazine. Each issue is presented, accompanied by the editor's pick of stories from past issues.

www.selfgrowth.com/articles/winnett2.html
This site features an article on empathy in communication.

www.uwinnipeg.ca/~epritch1/socperc.htm
This University of Winnipeg website examines how we see others and ourselves (social perception).

www.stresscanada.org
The site for the Canadian Institute of Stress's Hans Seyle Foundation.

JOURNAL AND DISCUSSION QUESTIONS

1. Eyewitness testimony is often very important in court cases. After reading this chapter, what do you feel about the accuracy of eyewitness testimony?

2. What are some classic stereotypes of police officers? Have these stereotypes changed? Once you are an officer, how can you go about changing some of the stereotypes the general public may hold about police officers?

3. What are some common examples of the self-serving bias? Can you think of any examples that would pertain to law enforcement? Do you think when people use excuses—such as a faulty speedometer—they are using the self-serving bias?

SKILLS PRACTICE 3-1

Designing a Script for Social Interaction (Class or Individual Activity)

Write a brief script for a daily activity. Examples could be greeting someone you know casually at the mall, going to the dentist to have your teeth cleaned, or asking a friend if he would like to go out after class for lunch. Make sure that your script includes you and another person. Share this script with another classmate, but do not give the person any lines. Simply outline the situation, saying that you are casual acquaintances who have just run into each other at the mall. Begin your lines (conversation).

Chances are that someone who has also experienced this situation several times can easily play the part without your script. Your lines may be slightly different, but there will probably be a number of similarities. Consider the influence of scripts on personal perception and interpersonal communication.

SKILLS PRACTICE 3-2

Stereotyping Exercise

It is important to learn about our own biases and stereotypes in order to change them. Complete the following sentences to get an idea of your own generalizations and stereotypes.

1. Canadians are_____

2. Woman are_____

3. Men are _____

4. Senior citizens are _____

5. Teenagers are _____

6. Lawyers are _____

7. Shy people are _____

8. People who look
me in the eye are_____

9. Attractive people are _____

10. Overweight people are_____

Now, select three of the above generalizations and try to explore why you think the way you do. What makes you think this way? Have you ever met people who proved the opposite? How might your generalizations affect the way you interact with people?

1. _____

_____

_____

_____

2. _____

_____

_____

_____

_____

_____

3. _____

_____

_____

_____

_____

_____

SKILLS PRACTICE 3-3
Perspective Shift Exercise

Try one or all of the scenarios listed below to challenge your assumptions of a particular group or profession—and perhaps to change your perspective and assist you in developing empathy.

1. Volunteer for a social service agency such as a homeless shelter, a soup kitchen, a newcomers-to-Canada group, or a women and children's shelter.

2. Spend the day with a journalist or set up an interview to see the world through her perspective.

3. Interview someone with a disability to learn what barriers or obstacles he may have had to overcome or deal with daily.

   Record your perceptions prior to the exercise and document your observations, insights, and new perceptions during and after the exercise.

PERCEPTIONS:

What did you think about _____ before?

_____

_____

_____

_____

_____

_____

_____

_____

OBSERVATIONS:

How have your perceptions changed?

_____

_____

_____

_____

_____

_____

What assumptions did you make that were inaccurate?

_____

_____

_____

_____

_____

_____

How has this exercise assisted you in developing empathy?

_____

_____

_____

_____

_____

_____

_____

_____

Chapter 4

Nonverbal Communication

After studying this chapter you should be able to:

- Define and explain the six functions of nonverbal communication.
- List and explain the six types of nonverbal communication.
- Explain four strategies to improve your interpretation of nonverbal communication.
- Define listening.
- Discuss five major barriers to effective listening.
- Explain six strategies to improve listening.

INTRODUCTION

Sarah has a new college roommate, Ming, who recently moved to Canada from China. As Sarah and Ming spend time together becoming friends, Sarah learns that the nonverbal communication between them is different. Sarah and Ming share the same Interpersonal and Group Dynamics class, and Sarah notices that Ming's nonverbal behaviour is different during interaction with the instructor. She observes that Ming does not make direct eye contact with the instructor. Sarah was raised to always look people in authority in the eye to show she was paying attention. Sarah asks Ming, "Why were you so rude to the instructor?" Ming, confused by Sarah's question, replies, "What do you mean?" Sarah responds "When the teacher was speaking to you, you did not look her directly in the eye." Ming replies, "In my culture, not looking directly in the eyes of someone in authority is a sign of respect." Sarah has learned a key element of nonverbal communication—that nonverbal behaviour varies among cultures, and reflects and is shaped by those cultures.

Interpersonal communication is much more than words. It involves a level of intimacy and self-disclosure, and through it, we manage our relationships through shared meanings and ideas. These meanings and ideas can be communicated verbally, but we communicate with much more than words. This kind of nonverbal communication uses gestures; facial and body expressions; and tone, pitch, punctuation, and volume of voice.

For law enforcement workers, paying attention to these nonverbal behaviours is critical in order to act and react effectively to potentially dangerous situations. How do you

Even on the phone, officers must be aware of nonverbal communication.
Mnjikining Police Services / © Lindsey Maier Inc., www.lindseymaier.com

know if a suspect is about to lose control or is about to attempt to flee from custody? Paying attention to cues will help you avert danger and keep your suspect in custody. As well, examining nonverbal behaviours will be of great benefit in interviews, to assess whether the individual is telling the truth, is nervous, frightened, or in some other emotional state. Similarly, you must also pay close attention to your own nonverbal behaviour and what it may be communicating to others. If you stand with your legs spread, hand on your holster, directly in front of a suspect, he may react to your aggressive posture.

In this chapter we will explore **nonverbal communication**, which is neither written nor verbal.

First, we will discuss the ways in which we use nonverbal communication. Then we will explore the types of nonverbal communication, the problems with relying on nonverbal communication, and how to improve both the sending and receiving of nonverbal signals. Finally, we will examine listening, which relies on learning both nonverbal and verbal skills. We will revisit listening in Chapter 5.

SIX FUNCTIONS OF NONVERBAL COMMUNICATION

You have probably heard the phrase "a picture is worth a thousand words." This statement highlights the power of nonverbal communication. Through nonverbal cues and signals, we communicate our emotions, agreement or disagreement, comfort level, level of intimacy, and many other things about who we are and what we believe or do not believe in our relationships. Some of these functions may be conscious—for example, the practised speaker who uses her hands to add drama to a speech. Or we may accidentally portray nervousness in an important job interview by wringing our hands or by fidgeting nervously. A hug from a friend or loved one when we are upset or sad says and does much more for us than just hearing that everything will be fine.

Nonverbal Communication Varies Among Cultures and Is Shaped by and Reflects that Culture.

Sarah is learning from her friendship with Ming that nonverbal behaviour varies between cultures and is shaped by and reflects those cultures (DeVito, Shimoni, and Clark, 2005). A nonverbal gesture in one culture may mean something totally different in another culture. It is important for police officers to be aware of differing nonverbal communication in different cultures. An officer could mistake what Ming considers a show of respect for authority (i.e., lack of direct eye contact) for a sign that Ming was hiding something. Such an assumption could lead the officer to communicate with Ming in a different way.

Nonverbal Communication Can Replace Verbal Communication

Nonverbal communication can *replace* verbal communication (Malandro and Barker, 1983). For example, you might nod your head to indicate "Yes" or "I agree with what you are saying." You can use signals at a loud party to indicate that you would like to leave. In some circumstances, an officer may not be able to speak directly to her partner and may use agreed upon signals to indicate that things are all clear or that a crisis may be developing.

Nonverbal Communication Can Emphasize Verbal Communication

To frown, talk loudly, and emphasize your words may indicate a depth of anger that simple words alone cannot illustrate to the listener—an example of how nonverbal communication can *emphasize* verbal communication (Malandro and Barker, 1983). We can also use touch to emphasize our verbal communication. When we are glad to see a friend, we may verbally express our happiness and then hug the other person, hold his hand or pat him on the shoulder. Most police officers know that a person who is very angry, who is yelling and intoxicated, requires intervention immediately to deter a physical confrontation.

Nonverbal Communication Can Contradict Verbal Communication

Nonverbal communication can also *contradict* verbal communication (Malandro and Barker, 1983). You may say to someone that you have time to talk, but if you keep looking at your watch, you indicate that you really do not have—or perhaps do not want to take—the time to talk. A friend may tell you that nothing is wrong, and yet you may pick up numerous signals that say otherwise.

Nonverbal Communication Can Regulate Verbal Communication

Have you ever started talking to someone who started talking at the same time? Often what has happened is that you failed to notice or to use nonverbal regulators. Nonverbal communication *regulates* interpersonal communication by subtle signals (Malandro and Barker, 1983). These signals include averting your eyes when you are speaking and do not want to be interrupted, and resuming eye contact to signal that it is now the other person's turn to talk. We are often not even conscious of these signals as we interact with others.

Nonverbal Communication Can Establish Relational-Level Meanings

Nonverbal communication also establishes *relational levels* with others. A **relational level of meaning** defines our identity and relationships with other people. Through nonverbal communication, three relational-level meanings are established (Mehrabian, 1981).

One relational-level meaning is *responsiveness*, or interest. Through nonverbal cues such as eye contact, body posture, spacing, and facial expressions, we can express our level of interest in another. If you walk into a restaurant and observe tables of patrons, chances are you will be able to distinguish who is interested in whom and who is just plain bored with a lunch or dinner partner. When we are interested in another person, we maintain eye contact, and may lean forward and reflect or mirror his facial expressions.

The relational-level meaning of *liking* is related to responsiveness. "Liking" refers to the positive or negative feelings that you have about another person. How can your friend tell if you like her? You indicate your feelings by smiling, by closing the physical distance between you, and by using other cultural indicators of liking. Because of gender differences, women are more likely than men to use nonverbal cues to indicate liking, tending to sit closer to others and to use more eye contact (Montgomery, 1988).

The third relational-level meaning aspect is *power*. We use nonverbal behaviours to communicate dominance. Men, more than women, are concerned about asserting dominance and control. Men use more space, use greater volume when speaking, and use more forceful gestures to assert dominance (Hall, 1987). Often, male officers have more difficulty with an angry male suspect than a female officer would, since the male suspect may not be as likely to try to assert dominance with a female officer. Many males who have been raised with the cultural assumption that females are less powerful believe that they do not have to assert such dominance in an encounter with a female officer.

GENDER DIFFERENCES IN NONVERBAL COMMUNICATION

According to a publication on interpersonal communication, men and women are socialized into different communication cultures (Wood and Henry, 2002). When children are very young, their play is often segregated and girls and boys learn very early to favour different games (Maltz and Barker, 1982). Girls tend to prefer games that rely on co-operation, sensitivity, and negotiation—games such as "house" and "school." Boys' games tend to require less negotiation and talking; the rules are clearer, as in baseball and soccer, and are often more competitive. It appears that this early socialization stays with us. Research suggests that there are distinct differences in how the two genders communicate as adults, especially if raised in a family with traditional gender roles (Aries, 1987; Beck, 1988; Tannen, 1990).

The following list outlines a few of the differences between male and female gender cultures. It is general in nature and the differences do not represent all women and men. Keep in mind that masculine and feminine roles vary between cultures and not all roles or cultures may be represented below.

Women:

- tend to use talk co-operatively to include others, to show interest, and to respond to others' needs

- tend to focus more on feelings and personal ideas and to discuss problems and maintain relationships

- are more likely to share personal feelings and secrets

- tend to touch more during communication

- require less personal space during a conversation with friends

- use more supportive verbal and nonverbal indicators of listening, such as utterances like "Uh-hmm" and head nodding

- also tend to use more eye contact (Montgomery, 1988; Roger and Nesshoever, 1987; Tannen, 1990)

- may often assume that men are not listening because men are less likely to ask personal questions, less likely to make comments, and do not tend to use utterances (Tannen, 1990)

Men:

- tend to talk more competitively in order to assert themselves, to show knowledge, to gain the upper hand, and to maintain attention on themselves

- tend to use talk to accomplish goals such as solving a problem, giving advice, or establishing their position on an issue or idea

- tend to prefer less intimate topics

We will not discuss the potential for conflict because of these different communication cultures, but you should be aware, as a professional, that men and women communicate differently.

KEY LEARNING POINTS

Six Functions of Nonverbal Communication

- Nonverbal communication varies between cultures and is shaped by and reflects those cultures.
- Nonverbal communication can replace verbal communication.
- Nonverbal communication can emphasize verbal communication.
- Nonverbal communication can contradict verbal communication.
- Nonverbal communication can regulate verbal communication.
- Nonverbal communication can establish relational-level meanings.

TYPES OF NONVERBAL COMMUNICATION

Much nonverbal behaviour is classified as nonverbal communication. We may use several types of communication at once in interpersonal communication, or we may rely on one mode or method of communication. According to Albert Mehrabian (1972), only seven percent of the meaning of a verbal message is verbal content. This means that 93 percent of what we communicate to others is through nonverbal channels (Figure 4-1). This 93 percent is broken down into nonverbal behaviours and paralanguage. Nonverbal behaviours account for 55 percent of our meaning, and include facial expressions and physical appearance, silence, body movement and gestures (**kinesics**), territory and space (**proxemics**), touch (**haptics**), time (**chronemics**), and personal objects (**artifacts**). Vocal cues are referred to as **paralanguage** and include

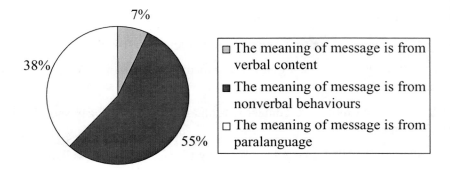

Figure 4-1   Communication of a message

voice volume, tone, pitch, and intensity. Paralanguage makes up the remaining 38 percent of communication.

In this section, we will examine types of nonverbal communication and divide them into discrete categories. Be aware, however, that nonverbal cues usually occur simultaneously. For example, an officer may feel that a suspect is lying because the suspect will not make eye contact or because she stammers, fidgets, or continuously rubs her arms. A second note of caution: much of the content below is based on North American studies that did not include cultural differences, so not all of these rules and examples will apply to all cultures.

Paralanguage

Paralanguage is communication that is vocal but that is not words. Voice volume (from whispering to shouting), tone, murmurs, gasps, sighs, rhythm, pitch, inflection, accents, sentence complexity, and how we pronounce words—these are all paralanguage. When we ask a question, we use inflection at the end of the sentence. Tactical communication relies on loud volume and inflection that indicates an order for compliance. Voices can also communicate many feelings. Sarcasm, for instance, is usually picked up because of paralanguage. For instance, saying, "Yeah, I really want to go," in a sarcastic tone conveys the opposite meaning of the words.

As a police officer, practise speaking in a professional voice that sounds firm and confident. Use correct grammar and appropriate vocabulary. Appearing frightened or unsure of what to do will undermine your credibility in the situation and might be potentially dangerous.

Nonverbal Behaviour

Facial Expressions and Eye Behaviour

The face deserves special consideration and in-depth analysis because it makes up a major part of our communication when we speak to others. Your face can assume a vast number of expressions, and much research has been devoted to its expression of emotion. According to research, the face can engage in 46 unique actions using the forehead, eyebrows, eyelids, nose, and mouth (Ekman and Friesen, 1978). It appears, however, that facial emotional expressions can be categorized into six broad categories: anger, fear, sadness, disgust, happiness, and surprise (Ekman, 1992). Obviously, since emotions occur in many combinations and occur at varying levels of intensity, we express more than these six emotions. For instance, if someone cuts you off while driving, you might be slightly annoyed—or you might suffer from road rage and produce a stream of obscenities to vent your anger. You might be happy and surprised at the same time if someone throws you a surprise birthday party.

While there is some evidence that these six themes of expression are universal, we need to be cautious when interpreting emotional expression (Carroll and Russell, 1996). A smile may not always indicate happiness; it may indicate other emotions depending upon the situation. Some people smile when they are embarrassed or when they get caught engaging in an illegal activity. You may smile because the social situation indicates that doing so is the appropriate behaviour—for instance, clapping and smiling at the end of a play you did not enjoy.

Our eyes have been called "windows of the soul," and in some respects this may be true. Eye behaviour, especially eye contact, provides a great deal of information about how we feel, and our perceptions and expectations (Nolen, 1995). Whether or not we choose to look at someone, how long we maintain eye contact, and how expressive our eyes are has a great impact on our interactions and relationships with others.

Eye contact has four functions, according to one text on interpersonal communication (Beebe et al., 2004). First, eye contact serves a *cognitive* function. Through eye contact, you can gain an understanding of another person's thought processes. For example, when someone is trying to remember a name or a place, he will glance slightly upwards to the right or left.

The second function of eye contact is to *monitor* the behaviour and reactions of others. When you are interacting with another person, you are trying to decide whether she is receptive to your message.

Third, eye contact functions as a *regulator* in communication. We use eye contact to signal when we wish to speak and when we are finished speaking. Eye contact also regulates other interactions and behaviour such as taking turns or indicating whether we want to participate in an activity. When a magician looks for a volunteer in an audience, those who do not want to be called on avert their eyes and may also use posture to say, "Please leave me alone."

As part of the regulative function, you can also learn what behaviour may occur next by observing the eyes and the direction in which they look. Before your roommate scoops the last cookie in the bag, he looks at the bag before reaching for it. Many officers have noted that when a suspect is about to flee, the suspect first glances in the direction she is going to attempt to run. A suspect may fleetingly glance at a place where weapons or other illegal goods may be hidden. And when lying, a suspect may break eye contact more often, over-sustain eye contact, or not make eye contact with the officer at all. For more information on lying, see the Law and Justice Perspective box on p. 64.

The fourth function of eye contact is an *expressive* function. The eyes and the area around the eyes are very versatile and can express a number of emotions. Eyes blink, cry, open wide, close, squint, and are an integral part of expressing feelings and their intensity. We express interest in what another person is saying by increasing eye contact, and we decrease eye contact if we are not interested. When trying to talk about something that is difficult or embarrassing, we may decrease eye contact (Knapp, 1978).

How Can You Tell When a Suspect Is Lying?

How can you tell when another person is lying to you? Is it possible to tell when someone is consciously deceiving you? Is it easier to identify lying from a stranger or from someone you know? People will lie to you, as an officer, to avoid trouble, to avoid turning in a friend, or to get someone other than themselves into trouble. Are lie detectors a valid tool for determining whether someone is lying? A great deal of research has tried to identify deliberate deception and the accuracy of lie detector tests.

Here are some *external* cues that research suggests may indicate lying:

- **basic discrepancies between various nonverbal channels** For example, a liar may manage facial expressions, but her body language may betray nervousness or tell a different story (Baron, Earhard, and Ozier, 1998).

- **variations in paralanguage, such as a rise in voice pitch, or lack of verbal fluency** (Zuckerman, Simons, and Como, 1981)

- **more sentence repairs** (Stiff et al., 1989) A liar may start a sentence, interrupt it, and then start all over again.

- **an unusually low—or high—level of eye contact** (Kleinke, 1986)

- **averting eyes before answering a question** This is often interpreted as an effort to hide something (Burgoon, Buller, and Woodall, 1989).

- **exaggerated facial expressions** (Baron, Earhard, and Ozier, 1998)

- **nervous mannerisms, such as excessive self-touching and fidgeting** Touching, scratching, and rubbing suggest emotional arousal that may be caused by lying to the officer (Baron, Earhard, and Ozier, 1998).

- **short and recurrent pauses that may signal that the liar has to be constantly thinking about what he needs to say next** (Anolli and Ciceri, 1997)

Internal responses that indicate deception are measured with polygraphs or lie detectors. Polygraphs record physiological reactions that occur during questioning. Research results are mixed regarding the accuracy of polygraphs. While many professionals believe that polygraphs are accurate, some research has indicated otherwise (Baron, Earhard, and Ozier, 1998). Under questioning, a person's nervousness or embarrassment may cause arousal that is similar to the arousal that is caused by lying. Also, people can intentionally change their level of physiological arousal (Zajonc and McIntosh, 1992). Accomplished con artists and other criminals can often control their physiological responses, just as the subjects in research have done. However, polygraph testing can be one method to detect lying and should not be ruled out as a method in crime investigation. In fact, one research report has pointed out that reviews of the reliability of polygraphs in introductory psychology texts may be negatively biased (Devitt, Honts, and Vondergreest, 1997).

Because of this ongoing debate and the question of their reliability, the results of polygraphs have not been admissible in Canadian courts since a Supreme Court ruling in 1987.

So how can you tell when someone is lying? Police veterans often rely on external indicators and use these indicators to increase questioning efforts. Also, past experience and gut-level feelings may help in the quest to find out the truth behind a crime. Since nonverbal cues and their meanings can vary between cultures and even gender, we need to be careful when interpreting others' nonverbal communication in order to ensure accuracy.

Kinesics (Body Language): Posture, Gestures, and Movement

Think back to a time when you were really happy—maybe it was the telephone call that landed you a job you really wanted. What did you do after you hung up the phone? Did you jump for joy? Your **body language** likely reflected your mood and feelings at that moment in time. Your body language can also indicate how you feel about yourself. People who walk and stand erect, hold their heads up and do not slouch appear calm and self-assured. On the other hand, people who shuffle along, slouch over and keep their heads down appear to be unsure of themselves. As with eye contact, body posture may indicate whether we wish to be involved in interaction. Students who do not want to participate in a discussion often slouch over, look down, and avoid looking at the teacher. We also use posture to let others know whether we wish to interact. We may sit slightly forward and smile to invite interaction. Flirting signals our sexual or romantic interest to a prospective partner and involves postures and other nonverbal behaviours, such as females swaying their hips and men swaying their pelvises (Rodgers, 1999). Specific postures and body movements may also be interpreted as threatening. Standing with legs apart and hands on hips, physically closing distance between yourself and someone else, suddenly standing from a sitting position, making fists, and clenching teeth are all possible signals of a physical threat. Officers will watch for these indicators and also pay close attention to any sudden and unusual movements.

Gestures are used to emphasize or replace verbal communication and are culturally determined. In North America, a thumbs-up gesture means "Great!" or "Way to go!" Making an "O" with your thumb and forefinger means "OK." Nodding your head up and down means "Yes." Holding up your middle finger is a gesture of aggressive contempt. But to illustrate the cultural determination of gestures, consider that the North American gesture for OK means a big zero in Germany, and indicates a part of female or male anatomy in Russia (Axtell, 1989).

Haptics (Touch)

Touch is the first sense we develop and is the primary way that we learn about our world. Touch can communicate the many emotions and feelings that we have about others. It can express affection, sexual interest, caring, dominance, aggression, and power. Due to the gender differences discussed earlier, women tend to touch in order to express affection, liking, and caring. They often hug other women, and young girls are more often seen holding hands in primary grades than are boys.

Some people are more "touching" than others. If you have been raised in a family where there was a lot of touching such as hugging, arm holding, and kissing, you may be comfortable doing the same. However, people raised in families that were more restrained may feel discomfort as adults with overt displays of affection. Cultural rules for touching may also lead to differing types of and comfort levels with touching. In some cultures, male friends greet each other with hugs and kisses on the cheek; most male college students in Canada would *not* do this when greeting a friend at the campus library. While North Americans use handshakes to greet each other, some cultures (for example, some Asian cultures), do not like to shake hands right away, particularly with strangers. East Asians also do not engage in interpersonal touching, and in particular, frown upon cross-sex touching in public (McDaniel and Anderson, 1998). We will discuss different cultural rules in Chapter 7.

Artifacts

Artifacts are the objects that we use to personalize our environments, to announce whom we are, and claim our space. Our personal areas are often jammed with objects that are important to us and reflect our values, ideas, and beliefs. If we value home and family, we may display pictures of family members and pets. If we are religious, we may decorate our homes and offices with religious symbols. One officer has his home office decorated with the mug shots of perpetrators he has personally helped to place behind bars. A doctor has decorated her office with pictures of the babies she has delivered. In residence, students decorate their rooms with objects from home, mementoes of their favourite bands, and other items in order to personalize an often plain room. The next time you are in the office of a teacher or other professional, see what artifacts are present and try to determine what they say about that person.

Appearance

Our appearance, physical attractiveness, and clothing send messages to others as well. Clothing is one of the most personal displays that we use to state things about ourselves to others. If you are a uniformed officer, the public will see and react to you based on your uniform. This reaction will be positive, negative, or neutral, depending upon the perception of the police at that time. Since you represent the whole police service, your unit commander will insist that your uniform be clean, pressed, and presentable at all times. Your uniformed presence is also a signal of authority and, as such, is the first level of use of force.

Chronemics

Chronemics—the way in which we perceive and use time—defines us, just as space does. We use time to define identities, interaction, and even status (Henley, 1977). In our fast-paced society, time is valued and therefore so is speed. We often talk about the fast pace of life and look for ways to manage this pace. We want faster computers, faster highways, faster food, faster drive-through banking, and so on. Being accustomed to this fast-paced lifestyle can mean frustration for Westerners who visit other cultures that do not place the same value on time and speed.

Proxemics: The Space Around Us

All of us travel in an invisible bubble that is called our personal space. Proxemics—the study of spatial communication—was pioneered by Edward T. Hall (1963). Often, we are not aware of our invisible bubble until someone gets too close or does not get close enough. In fact, many of our sayings use space to demonstrate feelings. "Get out of my face," "too close for comfort," and "get off my back" are just a few of the things we say when people overstep their boundaries in a relationship. When people we don't know get too close, we feel uncomfortable and we will attempt to increase the distance between us to feel comfortable.

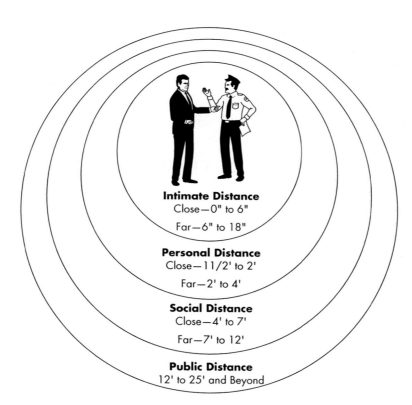

Figure 4-2   Four Interpersonal Distances
Source: Adapted from Andrew J. DuBrin and Terri Geerinck, *Human Relations for Career and Personal Success,* Third Canadian Edition, Prentice-Hall Canada Career & Technology, 2004, p. 180. Reprinted with permission of Pearson Education Canada Inc.

According to Hall, there are four interpersonal distances or circles that correspond to types of relationships: intimate, personal, social, and public (Figure 4-2).

- **Intimate Distance.** Intimate distance ranges from touching to 46 centimetres and is for close and intimate relationships where touching is important. When strangers cross over into our intimate distance, we feel threatened or very uncomfortable. For instance, in a crowded elevator we do not look at each other and we focus our eyes ahead on the floor numbers. To deliberately intimidate, we can invade the intimate space of someone else. Often, apprehending a suspect involves invading this space, and tempers can flare at this stage. Police officers are required to invade this space when handcuffing or subduing a person.

- **Personal Distance.** Within personal distance, your comfort zone is from 46 centimetres to a far range of 100 centimetres. Many of our friendly relations stay in this zone. At 46 centimetres, you can still touch a person by shaking hands or patting backs, but the zone is less intimate. The area is small enough for you to reach the person, and this zone is where the limits of physical control can be exerted. If you think a suspect may try to run, stay within this personal distance to maintain physical control without getting into the intimate area.

- **Social Distance.** Ranging from 1 metre to 4 metres, social distance is the distance where we conduct impersonal business and have less personal interaction. Conducting business across a desk is usually in this zone, and many office areas are designed to maintain this distance.

- **Public Distance.** Public distance ranges from 4 metres to 8 metres and beyond and is limited only when the speaker can no longer be heard. You will choose this as your safe distance from someone who is behaving in a bizarre manner, since this is the distance from which you can more readily flee from a situation. Stage productions, lectures, and speeches are presented at this distance.

These distances are general and are not always followed in interaction. For example, some cultures are more comfortable with closer contact. Also, as stated earlier, females are often more comfortable with touching, sitting, and standing closer together.

SKILLS FOR INTERPRETING NONVERBAL COMMUNICATION

Now that we have explored the types of nonverbal communication, how do we learn to interpret it accurately? By now, you probably realize that nonverbal communication is complex, and that because there are so many types used simultaneously, reading these messages can be difficult. Because they are symbols, nonverbal messages are often **ambiguous** and subject to interpretation based on culture, gender, age, and situation. When we look at a nonverbal signal, we interpret that signal based on how we select and organize the sensory input (remember the perceptual process from Chapter 3). Interpreting nonverbal communication relies on improving your communication in two areas: interpreting others' nonverbal messages and monitoring your own nonverbal communication. The following guidelines will help you develop the skills you need to avoid misinterpreting others' nonverbal communication and decrease the chance that others will misperceive your nonverbal messages.

Be Aware of and Monitor Your Nonverbal Communication

What nonverbal signals are you sending to the people around you? At times you may consciously control your movements, gestures, and other nonverbal messages, but you may often be unaware of what you are saying nonverbally to others. By paying closer attention to your nonverbal messages, you may become more aware of what messages you are giving others. Take a moment to try Skills Practice 4-1 on p. 76.

Seek Information to Confirm or Disconfirm Your Interpretation of Others' Nonverbal Communication

In Chapter 3 we discussed the ways we interpret others' behaviour in order to come to conclusions about their personality or dispositions. We also discussed the types of errors we make in interpreting this information. We make similar mistakes when interpreting nonverbal messages. Often, nonverbal cues are more believable than verbal ones, as we perceive that nonverbal cues are not as easily controlled. In other words, we choose what we say and may not be aware of the nonverbal aspects of the communication. Our true feelings may betray us if we attempt to hide them. A skilled observer may notice this *nonverbal leakage* (Beebe et al., 2004). To be more skilled at interpreting nonverbal messages, pay close attention to the entire body of the person with whom you're communicating. While facial expressions and eye contact are important, so are hands, feet, posture, space, and paralanguage. For example, a person may say he has calmed down after a fight, but fidgeting and a tense posture may indicate that he is not as calm as he says—and you, the officer, need to remain very alert for the possibility of further escalation.

Once you have gathered your nonverbal evidence, you need to decide if your perceptions are accurate. This is known as **perception checking**. Perception checking involves clarifying whether your initial perceptions and interpretations of another person's nonverbal behaviour are accurate. The better you know someone, the better the chances that your perception will be correct. As professionals, we may only encounter a person once, and this may lead to more inaccurate perceptions. After a car accident, a person may say she is fine. However, if you notice that she is still visibly shaking and rubbing her hands on her knees, you may want to ask again. Perception checking is done by using "I" language and asking directly, in a non-threatening and non-confrontational way. You might say, "You say that you feel fine, but I see that you are still shaking." Hearing this, she now has a chance to respond and may say, "You're right. I know I don't have any injuries. I guess it is all just sinking in." With "I" language, the key is that you *own* what you perceive to be happening and that you are tentatively checking this impression.

Sometimes you will be wrong, and the other person will then have the opportunity to tell you that you are wrong in a non-threatening way. If you feel someone is giving you the nonverbal message that she does not have time to talk, try saying something like, "I see you glancing at your watch, and I get the impression that you really do not have time to talk to me." You may be pleasantly surprised by the reply, rather than feeling rushed or having hurt feelings. The reply may be, "I don't mean to give you that impression. I really want to talk to you, but I have a meeting in five minutes. Maybe we could meet later?"

Because we do not want to appear rude or uncaring, we often reply in socially acceptable ways rather than in a totally honest way, but when given the opportunity, many of us would prefer to be honest. After interpreting or checking out another person's nonverbal communication, you can then use the corrected information to continue interacting with the other person.

Interpret Nonverbal Communication in the Right Context

In Chapter 1 we learned that interpersonal communication is conveyed through a medium within a situation or context. Where we are situated can greatly affect our nonverbal communication and change the meaning of the nonverbal communication. If someone sits beside you on a crowded bus, it does not mean the person finds you attractive and wants to get to know you. But imagine how different you would feel if you were the only person on the bus and a stranger sat next to you. We all react to the situations that we find ourselves in. Some situations, such as a dinner in a very expensive restaurant with your future in-laws, call for more formal behaviour.

Contexts may also include cultural, gender-related, and specific group norms of behaviour. If a female from Tibet does not look at you while you are talking, it may not signify boredom. If you are male, many women from Eastern cultures will not look at you when you are speaking and may not even talk unless you make a direct request for a response. Some individuals will not talk to police because of what the police were like in their country of origin. As an officer, you need to be aware that cultural views of policing do differ, and that not all police services have "to protect and serve" as their goal.

Remember Individual Differences When Interpreting Nonverbal Communication

People are individuals and may have nonverbal habits that do not necessarily mean what you would traditionally think they mean. For instance, shy people are often perceived as snobby because they are quiet and do not engage in many conversations. Someone who is shaking may not be nervous but may have Parkinson's disease. Before coming to conclusions that may be wrong, use perception checking to more fully understand why a person is communicating nonverbally in a specific way.

LISTENING

In this chapter we will explore listening, since much of listening is nonverbal. We have just explored perception checking, which relies on paying attention to nonverbal communication and then soliciting feedback on the accuracy of our perceptions. To listen effectively to someone is a skill that takes practice and the development of effective listening skills. Effective listening requires skill in both understanding nonverbal communication and in demonstrating that you have heard the other person. First, we will define listening and then examine the barriers to effective listening. Finally, we will end by discussing ways to improve listening skills.

Listening Defined

Hearing is the physiological process of sound waves entering the ear and hitting the eardrums. When we listen to someone, we are doing much more than simply hearing what he has to say. **Listening** is an active process whereby we try to understand exactly what the other person is saying and feeling. In **active listening**, we give feedback to the speaker that demonstrates that we truly are trying to understand what he is telling us. Active listening involves reflecting back to the listener the content and the feelings of the message (Devito, 2005). However, when we listen, we may not always have to engage in active listening, since we listen for a variety of reasons. We may go to a concert or listen to a favourite CD for our own enjoyment.

Another goal of listening is to gain knowledge and information, as students do in a classroom and as officers do when questioning witnesses to a crime. Active listening is more likely to take place in closer interpersonal relationships or in professional settings that involve counselling. A police officer may use active listening when interviewing a victim of violent crime or abuse, but often officers who are more fully trained in counselling skills will interview these types of clients. However, to be effective communicators in our personal and career lives, active listening is a vital skill. In this section, we will first discuss the barriers to effective listening. Next, we will explore strategies to improve our listening skills.

Barriers to Effective Listening

We are often not very good at listening to others. How many times have you misunderstood others or been misunderstood? If you are like most people, you have probably lost count. While not all the barriers to listening effectively are covered here, below are some of the main reasons we fail to listen properly to others.

- **Too much or too complex information.** At times we may be bombarded by too many messages at the same time. It can be difficult to pay attention to one message with so much else vying for our attention. A message may also be too complicated for us to understand. For instance, if you are shopping for a computer and know very little about computers, the terms "bytes" and "RAM" may be meaningless to you in the sales pitch. You may find yourself not listening to the salesperson and may even become frustrated and interrupt with your own questions. This kind of reaction ties in with the next barrier.

- **Emotions and other internal states.** Listening is hard work that requires energy from us. It is difficult to listen when you are angry, frustrated, bored, or nervous. If you become angry at the computer salesperson, you may launch in with your own questions such as, "Will it be fast on the internet?" or "Can you please explain in regular words?" When we are arguing, we have difficulty taking turns and may interrupt or internally formulate our reply. When we are angry, we may become defensive. If the computer salesperson tells us that we should know these terms as most intelligent people do, we may assume this person thinks we are stupid. We may also be thinking about other things, rather than focusing on the speaker. For example, you put on a favourite television program but start thinking about an essay you need to complete—and then you suddenly realize you have missed the first 20 minutes of the program. Other internal states such as hunger, illness, tiredness, or stress also interfere with listening effectively.

- **Prejudgment.** Sometimes we assume that we already know what the other person is talking about and feel we do not have to bother listening (Wood and Henry, 2002). If we believe that someone has nothing important to say, we do not make an effort to listen. Likewise if we do not particularly like the person, we may not listen. You may have heard negative reports about a professor, so instead of listening in class, you do other homework or sit and daydream. Having preconceived ideas about another person interferes with listening and devalues who he is as an individual.

- **Self-Centredness.** Constantly focusing communication on ourselves creates obstacles to effective listening. Self-centred communicators switch the conversation back to themselves by interrupting or telling a story similar to the speaker's story. Interrupting does not always mean a person is controlling a conversation unless the goal of interrupting is to re-focus the conversation on herself. Sometimes, however, we can show empathy by sharing a similar story to the speaker's.

Skills for Effective Listening

Being aware of the many barriers to effective listening is the first step in improving your listening skills. Rather than pseudo-listening, you can say, "I am really too tired to go over the vacation plans tonight. Could we talk about it first thing in the morning?" While you may not want to use all of the skills below, these skills will help you become a better listener. Always keep your goal in mind when listening to another person. This will help you choose the right skills.

- **Listen as if you have to write a summary of what you just heard.** If you listen as if you will have to accurately write down what you are hearing, you will increase your attention to what is being said. Such listening will sharpen your listening skills and assist you in accurate note taking as a police officer.

- **Use verbal and nonverbal feedback to demonstrate that you are listening.** When someone is telling you something that you find interesting, you can demonstrate your interest with cues. Verbally, you may say, "Wow" or "I don't believe it" or "That must have been awful" and so on. Leaning slightly towards the speaker, nodding or shaking your head, and using paralanguage also indicate that you are listening.

- **Seek clarification and ask questions when necessary.** Ask questions when you are confused or unsure about what the other person is saying, just as you would with nonverbal communication that you may not understand. Another way to seek clarification is to repeat back what you have just heard. For example, if you are interviewing a victim whose home has been broken into, you may say, "So you are saying that you saw three men running from the house when you pulled into your driveway, or was it after you got out of the car?" Often, when people are very emotional, words can come out in a rush, and you may have to help the person go over the incident several times to get the facts in order.

- **Demonstrate understanding by using empathy.** You can also demonstrate that you are listening by giving feedback on how you think the speaker is feeling. In the example above, the officer may help the victim by simply stating, "I know that you must be feeling very upset right now, so let's try to get everything straight so that we can get the facts." When we use empathy, we are trying to demonstrate that we understand the other person's perspective, which is a cornerstone of effective interpersonal communication.

- **Be aware of differences in listening styles.** Not all people listen the same way. Previously, we discussed some cultural and gender differences in nonverbal communication. These same differences also apply when listening. Women are more responsive when listening, nodding their heads and using more facial expressions than men do (Tannen, 1990). If a man does not engage in these behaviours, a woman may make the incorrect assumption that he is not listening. Similarly, in cultures such as the African Canadian community, interrupting may signal that the listener is listening (Wood and Henry, 2002). When we develop an understanding of different listening styles, we may be able to adapt accordingly if the situation warrants a change. For example, say you make a friend at college who is African Canadian and you spend a weekend with her family. You may find it comfortable to adapt to their listening style after a while, or at least learn to feel better when you get interrupted repeatedly at the dinner table with expressions like "Keep on talking" or "Way to go."

- **Use active listening if appropriate.** Active listening relies on **paraphrasing**, expressing understanding, and asking questions (Devito, Shimoni, and Clark, 2005). Paraphrasing is expressing in different words what the speaker has just said. Often when someone is upset, you want to launch into advice about how he should manage the situation. Instead, paraphrasing reflects back what you understand his thoughts and feelings to be. These paraphrases are worded tentatively so that he can correct, if necessary.

When you *express understanding*, you reflect back the feeling content of the message as well. For example, your friend has just had her home broken into and vandalized and has called you because she is very distraught about the incident. After she tells you about it, you say, "It sounds like you are very angry about being vandalized like this." She now has a chance to clarify and elaborate. Her reply may be, "I'm more than angry. I feel violated. The vandalism wasn't necessary. Why didn't they just take any stuff they wanted and leave?"

The third step of active listening is to *ask questions* to make sure that you understand the person's thoughts and feelings and to get additional information. Your next question might be, "So it's not just the vandalism that is upsetting you, it's the feeling of violation?" Active listening gives her the opportunity to express her thoughts and feelings and may help her clarify things in her own mind. Not all situations require active listening, but it is a good skill to have when others are upset or need to talk through an issue. If you decide to use active listening, remember that it takes time, energy, and effort. In many situations as a front line officer, active listening is not appropriate. But you may branch out into other areas of enforcement, such as victims' services and crisis intervention, or you may work in a community with few other support services, and you may be the only officer on the scene. Try Skills Practice 4-2 on p. 78 to enhance your active listening skills.

KEY LEARNING POINTS

Skills for Effective Listening

- Listen as if you have to write a summary of the content.
- Use verbal and nonverbal feedback to demonstrate listening.
- Seek clarification when necessary.
- Use empathy.
- Be aware of listening style differences.
- Use active listening in the appropriate situation.

SUMMARY

In this chapter we have explored nonverbal communication and examined the six functions of nonverbal communication. Nonverbal communication can replace, emphasize, and contradict verbal communication, and it also regulates interpersonal communication. It also establishes relational-level meanings of interest or responsiveness, liking, and power or dominance. These functions are accomplished through several categories or types of nonverbal communication, including paralanguage; facial expression and eye behaviour; body language (kinesics); touch (haptics); time use (chronemics); the things around us (artifacts); and how we use space (proxemics).

Paralanguage is any vocal expression that is not actual words. The face and eyes have significant impact in conveying how we feel in any situation.

After understanding the functions of nonverbal communication, we moved on to ways of improving our interpretation of nonverbal communication. First, we need to be aware of and monitor our own nonverbal communication. Second, rather than making assumptions, we should seek information to confirm or refute our assumptions. Third, we should interpret nonverbal communication in the right context and pay attention to the situation in which the behaviour occurs. Last, we need to remember that individual and cultural differences can change the meaning of nonverbal communication.

Although listening is not strictly a nonverbal area, it was covered at the end of the chapter. Listening is an active process of trying to understand what a person is saying. We listen for many reasons, ranging from pleasure to seeking critical information, but several barriers interfere with our ability to listen effectively. The message may be too complex, or we may be overloaded by too much information. Other barriers are more internal and include emotions and internal states, prejudgments, and self-centredness. Several techniques for improvement were presented to help you be a more effective listener. These techniques include listening as if you have to write a summary of the content; using verbal and nonverbal feedback to demonstrate that you are listening; seeking clarification when necessary; using empathy; being aware of listening style differences; and using active listening in the appropriate situation.

WEBSITES

www.culture-at-work.com/nonverbal.html
This site offers tips on nonverbal communication across cultures.

www.face-and-emotion.com/dataface/library/refroom.jsp
This site presents library articles on psychology, appearance, and behaviour of the human face.

www.members.aol.com/nonverbal2/diction1.htm
This site offers a dictionary of nonverbal terms and phrases.

http://stephan.dahl.at/nonverbal/non-verbal_communication.html
This is an article on nonverbal communication.

JOURNAL AND DISCUSSION QUESTIONS

1. What problems have you experienced in communicating with the opposite gender or with other cultures? What did you do about it?

2. According to many researchers, we spend at least half our waking time engaged in listening. If this is true and you are not a good listener, it means that you are a poor communicator 50 percent of the time. Why do you find listening so hard? What are some strategies that you are going to employ to try to improve your skill?

3. What skills do you need to develop or improve in order to become a more effective listener?

SKILLS PRACTICE 4-1

What Messages Are You Sending to Others?

For the next two or three days, identify three settings where you will be interacting with others. Use a setting where you can take notes easily (such as a class, at home watching television with your family, and so on). In these three settings, you will need to focus on your nonverbal communication more than usual and make notes about your behaviour. Try to make at least one note under each of the categories.

Setting 1:

Brief description of setting and others present:

List nonverbal behaviours that you engaged in using the following categories:

Posture:

Gestures:

Paralanguage (volume, tone, other sounds):

Eye contact and other eye behaviours:

Touching (a hug or pat on the back—done or not done):

Distance between you and others (personal, social, and so on):

Chronemics (use of time):

Setting 2:

Brief description of setting and others present:

List nonverbal behaviours that you engaged in using the following categories:

Posture:

Gestures:

Paralanguage (volume, tone, other sounds):

Eye contact and other eye behaviours:

Touching (a hug or pat on the back—done or not done):

Distance between you and others (personal, social, and so on):

Chronemics (use of time):

Setting 3:

Brief description of setting and others present:

List nonverbal behaviours that you engaged in using the following categories:

Posture:

Gestures:

Paralanguage (volume, tone, other sounds):

Eye contact and other eye behaviours:

Touching (a hug or pat on the back—done or not done):

Distance between you and others (personal, social, and so on):

Chronemics (use of time):

When you have finished all three interactions, go over your results. Did you behave differently depending upon the situation? Did you notice any behaviour that you were not aware of previously? Often, students report behaviour that surprises them, such as not being aware of the number of times they say "Umm" in a conversation. Was your behaviour interpreted correctly by the other individual(s)? Usually, we only notice misinterpretation if something does not go as planned in the interaction. Awareness of your own nonverbal behaviour is the first step in changing any behaviour that may be a problem in some situations. For instance, it may be fine to say "Umm" frequently in conversations with friends, but it may lead to a lower mark in formal class presentations. Record your observations:

SKILLS PRACTICE 4-2
Active Listening

Below are three situations. With a partner, take a turn as listener and speaker for each situation. This is an opportunity for the speaker to practise acting skills while the listener practises active listening skills. Try to incorporate at least two active listening responses to each situation.

1. A friend in his last semester is failing an essential course in the program. *I can't fail this course. If I fail, I can't do my placement. My parents will be absolutely furious with me!*

2. Your best friend has just broken up with a long-time lover (Sam can be male or female). *Out of the blue!! No warning, no discussion, just a phone call. I had no idea that Sam was so unhappy.*

3. A friend has been fired from his part-time job. *Alan is such an idiot. He calls himself a manager. I didn't do anything to deserve this. I really need the money from this job. My rent is due and I don't have enough to cover it without a full pay this week.*

When you are finished, discuss with each other what was easy and what was difficult when using active listening. In what situations is it appropriate to use active listening? In what situations is active listening inappropriate? Record your conclusions:

_____

_____

_____

_____

_____

_____

_____

_____

_____

_____

_____

_____

_____

_____

_____

_____

Chapter 5

Verbal Communication

After studying this chapter you should be able to:

- Describe four major characteristics of verbal communication.
- Identify barriers to effective verbal communication.
- Explain and differentiate between the two types of communication climate.
- Use several of the 10 strategies to improve interpersonal communication with others.

INTRODUCTION

The scenario: Two officers have been called to the home of a woman who has stated that she cannot get her drunken boyfriend to leave. As soon as the woman lets the officers in the door, her boyfriend begins a tirade of insults. Both officers notice that the man is extremely intoxicated and that the woman appears frightened as well as intoxicated. The man is standing behind his girlfriend and is swaying; when he speaks, his words are slurred. When the officers enter the room, one of them increases the space between the boyfriend and the woman.

> Boyfriend: *Here we go again! Don't you pigs have anything better to do? There must be some real crime out there somewhere.*
>
> Officer One: *Your girlfriend has made a call stating that you refuse to leave her home. I think she would feel better if you left now.*
>
> Boyfriend: *I haven't finished my drink yet. I'll go when I'm good and ready, not when YOU say so. Maybe I'll have to show the both of you who runs this place!*
>
> Officer Two: *Sir, we're not looking for a fight here. I just think your girlfriend has had enough for one night.*

Recall from what you learned in Chapter 1 that the communication process has three components: the sender, the receiver, and the situation or environment where the interaction is taking place. The sender encodes a message, transmits the message, and the receiver then decodes the information. The message is sent using both verbal and nonverbal channels, with face-to-face interaction being the richest source of information. The words we use have power, and as you learned in Chapter 1, they can influence how people feel about themselves and you. As an officer, the words that you choose when interacting with a citizen set the climate for how that citizen will respond (McKinnon, 1993). When we use words to interact, we also use nonverbal channels to communicate

This officer must choose her words carefully. She displays interest by leaning forward.
Barrie City Police Services / © Lindsey Maier Inc., www.lindseymaier.com

how we feel and to express content. As we learned in Chapter 4, the actual words comprise only seven percent of the message; the balance of the message is paralanguage and nonverbal behaviours (Mehrabian, 1972).

People react to police officers based on the verbal and nonverbal messages they receive from those officers. Uniformed officers wearing a badge and a gun are already conveying nonverbal messages of authority and control. With this in mind, officers must carefully choose how they will interact with the public. An understanding of verbal and nonverbal communication, both of which were discussed in the previous chapter, becomes essential to the effective performance of your professional duties.

Although verbal communication is emphasized in this chapter, both verbal and nonverbal communication must be addressed to gain a full understanding of this final chapter on the communication process. First, we will examine words and what they mean. We will then move on to barriers in verbal communication. Next, we will explore three types of communication climate where interaction takes place. Last, strategies to improve verbal communication will be presented to assist you in improving your verbal skills.

WORDS AND THEIR MEANINGS: CHARACTERISTICS OF WORDS

What are words? In our opening scene, the man calls the officer a "pig." Is this positive, negative, or does it have any meaning at all? Words have meaning because we give them meaning. The meaning we assign to a word can determine how we react to the person who spoke the word. In order to communicate effectively, two people must share the same meaning of a word. Let's examine some of the characteristics of words and what they can do.

Words Are Arbitrary Symbols

Words are **symbols** that represent something else, such as thoughts, concepts, or objects (Beebe et al., 2004). By themselves words have no meaning or real connection with what they idealize or represent. For example, when new things are created, we design words to symbolize what they are. New computer technology has created a whole new vocabulary for us to master with words such as "internet," "surfing," and "downloading." While many of these words are not new, new meanings have been created for them. As symbols, words obtain their meaning from the context or situation they are used in.

Because words are arbitrary, they may not mean the same thing to everyone. Being referred to as a real "hottie" may be sexually offensive to one woman, while to another it may not. Often, misunderstandings occur because the same word may have different meanings for different people. Have you ever asked a question and received an unexpected answer? It may be because of having different meanings for the words in the question.

Words Are Given Meaning within Social Groups and Cultures

The meanings of words are not always clear, and their meanings as symbols can vary from culture to culture (Beebe et al., 2004) and from group to group. In our opening scene, the word "pig" has a different meaning for the drunken boyfriend than it does for someone who may not have heard the term used to refer to a police officer. Within social groups and cultures, words are given meaning. For instance, in North America, the names of many occupations have been changed to reflect the emphasis on sexual equality. See the Canadian Perspective box below for some inclusive ways of referring to occupations.

Since words have different meanings for different groups and individuals, conflicts may arise because of different interpretations. If a teacher tells you that he expects regular attendance in his course, you may give a different meaning to the word "regular" than he does. The teacher may mean that he expects you to attend *every* class, while you believe that "regular" means *frequently, but not every class*. If the teacher mentions at the end of the course that you have demonstrated poor attendance, you may be angry because you feel that you have attended *regularly*.

CANADIAN PERSPECTIVE

Inclusive Workplace Communication

In the past, many occupations were labelled with titles that excluded the female gender. Obviously, most occupations are no longer specifically for men or women, since both sexes can perform a vast number of jobs equally well. Here are just a few of these changes:

Instead of:	Use:
waiter, waitress	server
policeman, policewoman	police officer, constable
chairman, chairwoman	chair, chairperson
cleaning woman	cleaner
stewardess	flight attendant
secretary	administrative assistant
fireman	firefighter
mankind	humankind, humans, humanity

Abstract language	Concrete language
Law enforcement personnel → Police officer → Constable John Smith, Badge # 123	

Figure 5-1   Continuum of Abstract to Concrete Language
The more specific we become in our language, the more concrete it becomes. Using specific versus abstract language in our communication reduces the potential for misunderstandings with others.

The Meaning in Words Can Be Abstract or Concrete

Words can be situated on a continuum from **abstract** to *concrete*. (Beebe et al., 2004). Words are considered concrete if they are more specific in nature. For example in Figure 5-1, "law enforcement personnel" is more abstract than "police officer." And "Constable John Smith" with a specific badge number from a specific service is more concrete than "police officer." As you will see in the section on improving verbal skills, reducing the abstract nature of communication also reduces the potential for misunderstandings.

Words Have Two Levels of Meaning

Think of the word "dentist." Although most of us know that a dentist is a person who looks after our teeth, the meaning of the word does not stop there. For many of us the word "dentist" also conjures up a host of other feelings. Some of us quake at the mere thought of "dentist"—perhaps the result of some unpleasant memories. Words can have both a literal or **denotative level of meaning** as well as a **connotative level of meaning**. The denotative meaning is the one you find in the dictionary and that is shared by a large culture. The connotative meaning is the subjective and personal level meaning of the word. The dentist's job is at the denotative level of meaning. How you feel about the dentist is at the connotative level of meaning. For many of us, the term "police officer" symbolizes safety and integrity, but for some it means brutality and prejudice. As you learned in previous chapters, connotative meanings can be shaped by our own self-esteem and our previous life experiences.

Words Can Have Power

If you have ever listened to a great speaker, you have little doubt that words can inspire us to change or to behave in certain ways. The words we choose can affect how people react to us and feel about us, and they can hurt and heal. The Law and Justice Perspective box on p. 83 discusses how words can terrorize others and have devastating effects. How we label words can affect how we react to a label. Many labels are symbols that reflect our values and attitudes, some of which take away others' individuality and group people into broad categories. To say "All cops are pigs" takes away the individual differences among officers and groups them into a negative category. The broad use of such generalizations and stereotypes can dehumanize people, leading to misunderstandings and prejudice. Think of other labels that may have negative or biased meanings and that stereotype people into categories. Calling young people "punks," elderly people "old geezers," and people who have broken the law "perps" are examples of using *loaded language* (Wood and Henry, 2002). This kind of language slants perceptions and dismisses individual differences.

We also generalize when we talk about others' behaviours. Saying "You are always late" may be an exaggeration and not reflective of true behaviour. You probably have had a similar experience, and if you are like most people, you reacted to this generalization with anger. Using this kind of "you" language with such a generalization of behaviour may lead to conflict.

LAW AND JUSTICE PERSPECTIVE

Words Have the Power to Terrorize

A recent Canadian news story about a British Columbia girl who was charged with and found guilty of uttering threats and criminal harassment demonstrates how words have the power to terrorize and have devastating effects.

In 2000, a 14-year-old girl named Dawn-Marie hanged herself after three teenage girls called her on the telephone; in her suicide note she said she believed death was her only escape from the bullies who had been threatening her. According to testimony at the trial, the girls had uttered threats like "You're dead," and had taunted and verbally tortured Dawn-Marie; one girl also admitted to physically assaulting the victim.

This story drew widespread attention across Canada, reminding us that words have the power to harm. Like the girl in the case who was found guilty of uttering threats and criminal harassment, we are accountable for the words we use. Bullying in schools and in the workplace has become a serious issue in Canada. To find out more about bullying, criminal harassment, and Canadian law, visit the websites listed at the end of this and other chapters.

Source: "B.C. girl convicted in school bullying tragedy," cbcnews.ca. Retrieved January 30, 2006, from http://www.cbc.ca/story/canada/national/2002/03/25/wesley020325.html.

BARRIERS TO EFFECTIVE VERBAL COMMUNICATION

Although we have briefly touched upon several problems with verbal communication, it is helpful to go over several of these barriers in more detail. When interpersonal communication breaks down, the problem can often be traced directly to how the two individuals were speaking to each other and what they were saying—or not saying. Here are seven barriers to effective verbal communication.

Same Words, Different Meanings

The same word can have different meanings. If you were not familiar with the use of the word "pig" to refer to a police officer, or of "old man" to refer to a parent, some conversation could be misunderstood.

Imprecision with Words

Sometimes signs or billboards are humorous because their content is unclear and so is their meaning. This sign was spotted at a highway service centre: *Cheap Food. Get Gas Here.* People assign their own meanings to words, and others do not always share the meanings or understand what those meanings are. Many people use **jargon** or abbreviations for specialized terms in their occupation. In law enforcement, we use terms such as "perp," "juvie," "snitch," "B and E," and "tact team" to refer to particular people and procedures and to abbreviate common language. While this kind of jargon may be fine to use in your professional circle, others may misunderstand it.

People who are intimate with each other also develop their own system of words, as do subgroups and cultures (Beebe et al., 2004). This system of words is referred to as a **restricted code**. In families, aspects of toiletry, hygiene, and lovemaking may all have restricted codes. Students at a college may also have restricted codes in the group that they socialize with regularly. Rather than saying, "Let's skip class and go to the pub," one group member may say to another, "Let's get down to some serious studying," thereby signalling that it may be time for a pub visit.

Making Generalizations and Using Extremes

Generalizing was mentioned earlier as a potential problem in verbal communication. Statements like "All women are poor drivers" and "All cops are pigs" deny individual differences, and such generalizations are untrue. There are poor women drivers, and there are excellent women drivers. There are officers who behave in less than exemplary ways, and there are officers who go above and beyond the call of duty.

Often when we generalize, we describe events, people, or objects using extremes. Generalizing by using extremes is referred to as **polarization**. When we use polarized language, we fail to communicate individual or subtle differences. When we polarize our perceptions and verbally describe these inaccuracies, we are on the path to conflict. Such statements as "You're either for me or against me," "You either love me or you don't," and "You're always lying to me" illustrate this type of polarized communication.

Biased and Loaded Language

The words that we choose can alter the perceptions of others and ourselves. Earlier we discussed loaded language and stereotyping. An example of loaded language is the sexist language that was once used to describe occupations. Referring to a position with a male-gender term negates the fact that women can or do perform the same job. Using biased or loaded language to refer to other cultures is also wrong. Loaded language can include emotional appeals and use language to conjure up images to make a point or to change another's perception. A political candidate dedicated to ending homelessness might refer to the "greedy rich," "the isolated and sobbing children of the streets," and "uncaring bureaucrats" rather than giving statistics, reviewing current practices, or using other less emotional tactics. Articles and advertisements in newspapers and magazines also use biased or loaded language to get your attention and convince you to buy the product.

Culture Makes a Difference

We all use symbols to communicate, though we may use them in different ways (Wood and Henry, 2002). Different cultures and groups use symbols differently as well. A culture's shared **norms** or shared expectations of how to behave may not be understood by non-members of that particular culture or group. Canadians from Italy may use more hand gestures and talk louder than Canadians of Anglo-Saxon descent. To those of Anglo-Saxon descent, the Italians' interactions may appear to be angry discussions.

In Chapter 4, we examined some of the differences in communication patterns between gender cultures. Failure to understand and to respect cultural and group differences can also create significant barriers for effective interpersonal communication.

Rigid Thinking Leads to Static Evaluation

Failure to see and adapt to change can pose a significant problem in the world of interpersonal communication. **Static evaluation** is a tendency to retain evaluations without changing them over time (Devito, 2005), rather like taking a snapshot of someone and then viewing that picture over time without incorporating the changes that take place as the person grows and changes. Realizing that time and people are not static will help you avoid the pitfalls of making a "one-shot" evaluation. For example, if you meet someone at college and become friends, and then meet that person years later after losing touch, this person will not be that same college friend. She will have changed as a result of many life experiences. You cannot assume that she still likes the same music or holds the same political views. You might say, "The last time we talked, you were voting Conservative. Whom do you support now?" Such statements allow her to show you how she's changed since you last met.

Voicing Inferences as Facts

"She is wearing blue pants" is a statement of fact. You can see the pants and the colour of the pants. However, saying "She is nervous" is an inference that you make by observing what you perceive as indicators of nervousness. **Inferences** are guesses, opinions, or ideas that you have about a person, object, or event. Inferences are not reality, and treating them as if they are reality can create barriers to communication. She may not be nervous—she may just be chilled or have a physical condition that causes her to shake or demonstrate other physical signs that can be misunderstood for nervousness. Police officers must interview witnesses carefully to uncover facts rather than accept inferences. Learning effective techniques such as perception checking (Table 5-1) to separate facts from inferences is essential to accurately interview witnesses to a crime.

Table 5-1 Indirect and Direct Perception Checking

People may feel attacked and become defensive when we make inferences or assumptions about them. This can lead to communication breakdown and increased conflict. To avoid making errors and jumping to conclusions, use the perception checking steps below (adapted from Beebe et al., 2004).

Indirect Perception Checking:

1. Passively seek additional information to confirm or refute your initial perception.
2. Ask questions and listen carefully with your mind open to the person's words.
3. Observe cues in nonverbal communication, such as eye contact and body movement. Be sensitive to cultural differences.

Direct Perception Checking:

1. Describe the behaviour you observed.
2. Describe two possible interpretations of what you perceive the behaviour meant.
3. Ask for clarification. Using tact and empathy, ask the person directly for clarification about how to interpret the behaviour from their perspective.

COMMUNICATION CLIMATES: DEFENSIVE VERSUS SUPPORTIVE

Interpersonal communication takes place within a climate that is created by the people involved in the exchange. You have most likely had the experience of feeling defensive when talking to someone. You may have felt put on guard, attacked, unimportant, inferior, and hurt. On the other hand, you have probably had experiences in which you found it easy to talk and you felt supported, encouraged, and valued as a person in your own right. The first experience took place in a defensive climate where **disconfirming responses** were made to you (Beebe et al., 2004). In this defensive climate, you may have felt devalued and may have responded similarly, resulting in a climate that was not conducive to honest interpersonal communication. The supportive climate was one where **confirming responses** were made to you (Beebe et al., 2004). In this kind of climate, people value themselves and others.

In the opening scene of this chapter, the boyfriend immediately makes the climate a defensive one by using derogatory terms and remarks. What are the differences between a supportive and defensive climate? Which types of communication foster one climate or the other? We will examine each one briefly (adapted from Beebe et al., 2004).

Describe Your Own Feelings Rather than Evaluating the Behaviour of Others

When someone calls you a name or assumes that you are similar to another person, you feel that you are being evaluated. When others evaluate you, they often use sentences that begin with or use "you." For example, saying, "Don't you pigs . . ." immediately labels the officers in unfair and negative terms. On the other hand, using descriptions from observations can also foster a more supportive climate. If you describe what you see without passing any judgment, you can keep the climate supportive. Using statements that begin with "I" is less offensive and does not lead to such a defensive climate. For example, saying "I feel hurt when you don't call to let me know you are going to be late" is much less defensive than saying "You never call when you're going to be late." Describing behaviour rather than evaluating it will lead to a more supportive exchange. "You" versus "I" language will be discussed in the next section as a method to improve communication.

Be Flexible Rather than Rigid Towards Others

Have you ever tried to argue with someone whose mind was already made up? Banging your head against a wall may be less painful! On the other hand, stating ideas as if they are not carved in stone can keep a discussion open. If you keep your discussion and your mind open and state your ideas in a provisional manner, the climate of discussion will be more supportive and open. For example, you might say, "I tend to view communication courses as essential for learning good communication skills." By using flexible statements, you are indicating that you are aware that other views, ideas, and ways to approach problems do exist. Such statements leave room for further discussion and other opinions.

Be Genuine Rather than Manipulative

When we think others are trying to manipulate us or are not being honest with us, we become defensive. If others appear to be planning what they are saying, we become suspicious of their motives. For instance, if a friend starts a conversation with you by saying, "Remember when I helped you with that essay you were having so much trouble with?" you may start to wonder what she is leading up to. On the other hand, genuine communication feels open, honest, and unrehearsed.

Solve Problems Rather than Controlling Others

When we attempt to control others, we do so by asserting that our solutions or ideas are the only acceptable ones. When we attempt to control another person this way, we are demonstrating that we feel superior, have more power, and have more rights, intelligence, and abilities than the other person. We may try to control others by pointing out what it is that we control and what they do not. For example, "I'm the one paying the bills here, so we are going to buy the stereo I want."

Communication that is problem-oriented rather than controlling helps to maintain a supportive climate. When we problem solve, we attempt to find a solution that is satisfactory to everyone involved with the issue. For example, you might say, "Why don't we take a look at both stereos and draw up a list of their respective features and choose based on that?" Regardless of who is paying for the stereo, making joint decisions as co-members of a household demonstrates respect and fosters a supportive climate. We can view differences as opportunities to reach mutually satisfactory solutions.

Empathize Rather than Remaining Detached from Others

According to Gibb (1961), when people react to us in a neutral or detached way, we become defensive with this lack of caring or concern. Using empathy demonstrates concern for other people's thoughts and feelings and fosters a more supportive climate. Empathy demonstrates acceptance of the other person, even if his opinion is contrary to your own.

Present Yourself as Equal Rather than Superior

When someone acts as if he or she is better than you are, communication between you is adversely affected. Just like someone who tries to assert control, a person who fosters a defensive climate asserts his or her superiority in a number of ways—trying to demonstrate superior knowledge, intelligence, and power. If a teacher says, "What do *you* know? You're only a student," she is trying to demonstrate that she possesses superior knowledge. What are the chances that you will have a second discussion with this teacher?

When people treat us like equals, a climate of support and mutual respect is created. If the teacher were to say instead, "That is a very interesting observation. You have taken some time to think this issue through," she would be demonstrating that your thoughts are valuable and deserve attention. You would feel more comfortable self-disclosing in this relaxed and supportive climate.

Avoid Sexist, Demeaning, and Ethnically or Racially Biased Language

As observed earlier in this chapter, our words have power and can shape our own and other people's perceptions. Words have the power to harm, and using words that reflect stereotypical attitudes, depict a group in a negative way, or demean them is disrespectful and dehumanizing. For example, words such as "policeman," "fireman," and "mankind" disregard women in the workforce—and the human race. Labels like "police officer," "firefighter," and "humankind" are gender neutral and inclusive of both sexes.

By removing demeaning language and bias from your speech, you will help confirm the value of all the individuals with whom you interact.

IMPROVING COMMUNICATION: LISTENING AND RESPONDING

Creating a supportive climate is a major step in developing a foundation for effective interpersonal communication. When we communicate with others, we engage in two processes that are intricately connected: we listen and then respond to what we assume or perceive we have heard. The person to whom we are speaking is engaged in the same process. We pay attention to nonverbal communication, verbal content, and our own thought processes and ideas.

The rest of this chapter is devoted to developing better communication skills. Many of these skills rely on both verbal and nonverbal abilities. Remember, it is not only what you say that matters, but also how you say it. Also, when studying these skills, realize that you would not use all of these skills for all situations. Depending upon the level of intimacy you wish to achieve, the purpose of the interaction, and the outcomes that you desire, you will vary the skills that you use for each encounter.

Create a Supportive Climate

So how can you create a supportive climate? Now that you know the difference between a supportive and defensive climate, you can actively work on ensuring that you create the supportive climate. Recall that a supportive climate includes *descriptive communication*, *flexibility*, *genuineness*, *problem-orientation*, *empathy*, and *equality*. Use the things you learned in the section on climate as your foundation, and then use the following suggestions to keep building the base for effective interpersonal communication.

Use "I" Language and Active Listening

We have briefly touched on "I" language versus "you" language as part of active listening and as a method of perception checking when interpreting nonverbal messages. When you use "I" language, you demonstrate that you are the owner of the statement and are accepting responsibility for your own feelings. You also demonstrate that your perception is open to reinterpretation. Often, we accuse others of making us feel certain ways. If I say, "You make me angry when you don't call to let me know you are going to be late," the statement suggests that it is you who is making me feel angry. It is your fault that I am angry. "You" language creates defensiveness.

The climate changes when we demonstrate that our feelings towards another's behaviour are our own. If I say, "I feel angry when you are late and don't call to let me know," the level of defensiveness decreases. Instead of saying, "You never give me a chance to pick out the new family car," say, "I would like an opportunity to help pick out the new car." We can use "I" language to demonstrate in a non-threatening way how we feel about another's behaviour, and demonstrate our needs in positive terms.

We can also use "I" language to check our accuracy when interpreting another's behaviour. This is the skill of active listening, and many barriers can be avoided by using it to check the accuracy of our interpretation of another's behaviours, feelings, or words.

If your roommate comes in, slams the door, throws down his books, sees you, and immediately says, "Well, I'm glad you're relaxed enough to enjoy a sandwich even though you haven't done the dishes as usual," your first reaction may be to defend yourself. But if you use "I" language instead, you may find out the true cause of the anger. Saying "I get the feeling that something is really bugging you" may be a better way to find out the real cause for the anger. After all, the door was slammed before the dirty dishes in the background were spotted.

By using "I" language, we can also check the depth and accuracy of our perception of a feeling. What if your roommate slams the door, throws down his books, and sits and turns the TV on? When you say, "Are you all right?" and the reply is "I'm just fine," you know that things are not "all right." Use "I" language to open up a dialogue: "You say that you are fine, but I still get the feeling that something is making you really angry." Only use "I" language if you really want to open the lines of communication. With people that we care about—even in a professional capacity—our goal may be to talk and find out more about the other person.

Skills Practice 5-1 on p. 98 is an exercise to help you improve your ability to use "I" language. Students often feel uncomfortable with this skill, saying that it feels phoney. But new skills often feel awkward or strange at first—and remember that you will not want to use "I" language in every situation. In many settings, "I" language would be inappropriate; for instance, when interrogating a hostile perpetrator.

Tie in your active listening skills as you use "I" language. Remember that active listening includes paraphrasing, expressing understanding, and asking questions (Devito, 2005). Review the active listening skills in Chapter 4, and use them to further your ability to communicate effectively.

Be Other-Oriented

In earlier chapters we briefly discussed being other-oriented as a skill for improving interpersonal communication. Rather than being self-focused in a conversation, we need to be able to focus on the other person's thoughts, needs, and feelings. We demonstrate other-orientation by decentring—being attentive and interested in the other person. There are several specific ways to do this (Devito, 2005; Wood and Henry, 2002; Beebe et al., 2004):

- Indicate, nonverbally and with paralanguage, that you are paying attention and listening. We enjoy talking to people who show us nonverbally that what we are saying is important. Smile, use facial expressions, and orient your body towards the speaker. As well, use paralanguage indicators such as "Uh-hmm" and "Oh" to indicate that you are listening.

- Ask the other person questions—for suggestions, opinions, and clarification. For example, asking such questions as "How do you feel about that?" and "What are your ideas to help?" and "What did you think about him reacting like that?" all encourage continued conversation from the speaker. Try to avoid "why" questions, because they can make the listener feel as though he or she is being judged—which increases defensiveness.

- Use **positive reinforcement** to help create a supportive climate with others. You can do this by encouraging people and by using praise statements during your interaction with them. Positive reinforcement rewards a desired behaviour and increases the likelihood that the behaviour will be repeated. Some people have difficulty talking, may be anxious about a topic, or may be shy or insecure. Using positive reinforcement such as "I appreciate your input" or "That's an interesting idea" encourages the speaker to participate further. Teachers of young children often positively reinforce a wrong answer to encourage the children to keep trying. An officer may use positive reinforcement with a victim who may be reluctant to speak. Even encouraging a small amount of talk may allow the officer to offer a supportive environment. You do not have to indicate that the person is right; your goal is to encourage a continued dialogue.

- Express your agreement if the situation is appropriate. You may say "You're right, that was a hard time for you," or "That's true." Making people feel that what they are saying is acceptable to you encourages continued interaction and confirms that person's right to feel his own feelings.

Use Empathy

Using empathy is part of developing a strong ability to become other-oriented. When we empathize, we understand the feelings of others and can predict how they might feel in a specific situation (Beebe et al., 2004). A friend once stated that she poured her heart out to her life partner after a particularly disturbing event at work. Her partner replied with a noncommittal "Uh-hmm," and she realized that her partner had the TV on without the sound and was watching a hockey game. When people react with neutrality, they dismiss our feelings. On the other hand, empathy demonstrates that we care enough to take the time to listen and to understand another point of view.

Demonstrate Respect

If you heard a police officer use the term "white trash" to describe a client, what would you think? Although the officer may not have meant anything negative with the use of the term, she certainly was not demonstrating respect or acceptance, and may have demonstrated a feeling of superiority. Asserting superiority over others also does not demonstrate acceptance or respect.

To demonstrate respect means to be non-judgmental in your interaction with another person. You may disagree with prostitution, but this does not preclude you from treating a suspected prostitute with respect. You may not personally believe in some of the values, beliefs, or orientations of others, but this does not limit your capability to demonstrate respect and acceptance of others.

Many citizens will respect your authority as an officer and sincerely believe and trust in the judicial system. This respect will place certain demands upon you when you are on patrol, interviewing witnesses, victims, and suspects, and when testifying in court. The Law and Justice Perspective box below discusses some tips to help you present yourself in court in a way that will maintain the respect of others.

LAW AND JUSTICE PERSPECTIVE

Presenting Yourself in Court

Part of an officer's duty is testifying in court. The courtroom can be an uncomfortable and adversarial environment. Whether you are called by the defence or by the Crown, testifying in court can be stressful and unpleasant. How you present yourself can make lasting impressions on the judge, the jury, other witnesses, lawyers, Crown attorneys,

LAW AND JUSTICE PERSPECTIVE (*Continued*)

and other onlookers in the courtroom. Captain David W. McRoberts (1993), a division commander and contributing author to many law enforcement publications, offers a few guidelines for an officer to be an "effective law enforcement witness."

- **Integrity** Don't lie. Often the testimony of an officer is given more weight and believed to be more credible than that of other witnesses. Lying puts you at risk and reflects negatively upon the whole law enforcement field.

- **Understanding** Understand your role as a witness for the defence or the Crown. Also understand that you will feel a certain amount of fear or nervousness when testifying, due to the rules of the courtroom. When you walk into the room, walk to the witness stand assertively, as you will be the focus of attention.

- **Preparation** Be as prepared as possible for courtroom testimonies.

- **Appearance** There are two separate issues regarding appearance: clothing and grooming. If you are in uniform, it should be clean and pressed. If you are out of uniform, your attire should be conservative. As part of the total package, you should also have a well-kept and groomed appearance.

- **Demeanour** Project self-confidence and positive self-esteem when you walk and with your posture. To appear unsure, arrogant, or indifferent will destroy the effectiveness of your testimony.

- **Delivery** Speak clearly, avoid "non-words" and phrases such as "Yeah," "Um," and "Well, uh...." Speak loud enough to be heard and concentrate on a smooth delivery. Stick to the facts and do not give additional information after you have given the appropriate answer.

A good performance in court will have a positive effect. It will reflect upon you the officer, upon the effectiveness of the court system, and upon the police force itself. As you read back over this list, notice that the tips include nonverbal and verbal communication skills.

Source: Captain David W. McRoberts. (1993). "Courtroom demeanor and testimony." In Ed Nowicki (Ed.). *Total Survival*, pp. 249–259. Powers Lake, WI: Performance Dimensions Publishing. Reprinted with the permission of the author and the publisher.

Don't Interrupt

How many times have you started to say something only to be interrupted? Sometimes, the interruption is legitimate—the phone rings or your two-year-old has to go to the bathroom. Often, interruptions are unnecessary. When you interrupt someone, you may be giving the impression that you believe what you have to say is more important than what someone else is currently saying. Rather than interrupting, practise listening carefully and then talking when it is your turn to speak.

Be Honest and Assert Yourself When Necessary

Many of us have difficulty being open and honest with others for any number of reasons. We might be afraid we are going to hurt someone's feelings. Maybe it is easier to give in rather than to open up for a potential conflict. We may feel someone has power over us, and we are genuinely afraid to engage in any confrontation at all. For whatever reason, being assertive can be difficult. And yet a lack of honesty may eventually erode an intimate and close relationship. Even in professional relationships, we need to be assertive and tell it like it is.

If we cannot assert ourselves, we may become **non-assertive**, letting things happen without making our feelings known or giving in to another person's requests. Or we may become **aggressive** and overbearing, pushing for what we want without concern for the feelings of others. There will be times when, as an officer, you need to be aggressive and use force. The key is to be able to choose the correct skill to match the situation. Responding assertively to others is a technique that assists you in everyday communication and is essential for conflict management.

Assertive people communicate in a direct and straightforward manner (DuBrin and Geerinck, 2004). Let's look at an example: A fellow student repeatedly borrows your notes and twice does not return the notes when exams are pending. You have decided that you will not let this student have your notes again. It is the night before a major exam, and you are studying in the library when this student approaches you. "Oh, thank goodness you're here! I need your notes right away. I missed the last two classes. I need them right now!"

> **Non-assertive response:** *Oh, okay. Here you go.*
>
> **Aggressive response:** *Forget it! Quit whining and complaining. You're an idiot and you are not touching any of my notes again.*
>
> **Assertive response:** *I will not be able to lend you my notes. I also need them to study for the test.*

To assert yourself in a conversation, maintain a straight posture, keep your body well balanced and use gestures that support your key words. Choose words that express your feelings and needs and that do not insult the other person. For example, if a classmate asks you out, you can say no in an assertive manner that should not hurt the feelings of that person. You can say, "Thank you for the invitation, but I would prefer not to go out with you." This is better than being non-assertive and going out when you don't want to, or making up an excuse for that evening—which only leaves you open to being asked again. Telling the person to get lost is aggressive and hurtful. Being open and assertive in your communication will help you keep honesty in your relations with others and have your needs met in a fair and non-manipulative way. Try Skills Practice 5-2 on p. 99 to improve your skills in assertiveness.

Use Self-Disclosure Appropriately

We have many different relationships in our lives. Some of them are close and intimate, while others are temporary, such as those in our professional lives. In Chapter 1, we examined the continuum of self-disclosure or intimacy. In some relationships, we disclose more than we do in other relationships, because of differing levels of intimacy. When communicating with others, especially in professional settings and relationships, we need to be aware of what we are telling the other person. For example, a victim of a violent crime does not need to hear about how you have apprehended such perpetrators in the past. Instead, while you interview for necessary details, concentrate on reassuring him that everything possible will be done to apprehend the suspect.

Be Accurate and Communicate Clearly

Sometimes people reply to a question incoherently. Others may use jargon or complex vocabulary that we cannot understand. When you talk to someone, speak clearly and be

Verbal Communication **93**

as accurate as possible with your choice of words, especially during a professional encounter. If you are the listener and do not understand the speaker, do not hesitate to ask for clarification. A teacher will seek to gauge student understanding, and if there is a sea of confused looks, she will backtrack and repeat the content in a different way or ask if clarification is required. You should do the same when you talk to others; if you feel you are losing your audience, ask if the message has been understood.

Make Allowances for Cultural, Gender, and Individual Differences

In Chapter 4 we discussed cultural differences that affect nonverbal communication. These same differences also have an impact on a verbal exchange. For example, East Asians do not touch as often; this does not mean they are cold and aloof. Many other Asian cultures do not engage in high levels of eye contact; this does not mean that they are not interested in the speaker. Women may engage in more touching than men.

Also, people are individuals. We grow up in different families and have unique personalities. When people are strangers to us, we can misinterpret their behaviour and what they say to us. Some people are shy and have a difficult time initiating and maintaining conversations (Hendersen and Zimbardo, 1996). Some people grow up in families where there is a lot of touching, hugging, and other verbal and nonverbal gestures of affection, while some people grow up in more reserved family atmospheres. As we meet people and get to know them in our personal and professional lives, we have to remember that these individual differences do lead to different reactions and ways of interacting in conversations. Therefore, before you become defensive or confused, take time to check out your perceptions by using active listening, seeking clarification, or asking other questions to increase your own understanding of the situation.

If you feel overwhelmed with the number of suggestions mentioned, remember that the purpose is to assist you in becoming a more effective communicator. Try adding a couple of skills to your current strategies until you feel comfortable with them. Then add a couple more. Effective communication is a learned skill. No one is a perfect communicator, but we can all learn to become better communicators through practice.

KEY LEARNING POINTS

Improving Communication

- Create a supportive climate.
- Use "I" language and active listening.
- Be other-oriented.
- Use empathy.
- Demonstrate respect.
- Don't interrupt.
- Be honest and assert yourself when necessary.
- Use self-disclosure appropriately.
- Be accurate and communicate clearly.
- Make allowances for cultural, gender, and individual differences.

SUMMARY

In this chapter we explored verbal communication, first by examining the characteristics of words. Words are arbitrary symbols that are given meaning within social groups and cultures. The meaning in words can be abstract or concrete. Words have two levels of meaning: a literal (denotative) level and a subjective (connotative) level. Words can also have power and influence how people view themselves. Therefore, we have a responsibility to be ethical in our communication and to use non-offensive, inclusive words.

We reviewed seven barriers that interfere with effective verbal communication: different meanings for words; imprecise meanings for words; generalizing and using extremes; using biased and loaded language; cultural differences; rigid thinking; and treating inferences as if they were facts.

Two communication climates were identified. The supportive climate allows for open and honest communication, whereas the defensive climate operates to destroy or impede true attempts at open and honest communication. Ways to maintain a more supportive climate were discussed. Establishing a supportive climate was the first of 10 strategies that were discussed to improve our ability to communicate more effectively with others. Other strategies are using "I" language and active listening; being other-oriented; using empathy; demonstrating respect; not interrupting; being honest and assertive; self-disclosing appropriately; being accurate and communicating clearly; and allowing for cultural and individual differences.

WEBSITES

www.shyness.com
This site contains research and information on shyness and social phobias.

www.open.gov.uk/home_off/prghome.html
This is a police site that contains information and some research on a variety of topics in social science.

www.oape.org
This is the site of the Ontario Association of Police Educators.

www.cjc-online.ca/sitemap.php
This is the Canadian Journal of Communication site.

http://pages.towson.edu/itrow/wmcomm.htm
This page presents an article on gender differences in communication, from Towson University's Institute for Teaching and Research on Women.

www.sideroad.com/Cross_Cultural_Communication/cross-cultural-communication
"Cross Cultural Communication: Basic Tips"

www.safety-council.org/info/OSH/bully-law.html
The Canada Safety Council site provides information on laws against bullies, as well as links to other related information.

www.workplaceviolence.ca/thm-bullying/discussion.html
This site will take you to "From Words to Weapons: An Anatomy of Workplace Violence in Canada."

www.workplaceviolence.ca/home.html
This is the Canadian Initiative on Workplace Violence site, with links to prevention strategies.

JOURNAL AND DISCUSSION QUESTIONS

1. What do you see as essential interpersonal skills for a police officer? Why? Which of the skills do you find the most difficult to practise? Why? Which ones are easiest for you? Why?

2. Research on shyness indicates that shyness is widespread in North America. Why can shyness be a problem in our society?

3. Identify a conversation that you have had recently that did not turn out the way you would have liked. Perhaps a conflict started or you did not get your points across as you had intended. What were the main causes of the problems in the conversation? What might you have done differently to avoid the problems?

_____

_____

_____

_____

_____

_____

_____

_____

_____

_____

_____

_____

_____

4. As an officer, many of your calls and dealings with the public will involve communicating with individuals who have been drinking. What do you view as essential skills for these types of contacts?

_____

_____

_____

_____

_____

_____

_____

_____

_____

_____

_____

_____

_____

_____

SKILLS PRACTICE 5-1
"I" Language

For the scenarios described below, reply using "I" language. Practise with a partner. The first scenario is completed for you, using two different replies. In order to become comfortable with "I" language, use sentences that begin with phrases such as "I sense...," or "I get the feeling...," or "I feel...," or "I hear...," or "I would like...." As you become more skilled, you will be able to use "I" language in more unique and individual ways. You do not have to solve the problem—just use "I" language in your reply and record your reply for reference.

Example scenario: You are home for a holiday, and your parents are delighted to see you since you have not been home for almost a year. You are very tired and are looking forward to a good rest. As soon as you walk in the door, your mother says, "Oh, we're so thrilled you're home! I have organized a family party, and we'll go visit your aunt and uncle for a couple of days, and then your dad needs help with some painting."

REPLY 1: *I'm really glad to be home too, Mom! I sense that you have a real schedule lined up for me, but I am really exhausted and looking forward to resting.*

REPLY 2: *I get the feeling that you have a real calendar of events lined up for me. I'm glad to be home, but I'm looking forward to some serious relaxing.*

1. You and your life partner have agreed to put money away every month and not to spend any major amount unless you both agree, because you are trying to save for a down payment on a house. Your partner walks in after work and says, "I can't believe my good luck!! I just bought that new stereo system that I have wanted for so long! It was on sale—only $600!"

2. At your part-time server job, your co-worker feels that you have put in very little effort on a particular night and have not helped enough with the cleaning up before closing. On your previous shift, this co-worker did very little, and you see this as payback time. The co-worker says angrily, "You're a useless good-for-nothing! I just did all the work and you did nothing! You never help out!"

SKILLS PRACTICE 5-2
Assertive Responses

Below are several statements. For each one, practise and record an assertive reply. You may want to practise with a partner who can help verify whether your responses are assertive, non-assertive, or aggressive. Tip: Remember that an assertive response makes your needs known without demeaning or belittling the other person.

1. You are at a shopping mall and are just about to leave to go pick up your friend from work. Just as you approach the exit, a person who is obviously conducting a survey approaches you and says, "Hi, my name is Jenny, and I am doing a consumer survey. It will only take a few minutes. If you would just come and sit over here, we can get started right away."

2. You are just about to approach your boss to book next Saturday off. You have worked every Saturday for three months, and your life partner is counting on you to attend a wedding for a very close friend next weekend. When your boss sees you, she says: "Great, there you are. I was just on my way to find you. We have a really big shipment coming in at the end of next week. You'll need to put in a few extra hours over and above your usual weekend time."

3. Your life partner is really excited and has asked you to join him at a concert of one of his favourite groups. You really hate this group and would prefer to have a quiet evening, but you do not mind if he goes to the concert. He says, "I'm so excited about this concert! I can't believe I actually got the tickets!"

_____

_____

_____

_____

_____

_____

_____

_____

Conflict Management and Problem-Solving Skills

LEARNING OUTCOMES

After studying this chapter you should be able to:

- Define and outline the major causes of conflict.
- Differentiate among five conflict management styles.
- Identify and compare effective and ineffective strategies for managing conflict.
- Differentiate between the processes of problem solving and decision making.
- Set effective goals to assist in problem solving and decision making.
- Explain barriers to effective decision making and problem solving in groups and teams.
- Explain the CAPRA model and PARE analysis methods of problem solving.
- Explain ways to improve decision making and problem solving in a group or team.
- Identify and define the four stages of a crisis, and explain strategies for preventing and managing a crisis.

INTRODUCTION

Situation #1: An officer has been dispatched to deal with a person who is creating a disturbance outside a small office building. When the officer arrives, he sees the person talking incoherently to himself. The person is wearing dirty clothes, is unshaven, and is acting as though he is intoxicated. The officer thinks to himself, "Another nut out on the loose." The officer gets out of his car and approaches the man.

Officer: *Hey there, how are you doing?*

Male: *Huh? You talking to me, officer?*

Officer: *Yes, I am, sir. Are you having any difficulty? You seem to be having a problem.*

Male: *I'm not having any problems. I am exercising my rights as a free man. I have every right to be on this street, and I can protest! That's legal too! These bums kicked me out of my apartment! And I'm doing something about it! I'm protesting!*

Officer: *You don't have any rights to behave this way! So move on down the street and attend to whatever other things you need to do.*

Male: *What other things? They took away my home! They don't care and you don't care either! You're just another guy out to hassle me!*

Good conflict resolution skills can lead to positive outcomes.
Sr. Constable Brad Filman, Ontario Provincial Police, Peterborough Detachment

Officer: *Calm down!*

Male: *Don't you go telling me to calm down!*

Officer: *You really need to take a few breaths here, buddy!*

Situation #2: An officer and her male partner have been called to a home where a loud party is taking place. It is just after 3 a.m. on a Tuesday night. After repeated and loud knocking, the door is finally answered by an individual who stares at the officers and is obviously intoxicated. There are voices in the background—some at shouting volume—and blaring music.

Female officer: *Excuse me, sir. We have had a report of a loud party here. We are going to have to ask that you please turn down the music and noise level.*

Male: *Oh, I'm sorry that it got so loud. I guess no one can have a good time in this neighbourhood. Probably, Ms. Busybody across the street is all upset. She's just dying to be part of the action, but I can't stand the ____! Why don't you come in and join us? Just leave that guy out here. We're low on girls to party with.*

Female officer: *Sir, I am not coming in. I am requesting that you turn the music down immediately.*

Male: *Or what? Going to bring that baboon in with you and start smashing heads? Hey fella, are you deaf or what? Got nothing to say?*

Male officer: *If you do not comply with the request, I'm afraid we will have to come in and assist you in ending this party.*

Male: *Try it!* (Attempts to fight male officer.)

After reading these two situations, can you identify what went wrong in each case—or did nothing go wrong? Both situations involve officers being called to handle disturbances, and both situations involve conflict.

Conflict is a part of life, but for many of us, conflict and managing conflict are also part of our professional lives. The very nature of police duties "requires police officers to participate in confrontational situations" (Dantzker and Mitchell, 1998). In police work, how you manage conflict can sometimes mean the difference between life and death. You are more likely than other professionals or citizens to find yourself in confrontations involving the use of force (Dantzker and Mitchell, 1998). Police officers commonly face situations involving individuals who have been drinking or who are under the influence of other drugs. They also face conflict with the public, co-workers, members of other agencies, and other law enforcement personnel—conflict which can be inconvenient and feel like just another daily hassle.

In this chapter we will look at what conflict is, its causes, conflict management styles and strategies, and how people manage conflict. We often do not manage conflict well, so it is important to improve conflict management skills.

We will also focus on decision making and problem solving in groups and teams. Teams and groups that make poor decisions or solve problems in ways that create more problems are headed for disaster. Unfortunately, innocent people sometimes pay the price for such decisions. As well, organizations can pay a high price for bad decisions by marketing products that should never have been marketed or recommending investments that never should have been made.

We will discuss how decision making and problem solving differ, and we will look at goal setting. Without being able to set good goals, you will have difficulty solving problems and making decisions in groups or on your own. In groups or on teams, decisions are made using a variety of methods.

We will also examine barriers to effective decision making and problem solving. There are many different models available to increase the effectiveness of decision making and problem solving in groups. Problem solving will be discussed as one way to manage an interpersonal conflict. We will explore a similar model that can be used when making a decision in groups. Then, several strategies will be introduced to help improve your effectiveness in problem solving and making decisions.

We will also examine crisis and crisis management. Situations can escalate very quickly into a crisis—or you may step into one already in full swing. Some crisis intervention techniques will be covered in this section.

DEFINING CONFLICT: IS CONFLICT GOOD OR BAD?

Both of the situations presented at the beginning of this chapter illustrate a conflict. **Conflict** is a condition that occurs when two sets of demands, goals, or motives are incompatible (DuBrin and Geerinck, 2004). In both situations, the police officers are interfering with the motives and goals of the two males. One male wishes to continue his protest and the other male wishes to continue his party. When people experience such differences, antagonistic or hostile relations may begin between them.

Conflict cannot be avoided. Even when we try to ignore the signs of an impending conflict, eventually we have to face it. Often we avoid conflict because we are fearful of the many negative consequences that accompany a poorly managed conflict. Prolonged conflict can lead to stress and may impair emotional and physical well-being (DuBrin and Geerinck, 2004). In conflict, we may ignore the needs of family, our profession, and society (DuBrin and Geerinck, 2004). Embroiled in conflict at work, we may be short-tempered at home and take out our professional frustrations on our family.

Unresolved or poorly resolved conflicts can lead to further problems in a relationship. An employee can make costly mistakes on the job by not paying attention and by letting his mind wander because of conflict. Violence is an extreme negative consequence of conflict at home or on the job. We have read about incidents where disgruntled employees engage in bullying, violence, or sabotage at the workplace. For more information on workplace violence, refer to the Canadian Perspective box on p. 108.

We may also hesitate to engage in conflict because of the type of family we grew up in and how conflict was managed in the home. If our family did not voice differences or voiced them in inappropriate ways, we may be unable to manage conflict when we are older. We need to realize, however, that conflict can have many positive consequences if managed constructively. When faced with conflict, we may come up with novel solutions and ideas, and new talents and abilities may emerge. We may become closer, as managing conflict may lead to a heightened understanding of others. Managed properly, conflict may be an opportunity to achieve personal and professional goals.

As future police officers, learning how to manage conflict with members of the public is an essential professional skill. Therefore, it is in your best interest to learn good conflict management skills.

CAUSES OF CONFLICT

While conflicts seem to be very individual, we can actually divide the causes of conflict into six major types. Often when we think about conflict, we think about people having heated arguments, but whatever the cause, conflict can be overt or covert. **Overt conflicts** are conflicts that are openly discussed. **Covert conflicts** are hidden. When a covert conflict occurs, people may hide their feelings and express them indirectly in a variety of ways. People may "play games" or deliberately hurt the feelings of another person when they feel angry or hurt. You may have had the experience in which an individual will not come out and tell you what the problem is directly, but expresses his discontent in more indirect ways, such as picking fights about unimportant or inconsequential things.

Although it is impossible to deal with all of the ways that covert conflict occurs, be aware it can and does happen. Eric Berne (1964) wrote a classic book on interpersonal games entitled *Games People Play*, which is well worth reading. Following are some of the major causes of conflict.

KEY LEARNING POINTS

Causes of Conflict

- Competition for limited resources
- Differences between personalities and cultures
- Different priorities and goals
- Role conflict
- The building of stone walls

Competition for Limited Resources

When there is only so much to go around and everyone wants at least part of it, conflict is bound to occur as people compete for those resources. Think of three children fighting over the last two chocolate chip cookies, adults in a business setting trying to allocate limited funding to a wide range of corporate needs, or police management trying to allocate too few officers over a wide area. Differences of opinion about allocation of limited resources may result in conflict.

Differences between Personalities and Cultures

Personality and cultural differences may also be a potential source of conflict. For instance, one police manager may be a strong supporter of crime prevention and may therefore want to assign more officers to prevention posts than another police manager does. This difference in beliefs may create conflict. In Canada, many conflicts have their roots in cultural differences and values. These conflicts become larger when entire groups adopt one attitude or belief over another.

At times, personal differences may result in a **personality clash** (DuBrin and Geerinck, 2004). A personality clash is an antagonistic relationship between two people who differ in characteristics and attributes, preferences, interests, values, and personal styles. It may be difficult for two people to work together in such an antagonistic relationship.

The type of policing style an officer adopts can be a source of conflict. American research shows that there are fundamentally different styles of policing (Greenberg and Ruback, 1982; Walsh, 1977). For instance, Greenberg and Ruback (1982) have identified four different styles: *crime fighter*, *social servant*, *law enforcer*, and *watchman*. The *crime fighter* focuses on capturing the perpetrator and does so in an authoritarian and aggressive manner. The *social servant* believes that the major part of her job is to help others. The *law enforcer* enforces the law rather than focusing on the more aggressive pursuits of the crime fighter. The *watchman* does no more than what is required and often displays an uncaring attitude. The crime fighter may not agree with much of what the social servant feels and may even be critical of the helping attitude. The social servant may disagree with the aggressiveness of the crime fighter. These different styles may sow the seeds of future conflict.

Different Priorities and Goals

In the scenarios presented at the beginning of the chapter, there are definitely differences between the priorities and the goals of the officers and the citizens. The priorities and goals of the officers are to uphold the law and maintain public peace. Both males are interfering with these goals and priorities as they have *different* priorities and goals. We may often share goals but place them in a different order of priority. A father may want his son to find a job immediately after finishing college. The son may share this goal—but not its immediacy. The son does not see finding a job as a priority, and having some fun may be higher on his priority list.

Role Conflict

Role conflict occurs when we experience two competing demands or expectations. These demands or expectations can cause internal conflict but may also create conflict between two people. On the one hand, your life partner wants you to earn good money, so you take as much overtime as you can get. Then he starts to complain that you are not home enough. So what can you do?

As an officer, do you really want to arrest the man in the first situation? He is disturbing the peace, but you may also feel sorry for him. As is often the case, you have to use discretion. Doing so may create an internal role conflict that may manifest itself in conflict with your partner or superior officer.

The Building of Stone Walls

Richard J. Mayer (1990) referred to the slow and steady growth of a conflict as the building of a stone wall. Some conflicts begin with something minor—a *pinch* that is not managed immediately or as it should be. The individual who receives the pinch starts to unconsciously gather evidence to support his viewpoint, and much of this information is distorted because of the perception of the person. In policing, this pinch could be an arrest that an individual does not feel the officer conducted properly. Incidents like this build up to become a *wall* that becomes difficult to overcome. The person who has been pinched may be unable to overcome this barrier and to have open and honest communication with the *pincher*.

In another example, a long-term stone wall may result when a police officer is praised for how she handled a situation when it was really her partner who handled the situation well. She does not mention that it is her partner who deserves the credit, and this omission becomes the minor incident or pinch. The officer who has been pinched now starts to notice other evidence that she is not honest. Before long, these two officers begin to argue, and it becomes more and more difficult for them to work together. If the officer who felt pinched had approached the other officer at the beginning, the rest of the situation might not have developed into a conflict.

CONFLICT MANAGEMENT STYLES

Regardless of the cause, we often manage conflict by relying on a particular style. A discussion of five styles or orientations will help you better understand the nature of conflict and the different ways that people handle it. Kenneth Thomas (1976) identified these styles as competitive, accommodative, compromising or sharing, collaborative, and avoidance. Each style is based on how concerned you are about satisfying your own needs and achieving your own goals, and how concerned you are about the other person's needs and goals. Figure 6-1 plots the five styles in a graph.

- **Competition.** Competition is based on the idea of **win-lose**. One party has his needs and goals met while the other party does not. There is very little concern about the other person's thoughts or feelings. People who rely on competition can be overtly aggressive and argumentative, which can be destructive to relationships. We can see this type of approach with bullies.

Some people are more covert or hidden about their aggression. They express built-up anger and resentment in hidden ways that are incomprehensible and very hurtful and confusing for the person they are communicating with. They play games to "get back" at others because they cannot be open and honest in their communications. This is referred to as passive-aggressive behaviour. When someone uses passive-aggressive behaviour they are attempting to punish another person without accepting responsibility for the punishment (Wood and Henry, 2002). Passive-aggressive communication and behaviour is very destructive to relationships. As we mentioned earlier in this chapter, Eric Berne (1964) wrote a classic book on interpersonal games entitled *Games People Play*. To learn more about these games you may want to read this book.

- **Accommodation.** When using accommodation, you are more concerned with satisfying another person's concerns than with taking care of your own needs and goals. You put the other person's needs ahead of your own and may be called self-sacrificing or generous. For instance, if you go along with a friend who wants to go bowling, even though you prefer going to a movie, you are accommodating your friend's needs.

- **Compromising.** When you compromise or share, you and the other party get at least part of what each of you wanted. You say that you will go bowling tonight if next week your friend accompanies you to a movie.

- **Collaboration.** Collaboration is based on the idea of **win-win**, in which both of you can get what you want. Here you are using assertive communication that is also constructive in order to have your needs met. When you use a win-win strategy, you are genuinely concerned with satisfying both your needs and the needs of the other party. You discuss the reason your friend does not want to see a movie—maybe he would prefer to do something more active than sitting. You state that while you don't mind being active, bowling doesn't exactly thrill you because you are not very good at it. After some discussion you both decide to go golfing. One party has her needs met and you get to do an activity that you are skilled at.

- **Avoidance.** People who rely on avoidance can be both uncooperative and unassertive (i.e., they do not voice their needs). This type of person may withdraw physically or mentally from the conflict and has little concern for his needs or the needs of the other person. This person may adopt a Who cares? attitude. For example, you propose bowling, and your friend replies, "Yeah, whatever." You press for a commitment to a plan, and your friend says, "I don't care." This type of conflict is *lose-lose*, since neither of you gain anything from the conflict.

These styles are neither correct nor incorrect. Any style might be correct if it coincides with how important the goal is to you (i.e., satisfies your own concerns) and how important it is that you also satisfy the goals and concerns of the other person. For example, if the relationship and the individual goals of each party are very important, collaboration is the right strategy to choose. If your goals are not that important, but those of the other person are, you might choose to use accommodation. If you don't care

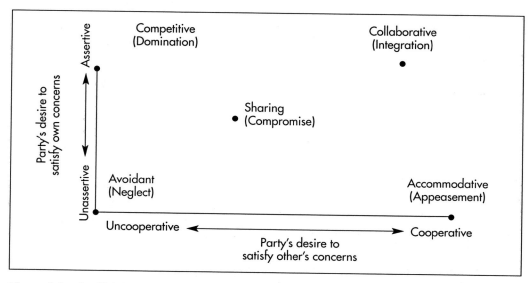

Figure 6-1   Conflict Styles

what you do as long as you get out for an evening, you can go along with your friend's choice of activity. We could relabel the X-axis "Importance of the relationship" to assist you in your choice of strategy.

In reality, we often do not make a conscious choice of style, and many of us rely on a preferred style that may not always be appropriate. One essential conflict management strategy, therefore, is to choose a style that suits both the conflict and the relationship.

CANADIAN PERSPECTIVE

Workplace Violence in Canada

Workplace violence has become an internationally recognized occupational health and safety issue. A 1999 International Labour Organization (ILO) report on workplace violence emphasized that physical and emotional violence is one of the most serious problems facing the workplace in the new millennium. The ILO definition of workplace violence includes bullying:

"... Any incident in which a person is abused, threatened or assaulted in circumstances relating to their work. These behaviours would originate from customers, co-workers at any level of the organization. This definition would include all forms of harassment, bullying, intimidation, physical threats/assaults, robbery and other intrusive behaviours."

The OC Transpo tragedy in Ottawa, in which a former employee of OC Transpo went on a shooting rampage that left four employees dead, and then took his own life, is an example of the seriousness of workplace violence in Canada. The killer himself had been the victim of workplace harassment. One of the recommendations resulting from a coroner's inquest was that the definition of workplace violence include not only physical violence but also psychological violence such as bullying, mobbing, teasing, ridiculing, or any other acts or words that could psychologically hurt or isolate a person in the workplace.

Prevention is the foundation of any workplace initiative aimed at curbing violence and aggression on the job. To find out more about workplace violence, visit the websites noted below and at the end of this chapter.

Sources: Adapted from Canada Safety Council, "Bullying in the workplace and targeting workplace bullies," www.safety-council.org/info/OSH/bully-law.html. Canadian Initiative on Workplace Violence, "An anatomy of workplace violence in Canada," www.workplaceviolence.ca/thm-bullying/discussion.html.

CONFLICT MANAGEMENT STRATEGIES

In this section we will review effective methods of conflict management from a variety of texts and articles (Beebe et al., 2004; Devito, Shimoni, and Clark, 2005; Devito, 1996; DuBrin and Geerinck, 2004; Tannen, 1998; Wood and Henry, 2002). When you become involved in a conflict, you may choose one or several strategies to help you. It should be noted that not all conflicts *can* be managed or solved; you and the other person may have to accept that some issues may never be resolved. You may have to reconcile yourself to the notion that you have areas of disagreement in even the closest relationships and that such differing views do not mean the end of the relationship. For example, you and your friend may have differing opinions on the issue of abortion. Rather than continue with heated debate about who is wrong or right, you may agree to disagree. However, armed with good strategies, you will be able to solve more interpersonal problems and conflicts than you would without having these strategies available.

KEY LEARNING POINTS

Conflict Management Strategies

- Choose an appropriate conflict management style.
- Control your emotions.
- Use empathy and practise being other-oriented.
- Be open and honest.
- Maintain your focus on the present.
- Be assertive, not aggressive.
- Use effective responding and listening skills.
- Manage the conflict using a problem-solving approach.

Choose an Appropriate Conflict Management Style

When experiencing conflict with another person, you need to ask yourself a couple of questions. First, how important is this relationship to you? Second, how important is the issue or goal? If the goal and the relationship are important, then you will want to use collaboration or compromise to manage the conflict. If the issue is more important than the relationship, you may need to adopt the competitive and more aggressive style. For example, if an individual refuses to comply with a police officer's order to stop a loud party, the officer will have to use more force to gain compliance. If an issue is not important to you and neither is the relationship, avoidance may be the most appropriate strategy. For example, if you are at the supermarket and a stranger "butts" in front of you, should you engage in conflict? If you are in no hurry and your ice cream is not going to melt in the next 30 seconds, it may be better to simply avoid the situation.

Accommodation is used when the relationship is more important than the issue or your goals. If a friend really wants to go to a concert that you're not interested in, you may go along just to please your friend. The real key is to choose the right style to match your goals and what you want from the exchange.

Control Your Emotions

When we experience strong emotions, we also experience heightened physiological arousal (Baron, Earhard, and Ozier, 1997). Anger, frustration, fear, sadness, and happiness all create physiological responses. For example, when you are angry, do you feel your heart rate increase, does your face turn red, or do you clench your teeth? When you are in this state, your perceptions are altered and you may not think clearly or be objective. Counting to 10 may be good advice when you want to manage your emotions. If you feel that your emotions are too intense for a discussion, you may want to suggest discussing the issue at another time and set a time to meet again. This will give you time to cool down and think clearly, and plan what you want to say. Remember from Chapter 3 that perceptions and the meanings we assign to an event or action can shape our emotions. With that in mind, another strategy to control your emotions could be to re-think your perceptions and try to look at the situation in another way. Recognize that at times you respond emotionally to events because they remind you of painful feelings from your past that may have little to do with the current situation. Remember too that you have choices and are responsible for controlling your own emotions.

If you do not give yourself time to control your emotions, you may regret the things that you say and do. Some people in the heat of debate launch into name-calling, engage in personal attacks, and become overly emotional, losing all objectivity. Some people become physically violent and may lose control. Such displays may escalate the conflict into something that is hard to back out of later.

In the second scenario presented at the beginning of this chapter, the male has decided to fight, which may lead to legal consequences for him. Police officers often have to work hard to control their body language and display a neutral demeanour in a conflict situation.

Use Empathy and Practise Being Other-Oriented

According to Devito (1996), a "frequently used fight strategy is to blame someone." In a relationship, we try to determine who is at fault and may attribute motives to the other person. When one officer blames the other officer's style on a liberal upbringing and lack of discipline, this blaming does little to resolve the conflict. These motives and attributes are not necessarily true and may further remove the two parties from actively trying to resolve the problem at the root of the conflict.

Instead of blaming the other person, use empathy and be other-oriented. Try to understand what the other person is really feeling, and what her thoughts and motives could be. Ask yourself, "Can I see why she behaved the way she did?" Looking at a situation from the other person's perspective can help to decrease the potential for conflict. Verbally express your empathy, "I can understand your being angry. I really should not have called you a bleeding-heart liberal. It was an unkind thing to say." Empathy does not mean that you agree with the other person; it does form a basis for further understanding and interpersonal communication.

Be Open and Honest

We are often reluctant to engage in conflict for many reasons. We may lack assertiveness, we may be afraid of hurting another person's feelings, and we may even be afraid of retaliation. When we are reluctant to manage a conflict, we may not be open and honest about the issues and about our feelings. Instead, we do not tell the truth. We say nothing is wrong and keep our feelings to ourselves, refuse to talk about what is troubling us, talk about irrelevant concerns, or downplay the conflict. The consequences of not dealing with conflict range from health issues to the destruction of a relationship. The building of stone walls may also result, and the conflict may become more difficult to manage as feelings become hardened, resentment builds, and anger develops. If people do not discuss their differences, doing so may become harder as time passes.

If an issue is important and maintaining the relationship is also important (whether it is a personal or professional relationship), conflict needs to be dealt with openly and honestly. When referring to conflict management styles, collaboration should be used, or, depending upon the level of importance, compromise may be another option. Both strategies rely on expressing what you want in an open and honest manner.

Maintain Your Focus on the Present

In the first situation presented at the beginning of the chapter, the male starts to discuss what has happened in the past. Have you ever had the experience in a conflict where suddenly everything that you ever did wrong is brought up? You may be late picking up your life partner today, but an old grievance from last summer is suddenly being discussed.

During a conflict, it is important to stay in the present and discuss the current conflict. Now is not the time to discuss other issues. You might try saying something like, "I understand that last summer is still bothering you, but let's continue with what the current problem is. We can discuss last summer at another time if you wish."

Be Assertive, Not Aggressive

Many strategies rely on your being able to express yourself in an assertive way. Remember that people who are assertive state what they want in a direct way and can express themselves without infringing upon another person's rights. During a conflict, assertive people express their feelings, thoughts, and views in a straightforward manner. See Table 6-1 for a crash course on how to be assertive.

Unfortunately, many people use aggression when faced with conflict, anger, and frustration; police officers often deal with angry and aggressive people. *Anger* is an emotion that includes feelings of hostility, indignation, and frustration. When people become angry, they can become highly argumentative, openly hostile, and physically aggressive. Judgment can become impaired (DuBrin and Geerinck, 2004). We will deal with the hostile and physical consequences of anger later in the section on crisis management.

Many people engage in verbal aggression when they are angry. According to Deborah Tannen (1998), North America has developed "an argument culture" that has led many of us to approach any issue in an adversarial way—recognizing only two sides to an issue rather than grey areas or middle ground. The ability to argue is not necessarily negative, but people who are highly argumentative may argue unnecessarily and too forcefully (Devito, 1996). Becoming highly argumentative may lead to managing a conflict in a competitive style wherein the goal of winning is sought at the expense of the relationship. Before getting into a heated debate, ask yourself whether it is worth it. How important is maintaining the relationship? Sometimes the risk may be necessary if the issue is extremely important to you. For example, if you truly believe that child pornography should be illegal, you may argue strongly for your view. But even if you engage in an argument, you can keep from becoming verbally aggressive by focusing only on the issue, avoiding personal attacks, taking turns and refraining from interrupting, expressing interest in the other viewpoint, and allowing for *face-saving* (Infante, 1988).

These are just a few strategies. Shyness can be more difficult to change and requires more time, effort, and strategies. However, we can all benefit by being more assertive when standing up for our rights and ideas. If people can practise being assertive, they are less likely to use aggressive strategies or give in to others.

Use Effective Responding and Listening Skills

During conflict we do not always pay attention to how we are saying things. We interrupt, misinterpret, make assumptions, and generally do not use very good responding

Table 6-1   Using Assertiveness to Manage Conflict

Many people struggle with shyness and the inability to be more assertive. Do you ever back down when you don't want to? Do you have trouble telling someone what you truly feel or think or keep pretending that you feel the way he thinks you do? Do you have trouble expressing your view on a certain issue or idea? If so, you may be having difficulty being assertive. Working in law enforcement requires that you have the ability to be assertive with the public and project an attitude of competence and authority. Below are some tips, adapted from several texts and sources, which should help you become more assertive (Beebe et al., 2004; DuBrin and Geerinck, 2004; Zimbardo, 1977; Shyne, 1982).

1. **Rehearse a difficult situation.** If a particular situation is one in which you need to develop your assertiveness, rehearse what you are going to say. Memorizing your lines like an actor may help when you get nervous. If it is helpful, rehearse with someone who can give you feedback on your lines. For example, a student was convinced that a mark she received on a paper was much lower than necessary. She wanted to talk to the teacher about it, but was afraid of questioning the grade. By rehearsing what she was going to say with the help of another teacher, she was more confident in approaching the teacher who gave her the low grade.

2. **Practise the broken record technique.** Some people do not take no for an answer, and it can be difficult to maintain your position against this onslaught. Using the broken record technique, you continue to repeat your viewpoint without showing frustration or anger. For example, if an individual is trying to get you to assist with homework that he should complete by himself, you calmly state, "No, you must do it on your own." At every angle and corner, simply repeat the statement. Usually the person will stop making the request.

3. **Know your rights and know where to go if your rights have been violated.** You have rights as a person and as a citizen. For instance, if approaching your landlord has not solved the problems with your apartment, you can get assistance from agencies that will be assertive for you. Read the Human Rights Act and other documents so that you know where you stand on a wide range of rights.

4. **Practise conversations with strangers.** If you are shy and find yourself stumbling over words when trying to meet people you would really like to get to know, practise with strangers where it does not matter so much if you stumble. In a long line, comment on how long you have been waiting. Such small exchanges may help you with the bigger and more important ones later.

5. **Monitor your nonverbal and verbal communication.** Part of being assertive is to look assertive. Walk confidently with head high, shoulders back, and a purposeful stride. Speak clearly, loudly enough to be heard, and do not use "Ums" and "Uhs." Do not end statements as if they were questions. For example, a non-assertive person might say, " I, ah, think I would, ah, like, ah, a coffee?" An assertive person states, "I would like to have a coffee."

6. **Use "I" statements and state your feelings and goals.** Assertive people state their feelings and goals directly, without violating the rights of others. They do not allow others to play games, or use intimidation or other ploys to get their way. "I do not wish to go out on a date with you" is an assertive statement. When necessary, assertive people simply repeat their position (i.e., use the broken record technique).

and listening skills. Although we have discussed some of these skills in prior chapters, we will briefly list them here again:

- **Use "I" language.** The feelings that you have are *your* feelings. You and only you are responsible for your feelings. Avoid statements such as "You make me so mad," "You don't understand," and "You never...," which blame the other person for your feelings. Instead, describe what you feel and what your perceptions are with "I" language; for instance, "I feel really mad when you don't call to say you are going to be late."

- **Describe the conflict-producing events clearly.** When emotions are high, we are not always very coherent. Stay calm and state clearly what is on your mind. Ask for feedback if the other person looks puzzled or does not appear to understand.

- **Pay attention to nonverbal language.** During conflict, nonverbal cues are important. For example, someone may say that she is not angry, but nonverbally she may be demonstrating anger or defensiveness. Use nonverbal language to check and maintain the communication. For example, you might say, "You tell me that you are not upset, but you keep wringing your hands. Is something still bothering you?" In addition, be aware of and watch your own nonverbal messages. You may be sending a message that escalates a conflict situation. For example, if you have your arms crossed in front of you in a closed-off position, you may be sending the message that you do not care about what the other person is saying to you.

- **Use effective listening skills.** When we are upset, we need to use effective listening skills. You may want to use prompters to signal your interest in hearing the speaker's message, or paraphrase what the speaker has said to verify that you have heard the message correctly. For more information on listening skills, refer back to the section on listening and responding in Chapter 5.

Manage the Conflict Using a Problem-Solving Approach

One way to view a conflict is to see it as a problem that requires a solution. If both parties can agree to sit down and solve the problem, a better understanding can be reached with a mutually made and agreed upon solution. If you can structure conflicts as problems to be solved, you are well on your way to seeking strategies to manage the issues that confront you and the other person involved with the conflict. There are many models of problem solving that can be used to arrive at a solution. Most models rely on a set of defined steps. These models can be found in business and counselling texts and are actively used by many organizations, including police services. See the Law and Justice Perspective box on p. 115 for the RCMP and OPP problem-solving models.

We will focus on a very straightforward model that can be used for interpersonal conflict. Define the problem, analyze the problem, generate many possible solutions, select the best solution that achieves the goals of the conflicting parties, implement the solution, and then finally evaluate the solution at a mutually agreed upon date. For purposes of understanding the model, we will use the example of policing style differences that are creating a problem for two officers who have recently been partnered. In the first two weeks of working together, one officer has twice responded to a call that should have been covered by officers closer to the scene. This officer, Tara, appears to be more of a crime fighter, is very aggressive, and has little patience for the social aspects of the job. On the other hand, Chan is very caring with victims and uses very little force with perpetrators. A few arguments have followed after several arrests, and Chan is becoming frustrated with Tara's behaviour. Tara has accused Chan of being too soft on several occasions.

1. **Define the problem.** Most conflicts and problems boil down to something you want more or less of. You can think of a problem as a deviation from where you would like to be or what you want regarding a specific issue. Chan prefers a higher focus on treating people with respect and answering a wide variety of calls. Tara is a crime

fighter and wants to go after the offenders. Chan wants Tara to be less aggressive and more humane in her approach to policing.

Make sure that you define the real problem and not just the symptoms. Lately, Chan and Tara have been fighting over small arrests, so they may need to spend some time talking about what is wrong and trying to understand each other. Rather than just dealing with symptoms (like a specific arrest or incident), they will need to get at the larger issue responsible for the conflict.

2. **Analyze the problem.** Next, analyze the problem to determine the cause of the conflict. When we analyze something, we reduce it or break it down into smaller pieces. Begin by describing the conflict-producing events in the order you feel they have happened. Describe the events in an unbiased way without evaluating the other person. Chan can describe the events that made him feel uncomfortable during the last couple of weeks, and Tara can do the same. You do not want to start an argument—remember that you are trying to get at the root of the conflict not start a new one. Is the conflict centred on one major issue or are there several issues? As Chan and Tara discuss the events, they discover that the conflicts they are experiencing are being generated by a basic philosophical difference in what they feel are the major goals of policing.

3. **Generate solutions.** For any problem there may be multiple solutions. Part of resolving a conflict using the problem-solving approach is to list as many solutions as possible. One or both of them could request a new partner. They could continue as they are and do nothing. They could try to be more understanding of their differences and learn to work together effectively. Chan could apply for a social worker position. Tara may want to try to get on a force, such as a tactical unit, where she could enjoy more opportunities for fighting crime. The key at this stage is to generate solutions. Some of them may be strange, impossible, or highly improbable; just keep up the momentum. You may even want to write them down.

4. **Evaluate the solutions.** Once you have a few solutions, you need to evaluate them based on the goals of the individuals. For instance, Chan's goal is to remain a police officer, so applying for social work positions would not help him with this goal. Either of them could request a new partner, but how would that reflect on both officers in the future? Would they be evaluated as unable to get along with team members, or might there be other negative side effects of making this request? The two partners then decide that they will need to become more understanding of their different styles and philosophies of policing. But this is not a very concrete solution. Generate objective criteria for a solution. The more measurable, verifiable, and objective the criteria, the greater the likelihood that both parties will be able to agree to the solution and implement it. They will need to refine this solution so that they both have a firm grasp of how they will behave differently with each other. Tara agrees that they will answer crime-fighting calls only when the calls are in their area. Chan says that, while he will continue to be concerned with victims, he will end his conversations sooner by notifying an appropriate agency or by giving out the number of such an agency.

5. **Implement the solution(s).** Once you have defined the solutions in clear terms, implement them.

6. **Set a time to re-evaluate the chosen solution(s).** It is not enough to agree to a solution. Both parties must live up to their end of the agreement. Once a solution has been agreed upon and implemented, many variables can get in the way of the intended goals.

Therefore, particularly with long-term solutions, periodic checking is necessary to keep the parties focused and to determine whether other problems are creeping into the solution. Chan and Tara agree to try their solutions for two weeks and set a time to discuss progress after work at that time.

LAW AND JUSTICE PERSPECTIVE

Problem-Solving Models in Policing

To improve a team or group's ability to solve problems and make decisions, models or processes have been developed and used by many researchers and organizations. The RCMP uses the CAPRA model, and the Ontario Provincial Police uses PARE analysis. A brief outline of each follows. As with most such models, these two have some common components.

The RCMP's CAPRA Conflict Management System

The Royal Canadian Mounted Police have developed a problem-solving model called the CAPRA conflict management system. The following is a very brief outline of the model.

The "C" in CAPRA stands for client and communication. A client is anyone who is directly or indirectly involved in an occurrence, or affected by it. Effective communication skills are essential for solving any problem.

The "A" stands for acquiring and analyzing information. Gathering relevant information and then analyzing that information requires skill.

"P" stands for partnerships, which are required for problem solving. These partnerships may be internal or external to the police service. Some examples of partners include community agencies, citizens, and experts in or outside the organization.

"R" stands for response, and includes prevention, incident management, officer and public safety, decision making, domain, parameters of legislation, policies and procedures, risk management, and use of force.

"A" stands for assessment. Assessment includes learning from experience, evaluation, self-reflection, thinking through potential consequences, and making good choices.

The Ontario Provincial Police's PARE Analysis Problem-Solving Model

The Community Policing Development Centre has developed a problem-solving model referred to as PARE. For a complete look at the model, visit the website listed at the end of this section.

The model consists of four steps:

1. Problem Identification and Analysis. A key step in problem solving is to accurately identify the problem. This step includes listing everyone's perceptions of the problem or events. Continue to discuss these perceptions by asking "why" questions.

2. Analysis. This step includes analyzing the impact of the problem, the seriousness of the problem, its complexity, and its solvability prior to determining the response. Examine the problem using the five Ws: who, what, where, when, and why. Obtain

information on the victims, offenders, and the situations. Prioritize (give weight to) the problems by determining their impact, seriousness, complexity, and solvability. At this end of this stage, the target problem is identified and a goal developed. The goal has one of four intentions: to eliminate the problem, reduce the problem, reduce the harm or impact of the problem, or redefine the problem responsibility.

3. **R**esponse. Response options can include but are not limited to investigation and enforcement, community education, crime prevention programs, and other strategies. Based on the goal, an action plan is developed, and strategies are chosen. The PARE document lists nine different strategies that range from enforcement and investigation responses to educational responses, to community and social development.

4. **E**valuation. Evaluate the effectiveness of the chosen response and make recommendations and improvements for future similar responses. Develop a system for evaluating and monitoring the effectiveness of the responses. Evaluation consists of process evaluation, where an analysis is done on the implementation strategies (Was it difficult? Were there easier ways?), and impact evaluation, which evaluates whether the strategies worked (i.e., had an impact).

The results of a team's problem-solving efforts should be documented and stored so that interested parties can share them.

Source: Adapted from The OPP Community Policing Development Centre, *How Do We Do It* manual, May 1997, http://www.opp.ca/cpdc/english/how/output/how.html; and www.rcmp.ca.

PROBLEMS VERSUS DECISIONS

The terms "problem solving" and "decision making" are often used interchangeably, but problem solving differs from decision making in that the problem is analyzed to determine causes and effects. Decision making, although it is certainly an important part of problem solving, is choosing one alternative from several. A **problem** can be defined as a gap between what currently exists and what you want to exist. When we encounter a problem, we try to solve it (or have somebody else solve it for us). If you are hungry and there is no food in your fridge, you have a problem, and what you want is food in the fridge. There may be many solutions to the problem. If you have money, you can buy food at the grocery store. If you have money but you can't wait that long, you can go to the nearest fast food restaurant and eat within minutes. You can even go to your neighbour and beg. You can tell yourself that you are not hungry and that hunger is just a state of mind. Coming up with all the alternatives is part of **problem solving** and **decision making**.

Problem solving is actually a complex decision-making process whereby a group or person analyzes a problem and develops a plan of action to solve the problem or reduce its effects (Engleberg and Wynn, 1997). Not all problems will have a number of alternatives or solutions from which to choose. For example, if you get a sliver in your thumb, the only real solution is to remove it. But many problems do have a variety of solutions or alternatives, and this is where the decision-making process comes in. When you choose from all of these options, you have made a **decision**. A decision is the solution, course of action, or selection that you make from several alternatives. When you choose to go to a certain college, you make a decision.

Goals and Goal Setting

Being able to set goals is an integral part of decision making and problem solving, as well as an important part of motivating you and the team towards larger organizational goals. Later, you will see that goals and reaching goals are important components of effective decision making. Here we will look at goals in general.

If you had not decided on a career in policing, where would you be right now? When you chose to go into law enforcement, you not only made a decision, but you also set a goal for yourself. Some students enter college or university with no real idea of what they want to do or where they want to be in five or ten years. **Goals** are events, circumstances, objects, conditions, or purposes for which a person (or group or team) strives. Purpose and meaning become unclear without goals. Have you ever been to a meeting and wondered what the point was? Goals direct our behaviour. Effective goals help us or our group get where we want to be. Let's look at how we can design effective goals.

Effective Goals

Goals can be thought of as motivational tools, and setting effective goals has several advantages. Research indicates that setting specific and reasonably difficult goals actually improves performance. If we set effective goals, they serve as self- and group motivators that energize us into action (DuBrin and Geerinck, 2004). Properly defined goals increase our chance of success.

Guidelines for Effective Goals

Here are some guidelines to help you and your group or team set effective goals (from DuBrin and Geerinck, 2004):

- **Formulate clear or specific goals.** When you formulate a goal, you or your group should have no doubt as to what the goal means. If your task force wants to decrease impaired driving in the area, the goal needs to state specifically by how much the crime should decrease, based on current statistics—for example, "The OPP in this area will reduce impaired driving by 20 percent over the next year."

- **Formulate concise goals.** Use a short statement that gets right to the point. Goals that are too lengthy can become confusing to you, other group members, and outsiders.

- **Describe the desired outcome when your goal is reached.** An effective goal states the outcome: what will actually be happening, how things will have changed, or what the new event or object will look like. If your goal is to graduate from college with an average of 80 percent, you have a good idea what your final transcript should look like.

- **Set realistic goals for yourself and for the group.** On a good team, members understand each other's strengths and weaknesses. Teams will set goals that members know the group can reach. This does not mean that the goals are easy; on the contrary, while goals should be realistic, they should also be challenging and stretch members' abilities, imagination, and creativity.

- **Set goals for different time periods.** Part of planning for a major goal is setting a series of smaller goals. Goals should range from short-term to medium-term and finally to long-term or long-range goals.

- **Allow some room for imagination and dreams into the goal.** What would the ideal police service look like? Visions of *what could be* can guide people to set their sights a little higher and diminish rigid thinking. Envisioning the goal also helps us stay focused, motivates us, and creates momentum. Envisioning is like positive thinking but is more extensive and is used by many coaches to help athletes reach their goals.

- **Specify the Who, What, Where, When, and How of goal accomplishment.** Some groups and teams design great goals and then look at each other around the table. Each goal requires an *action plan* or a description of how the group is going to reach the goal. The action plan needs to include *who* is going to carry out the action. For example, if a police service management team decides that officers need more crisis intervention training, one person may be responsible for researching various related groups in the community. The *what* refers to the activities that each member will carry out. The identified officer is the *who*. *Where* refers to location, although it may not be a part of all goal setting. But if you choose a specific college, the college becomes the *where* of your goal attainment. *When* usually refers to the deadline for accomplishing the goal. For some goals, one person may have to wait and rely upon another member's task completion before doing her portion. For instance, one officer may research the available training in the area. Another officer may be responsible for advertising or designing the process that organizes who will attend the training, based on the numbers the chosen training group can train at any given point. Can the training group train 30 at once, or 40, 80, or 100? The methods used for achieving your goal comprise the *how*. In this example, the *how* is formal training. Other methods exist, such as arranging time for officers to do self-study or having officers pay for their own training during their time off. Usually the methods that the group chooses are the ones that should lead to the best probability of reaching the goal.

- **Monitor your progress.** Groups need to monitor both individual and group progress. Part of this review is examining the timelines of tasks and activities to ensure that the group is on track, as well as to handle difficulties before they become major barriers or group problems.

- **Review your goals at specific times.** Sometimes, as a group (or individual) works towards a goal, questions may start to crop up. Why are we doing this? Is this goal still relevant? For example, outside influences can change the environment of the group and its goals. While the group is busily arranging the crisis intervention courses, the department may experience a massive budget cut that affects the training budget. The group may have to change its strategy or maybe even cancel its activities. Goals need to be reviewed to see whether they are still relevant, whether they can still be managed, and whether the group or team can proceed.

Barriers to Effective Group Problem Solving and Decision Making

When groups get together to solve problems and make decisions, a number of problems can influence the process. In the last chapter we concentrated on personal characteristics, time constraints, and several individual factors that create barriers. Here, we want to concentrate on problems that affect the group processes. We will examine group polarization, groupthink, organizational and external pressures, politics, pre-existing preferences, and power differences.

Group Polarization

When groups make a decision or choose a solution, the choice may sometimes involve *risk*. Some solutions may be very risky, while some have very little risk or are extremely conservative. Think of some of your own personal decisions. At times, you may have chosen the more risky alternative—going to university in a foreign country, for instance. A much less risky choice would have been to stay in your hometown and attend the local college, and there are many alternatives in between theses two extremes. Groups engage in the same process of choosing from a set of alternatives.

In a group, the process may lead the group to make a more extreme decision than individuals would have made if they had been working alone. This process is known as **group polarization**. Why does this polarization occur in some groups?

First, members engage in using persuasive arguments that help to convince doubtful members. Remember public compliance and personal conformity? Some members actually change their beliefs to go along with the dominant group members' persuasive information.

Second, when a team makes a decision, members may feel less personally responsible for the outcome and consequences of the decision.

Third, people compare themselves to others in the group. In the process of **social comparison**, we try to see and present ourselves favourably (Alcock, Carment, and Sadava, 2005). In order to maintain this favourable image, we carefully observe others and ourselves in the group. When we see the group shifting its decision, we go along with the shift.

Last, the process of **social identification** may also account for polarization. Social identification is a process whereby we define ourselves in relation to others and thus conform to the norms and stereotypes of the group. Individuals may hold an extreme stereotype of their group and become motivated to conform to this perceived extreme norm (Alcock, Carment, and Sadava, 2005). For example, if you see your decision-making group as extremely creative and innovative, you will go along with decisions that are "far-out" and "weird" to maintain this image. All of these processes operate to push a group towards more extreme attitudes and more extreme decisions.

Groupthink

In the early seventies, the research of Irving Janis (1972, 1982) led to the popular use of the term **groupthink** to identify a process of faulty decision making in a group. Groupthink is the tendency for cohesive groups to value consensus more highly than making effective decisions. As a result, the group experiences a deterioration of mental efficiency, a lack of reality testing, and assumptions about the morality of the decisions. See Table 6-2 for a summary of the eight symptoms of groupthink.

Organizational and External Pressures

A group may experience many external pressures that affect what goes on inside the group or team. Some pressures may come from within the organization itself. Managers may be impatient or may pressure the group into making a decision or coming up with a solution when the group is not yet ready. Other groups may also exert pressure on the group. One group may have to wait to continue its own work until another group has completed its task.

Pressures can also be exerted from outside the organization. The media and victims' families may pressure the Solicitor General's office for new guidelines and methods of pursuit. Minority groups have successfully pressured the government at all levels for changes and for recognition of their rights as citizens and human beings. Special investigation units often feel pressure from outside parties who are waiting for the results of decisions regarding a shooting or other incidents. Some groups may be fearful of the

Table 6-2   The Eight Symptoms of Groupthink

1. **Illusion of invulnerability**   A belief that the group is above attack and reproach.
2. **Collective rationalization**   Rather than exploring the decision, the group justifies its actions.
3. **Illusion of morality**   The group members believe that they are right, and that therefore, their actions are moral.
4. **Shared stereotypes**   The group shares stereotypes of outgroups, such as "They are just scientists."
5. **Direct pressure placed on dissenters**   In order to preserve cohesiveness, pressure is applied to those who express contrary views.
6. **Self-censorship**   Rather than expressing their doubts and assuming everyone else is in agreement, members go along with the decision.
7. **Illusion of unanimity**   By suppressing dissension, the group produces the appearance that everyone is in agreement.
8. **Mindguarding**   Certain group members act as mindguards, making sure that the group is protected from dissenting information.

Source: J. L. Janis (1982). *Groupthink*, 2nd edition. Boston: Houghton Mifflin.

reaction to their decision, especially in light of past decisions, such as the jury decision in the beating of Rodney King.

When a group's decisions affect members outside an organization, there is bound to be reaction to the decision. This reaction may be positive or negative.

Politics

Some of the previous examples illustrate a significant barrier for groups and teams. There is usually a political component to all decisions, including organizational politics. Members may react and come into a group with political interests, as well as with **hidden agendas**. For example, in a political climate of cutbacks, it may not be prudent for members of Parliament to make decisions that involve large pay raises or other perceived extravagances.

Pre-existing Preferences

No matter what method the group or team uses to make its decision or solve its problem, there may be people on the team who have their minds made up from the very first day. For example, as a teacher, I may favour a particular textbook for a course. I may go through the motions of examining other texts with the group, but my mind is already made up.

Power Differences

Individuals differ in the amount of **power** they hold in a group. These power differences will affect problem solving and decision making within the group. In Chapter 9 the different sources of power will be discussed. As power shifts, members may change their minds or have difficulty committing to one member's ideas over another's. This is one reason why ideas need to be separated from ownership of ideas. In other words, members need to commit to ideas and not to the people who voice them.

OVERCOMING BARRIERS TO EFFECTIVE GROUP DECISION MAKING AND PROBLEM SOLVING

Here we will examine ways to reduce polarization, groupthink, and other group processing problems. Another strategy for effective decision making and problem solving is to rely on a model to guide the group through the process. Although using a model is an effective method for improving group and team decision making and problem solving, we will discuss models as a separate topic.

Encourage Constructive Controversy

When discussing problems, solutions, and making decisions, teams should encourage constructive controversy. With **constructive controversy,** team members feel free to openly debate their different opinions (McShane, 1995). One person or part of the team could also be appointed to play devil's advocate and, using constructive criticism, point out flaws or weaknesses of a team decision, solution, or action plan. The emphasis here is on "constructive." Constructive controversy is issue-oriented, not person-oriented. People on the team share ideas and critique those ideas. Personal feelings of idea ownership are not part of this process.

Use Brainstorming and Other Methods to Encourage Creativity

Often unique problems or difficult decisions are a challenge to even the best teams or groups. Like many professionals, police officers have standard procedures for much of their everyday activity. Police services, like other organizations, struggle with new issues and will continue to do so. For example, the increase of bystander deaths in car pursuits has created the need for new guidelines for pursuits and the examination and creation of new methods for apprehending fleeing suspects. As another example, when bulletproof vests were first issued, there were no vests designed for women!

Good ideas and solutions don't always come down through the channels—many are thought of by front-line workers, the people who deal with customers or clients on a daily basis. Organizations that want their workers to find solutions and make important decisions need to provide the resources to encourage creative thinking.

Creative thinking is the ability to process information in a way that results in a product that is new, original, and meaningful. The product can be an actual thing, such as Velcro, or it can be a new procedure, a novel solution, or a different angle. Edward De Bono (1972) coined the term **lateral thinking** to describe thinking that is non-logical, non-sequential, generative, explores unlikely paths, and escapes traditional patterns. **Vertical thinking** is analytical, sequential, logical, stays on tried and true paths, and stays within traditional and rigid patterns. Vertical thinking is often referred to as left-brain thinking because it is the left hemisphere of the brain that controls such functions as speaking and numerical skills, and that is the analytical half of the brain. Creative thinking is more of a right-brain process, because the right brain is the non-analytical and more feeling side of the brain. So how can organizations encourage employees to be more creative and to get away from vertical and rigid thinking when the organization needs to solve problems and make decisions?

One strategy is to encourage brainstorming. **Brainstorming** is an excellent tool for coming up with alternatives in a group or team and for improving group creativity. It is a process whereby a team meets and generates as many alternative solutions to a problem as possible. Most models of decision making and problem solving rely on brainstorming during the stage of generating alternatives. The primary goal of brainstorming is idea generation; evaluation and other analyses are done at a later time. Because there is no evaluation component in brainstorming, even the quietest group members may feel free to participate without any evaluation apprehension. There are four main rules in brainstorming (Adams, 1979):

1. There is no criticism, defence, evaluation, or judgment of ideas. The focus is to generate as many ideas as possible within a given amount of time.
2. Free association is encouraged. All ideas are to be voiced, no matter how "far out," wild, or weird they are.
3. Quantity is the goal, not quality. The more ideas there are, the more ideas there will be to evaluate later on.
4. Building on ideas, or "piggybacking," is encouraged. Ideas can be expanded on or put together with variations on the ideas.

It is best if all ideas are written down so that the whole group can see them, and time limits may be useful. Brainstorming stimulates creativity, an essential part of effective problem solving and decision making.

Get an Outside Opinion and Have Outside Experts Join the Group

Groups and teams may benefit from outside expertise. Rather than mindguarding or trying to protect the group from outside interference, using outside experts may give the group new ideas or new perspectives. An outsider may be able to point out fresh approaches and more objectively assess solutions. For example, when a police committee is making decisions about new educational initiatives, it may have members of a particular social agency join the committee.

Now that we have looked at problem solving and decision making, we will turn our attention back to conflict that becomes a crisis.

CRISIS MANAGEMENT

Occasionally, a routine call can turn into a conflict that can then become a **crisis,** as many police officers and others in law enforcement can verify. There are several definitions of a crisis, but the common thread is that a crisis is a reaction to an event that goes beyond the individual's capability to cope with it at that time (Arnold, 1980; Golan, 1978). A crisis can be a sudden change or turn in behaviour that has the potential to become violent, or may already be violent when officers arrive at the scene. Just by showing up officers can often precipitate or escalate a situation.

The second situation presented at the beginning of this chapter escalated into physical confrontation and a state of active crisis. Could the officers have prevented this? This last section will examine the stages of a crisis, discuss preventative strategies to avoid a crisis, and offer crisis intervention techniques.

Crises appear to go through a set of identifiable stages (Arnold, 1980; Golan 1978); see Figure 6-2. Although labelled differently by different sources, there are essentially four stages to a crisis. First, there is the *hazardous event,* which may be one event or a series of events that trigger stress. Second, the impact of this event throws a person off balance and places her in a *vulnerable state.* If the problem continues, tension continues to rise, and a *precipitating factor* (sometimes called a turning point) can occur that no longer allows her to use her current coping mechanisms and places her in the third state of *active crisis.* During an active crisis, she may act out aggressively or turn inward and withdraw. The fourth phase is *adaption*, in which an individual adapts and changes to cope with the crisis.

Indicators before a Crisis

How can you tell if a conflict or intervention is about to turn into a crisis? There are many signs to be aware of that will help gauge whether a crisis is imminent (Ouellette, 1996;

Crises appear to go through a set of identifiable stages
Stage 1: *the hazardous event*
Stage 2: *the vulnerable stage*
Stage 3: *precipitating factor of an active crisis*
Stage 4: *adaption*

Figure 6-2   The Four Stages of a Crisis

Source: Adapted from William Arnold (1980). *Crisis Communication.* Dubuque, IA: Gorsuch Scarisbrick Publishers; and Naomi Golan (1978). *Treatment in Crisis Situations.* New York: The Free Press.

McKenna, 1998). First, *the nonverbal language* of the attacker will change. The person may move into a defensive stance with the feet moving to shoulder distance apart and the strong foot moving back. The eyes may shift to an escape route or glance at a target such as the officer's chin or gun. The person may appear more agitated, may use more gestures, and may engage in more fidgeting. He may begin to talk louder or may begin shouting. Personal space may change as he tries to get closer for an attack or tries to get further away for flight.

The *verbal content* of the conflict may also change as the person starts to swear, engage in name-calling, and attempt to verbally aggravate the officer for a confrontation, using such statements as "Throw down your gun and I'll show you who's the boss." The individual may also start to talk about weapons or acts of violence. At this point, you want to engage in **crisis prevention** to avoid a continued escalation and possible physical intervention. Figure 6-3 outlines 10 tips from the Crisis Prevention Institute (1986) that will help prevent a crisis.

Crisis Intervention Strategies

Often, no matter how hard you try, a situation will escalate into a crisis. As an officer, you may enter a crisis that is already taking place—such as a domestic incident, an incident involving impaired individuals, or another violent crime scene. Other courses will go into more detail about tactics and strategies to defuse violence, but in this text we will concentrate on the interpersonal components of managing a crisis.

First, you must quickly assess the situation. If the individual is an immediate danger to himself or to others, you may need to react quickly with physical force. You may need to immediately call for emergency assistance such as back-up, specialized force units, the Children's Aid Society, or an ambulance. If no other assistance is required and the crisis is non-violent, you can apply the strategies listed here that rely on the ability to communicate effectively.

Nonverbal Skills

Be Aware of Personal Space In a crisis, people who are agitated or hostile may need more personal space. You can allow as much as six feet unless you feel the person may attempt to flee.

Use Eye Contact Appropriately The proper use of eye contact is an important nonverbal strategy. Eye contact by the officer can convey concern, support, confidence, and authority. By reducing eye contact, the power role is lessened and the helper role is increased. Maintain eye contact, but break it occasionally when the other person is speaking (Ouellette, 1996). Eye contact is a powerful tool to use for assessing potential aggression.

1. **Be empathic.** Try not to be judgmental of the other person's feelings. They are real, even if not based on reality, and must be attended to.
2. **Clarify messages.** Listen to what is really being said. Ask reflective questions, and use both silence and restatements (paraphrasing).
3. **Respect personal space.** Stand at least one and a half to three feet from the acting-out person. Encroaching on personal space tends to arouse and escalate an individual.
4. **Be aware of body position.** Standing eye to eye and toe to toe with the person sends a challenging message. Standing one leg length away and at an angle off to the side is less likely to escalate the individual.
5. **Permit verbal venting when possible.** Allow the individual to release as much energy as possible by venting verbally. If this cannot be allowed, state directives and reasonable limits during lulls in the venting process.
6. **Set and enforce reasonable limits.** If the individual becomes belligerent, defensive, or disruptive, state limits and directives clearly and concisely.
7. **Avoid overreacting.** Remain calm, rational, and professional. How you the officer or other personnel respond will directly affect the individual.
8. **Use physical techniques as a last resort.** Use the least restrictive method of intervention possible. Employing physical techniques on an individual who is only acting out verbally can escalate the situation.
9. **Ignore challenge.** When the client challenges your position, training, etc., redirect the individual's attention to the issue at hand. Answering these questions often fuels a power struggle.
10. **Keep your nonverbal cues non-threatening.** Be aware of your body language, movement, and tone of voice. The more an individual loses control, the less he listens to your actual words. More attention is paid to your nonverbal cues.

Figure 6-3 Ten Tips for Crisis Prevention

From www.crisisprevention.com, Crisis Prevention Institute Inc., © 1986. Reprinted with permission.

Use Non-threatening Body Positions Do not stand directly in front of the individual. A sitting position for both parties is not aggressive and can help open the door to verbal interaction (Ouellette, 1996). Not only is the probability of aggression reduced, people who have been victimized are more approachable if you let them sit down. Sitting has a calming effect since it is usually related to relaxing activities such as eating and watching television.

Monitor Other Nonverbal Behaviour What are your hands doing? Are they clenched into fists, resting on your hips? Are your arms crossed? During a crisis, it may be easy to forget many of the nonverbal communicators and what they appear to say. Gestures should be natural—as if you were speaking to a friend. This does not mean that you are not wary of the individual but rather that you do not want to display any signs of aggression. Pay attention to your nonverbal behaviour.

Demonstrate That You Are Listening The man in our second scenario may have only needed time to vent his frustration and anger. Telling him to calm down only cut off and interrupted this venting. Sometimes you need to listen, and listening takes time. But time spent listening is better than time spent trying to defuse a violent attack. Use the strategies from Chapter 4 to demonstrate listening. Listening is a sign that you care on a professional and personal level.

Verbal Skills

What you say is also important and can escalate or defuse a crisis situation. You should remain courteous—although this may be difficult if you are being verbally assaulted.

Use Paraphrasing of Content and Feelings Both of the situations at the beginning of this chapter might have been handled more effectively if the officers had used some paraphrasing. For example, saying something like, "I know when you're having a good time, it can be hard to call it to a close" could have helped defuse the second situation. In the first situation, paraphrasing and reflecting feelings might have helped. Saying, "It must be really upsetting to lose your home" instead of telling the individual to calm down might have reduced his anger. Saying something like "calm down" rarely produces the desired effect in a crisis.

Use Direct and Simple Language During a crisis, people may not be thinking clearly, so it is best to use direct, clear, and simple language. Keep your sentences short. If you need to issue a directive, state it firmly and clearly. Most tactical communication follows this simple rule.

Use Verbal Instructions to Remove Onlookers Having people watch what is going on may antagonize the person who has lost or is about to lose control. If possible, firmly ask onlookers to remove themselves from the immediate area. In the first scenario at the beginning of the chapter, the officer should ask the people who have come outside to watch to go back inside.

Use Humour if Appropriate Sometimes laughter really is the best medicine—when used wisely. Make sure, however, that the humour does not mean laughing at the person in crisis. For instance, a domestic violence victim who was in a lot of pain was lying on the floor waiting for an ambulance. The officers did not want to move her in case she had a back injury. One officer kept her company. From her position on the floor, she suddenly noticed some dirt on her ceiling and made a funny comment to the officer. Humour helped to reduce the emotional level of the incident for her and the officer.

SUMMARY

This chapter gave you an overview of conflict. A conflict occurs for many reasons, including competition for limited resources, personality and cultural differences, different priorities and goals, role conflict, and the building of stone walls. People manage conflict by adopting one of five styles: competitor, accommodator, compromiser, collaborator, or avoider. The appropriate style that an individual should use is based on assessing the importance of the goal or issue and the importance of the relationship. Inappropriate use of a style occurs when the two are not assessed correctly.

There are several conflict management strategies that you can use, depending upon the nature of the conflict and what you want out of the conflict. The first and most basic strategy is to choose a conflict management style that matches your goals and what you want from the exchange. When involved in a conflict you should also control your emotions, use empathy and be other-oriented, be open and honest, maintain a present focus, be assertive, and use effective listening and responding skills. Managing the conflict as a problem situation may also be beneficial and may lead to a mutually agreed upon solution. The six steps of problem solving are defining the problem; analyzing the problem; generating solutions; evaluating the solutions; implementing the solution; and then re-evaluating the solution at a later time.

We examined how teams and groups make decisions and solve problems. Problems and decisions were defined, with problem solving being a more complex decision making process. To assist in problem solving and decision making, effective goal setting and its steps were discussed. Setting effective goals with an action plan is an important skill for individuals and teams to develop.

There are many barriers that interfere with effective group decision making and problem solving, including group polarization; groupthink; organizational and external pressures; politics; pre-existing preferences; and power differences. To improve group decision making and problem solving and to reduce these barriers, groups and teams should encourage constructive controversy; use brainstorming and other techniques to encourage creativity; and get an outside opinion and have experts join the group.

A conflict that has become a very difficult crisis situation may have to be managed by police officers. There are several indicators that a crisis may develop, including a change in nonverbal language and changes in the verbal content of the individual(s). Crisis intervention strategies include both nonverbal and verbal strategies.

WEBSITES

www.workplaceviolence.ca/home.html
This is the Canadian Initiative on Workplace Violence, with links to prevention strategies.

www.otworks.ca
This is Canada's occupational therapy resource site. Take the quiz to assess your workplace mental health.

www.nobullyforme.org
This British Columbia site deals with workplace bullying laws.

www.crisisprevention.com
This is the site of the Crisis Prevention Institute. It offers good strategies, and copies of some of these strategies are available by sending away for free posters.

http://insight.mcmaster.ca/org/efc/pages/law/cc/cc.html
The Criminal Code of Canada is posted here.

www.ncjrs.org/txtfiles/ppsyc.txt
This is the National Criminal Justice Reference Service.

www.shyness.com
This site is devoted to shyness and helping those with shyness or social phobia.

www.lineofduty.com
This is an interesting site with a number of links. One of the links, "From the Blotter," has articles from the United States and Canada about policing actions and issues.

www.opp.ca
This is the site for the Ontario Provincial Police.

www.rcmp.ca
This is the site for the RCMP.

JOURNAL AND DISCUSSION QUESTIONS

1. What are the major causes of conflict in the life of a college or university student? Identify several sources of conflict.

2. Identify a current conflict that you are trying to manage. Using the problem-solving method, outline a strategy that could be used to solve this conflict.

3. What are your views on the use of force by police officers?

4. This chapter offers models for problem solving and decision making. What do you see as advantages of using models? What do you see as disadvantages of using models?

5. Use either of the two models and design a simulation for a real problem that must be solved or a decision that must be made in policing. Ideas to consider include increasing the number of women and visible minorities in policing, youth involvement in crime, and amalgamation of police forces.

6. You and your team have been selected to identify the characteristics of the ideal policing candidate. How will your group do this? Plan a strategy that your group can use to identify what the ideal candidate will be like.

SKILLS PRACTICE 6-1
Personal Goal Setting

Personal goal setting is similar to group or team goal setting. By practising personal goal setting, you will be better able to assist a group or team in setting and achieving goals. Below are several goals that do not adhere to the previous guidelines. Rewrite the goals to meet the criteria above. Remember that effective goals are specific, concise, have specific timelines, are realistic, and describe what the outcome of the goal will achieve. Feel free to use your imagination.

1. I want to do better at school.

Revised goal:

2. I'm going to get into better shape.

Revised goal:

3. I'm going to save money for a new car.

Revised goal:

Share your goals with other classmates. Were your goals identical? Did the goals meet the criteria for being effective goals? How could you improve your goals?

_____

_____

_____

_____

_____

_____

_____

Understanding and Managing Diversity

Chapter 7

After studying this chapter you should be able to:

- Define culture.
- Define beliefs and values.
- Identify five major differences among cultures.
- Be more aware of the diversity and types of groups in Canada.
- Identify barriers to effective intercultural communication.
- Identify and be able to practise various strategies to reduce communication barriers in a diverse society.
- Explain the challenge of diversity for policing.

INTRODUCTION

The face of Canada is changing. Data from past censuses show that visible minority populations are growing much faster than the total population (Statistics Canada, 2001). Our populace is aging, our birth rate remains at around 1.5 children per woman, and visible minorities now make up a high proportion of immigrants to Canada (Statistics Canada, 2001). According to ethnocultural projections, when Canada celebrates its 150th anniversary in 2017, roughly one out of every five people in Canada (between 19 and 23 percent) may be a member of a visible minority. According to a 2001 study by Statistics Canada, immigrants are also changing the face of Canada's largest urban centres (Statistics Canada, 2001). The Canadian Perspective box on p. 132 illustrates the powerful changes in cultural diversity that are occurring in our population. There is little doubt that Canada is a diverse nation, made up as it is of people from different cultures and lifestyles—people with a wide range of needs and challenges. As a future law enforcement officer, you will have little choice about whom you have contact with professionally.

The focus on diversity in textbooks and teaching reflects the changing nature and diversity of this nation. Understanding and managing diversity will help you be a better police officer and citizen. With the skills and increased depth of understanding you will have after completing this chapter, you will be better equipped to manage the diverse relationships that you undertake both on and off the job.

To begin, we will explore cultural differences and then look at other diverse populations, continuing with examinations of the family, the implications of an aging population, and issues of people with disabilities and other physical and emotional challenges. Some of these groups are referred to as **co-cultures**, or cultures within a culture. We will also touch on diversity in policing and conclude with several strategies to assist communication with people from diverse backgrounds.

UNDERSTANDING CULTURE

Culture, which comes in many shapes and sizes, can be defined as a learned and shared system of knowledge, behaviour, beliefs, attitudes, values, and norms. Cultures and co-cultures in many ways refer to a group's lifestyle or way of living. **Beliefs** are the ways in which cultures structure their view or understanding of what, to them, is true and what is false—for example, religious beliefs. **Values** are more enduring than beliefs and are central to who you are. Values can be defined as a set of central and enduring goals in life and ways of living that you feel are important, right, and true.

Religions are part of a cultural heritage for many people, and others may have different religious beliefs and a different religious value system. Your cultural background and all the things that make up your culture affect and impact how you communicate with others.

CANADIAN PERSPECTIVE

The Facts and Statistics of a Culturally Diverse Population

- In 2001, 95 percent of Canada's population comprised Canadian citizens. The majority were born in Canada, while 13 percent were naturalized citizens.

- Europeans made up the largest share of all immigrants living in Canada and accounted for 47 percent of all immigrants. However, the proportion of new immigrants from Europe has been steadily declining since 1961. Before 1961, 91 percent of new immigrants were from Europe, but this proportion dropped to 20 percent between 1991 and 1996.

- Data from past censuses show that the visible-minority population is growing much faster than the total population. Between 1996 and 2001, Canada's population increased 4 percent, while the visible minority population rose 25 percent, or six times faster.

- Between 1991 and 1996, Asian-born people represented 57 percent of immigrants. Most came from Hong Kong, the Philippines, China, and India. In 2001, Chinese and South Asians were the largest visible minority groups in Canada.

- Virtually all the immigrants who arrived in Canada during the 1990s—some 1.8 million people—settled in one of Canada's large urban centres (Toronto, Vancouver, or Montreal). Recently, however, some smaller urban centres have seen a considerable increase in their population as more immigrants choose to settle outside of the large urban centres.

CANADIAN PERSPECTIVE (*Continued*)

As part of this new diversity, the number of mother tongues in Canada is also changing, though English and French remain predominant. Here are the top 15 languages in Canada—excluding English and French—according to the Statistics Canada 2001 Census:

1. Chinese
2. Italian
3. German
4. Polish
5. Spanish
6. Portuguese
7. Punjabi
8. Ukrainian
9. Arabic
10. Dutch
11. Tagalog (Filipino)
12. Greek
13. Vietnamese
14. Cree
15. Inuktitut (Inuit)

Sources: Immigration statistics adapted from Statistics Canada, *The Daily*, "Demographic statistics," September 28, 2005; *The Daily*, "Study on immigrants in Canada's urban centres," August 18, 2004; *The Daily*, "Population projections," December 15, 2005; and *The Daily*, "Study on Canada's visible minority population in 2017." Languages adapted from *The Daily*, "Population by mother tongue," 2001 Census.

Through the process of **enculturation**, culture passes from one generation to another. We learn our culture from our parents, teachers, and peers, and from institutions and government agencies (Devito, Shimoni, and Clark, 2005). **Acculturation** occurs when one culture is modified by contact with another culture. Through such contact with people from other cultures, our own beliefs, values, attitudes, and ideas may change.

North American culture today is full of examples of acculturation. For example, many of us undergo acupuncture, practise karate and judo, enjoy East Indian foods, eat hot dogs and watch baseball, or do other things that were not initially part of our home culture. Intercultural communication can occur among many different types of cultures and co-cultures. Communication can occur among different religions, different cultures, different races, different nations, different co-cultures, and different groups within a culture.

We need to be aware that as we communicate with others from different cultures, we are always communicating from our own cultural perspective. For example, some Western women criticize the wearing of hijab by Muslim women. But some Muslim women who wear hijab believe that Western women are slaves to their appearance, and they see the wearing of hijab as being more liberated. Both sides are expressing their beliefs based on their cultural perspective.

The advance of globalization and technology, changing Canadian immigration patterns, and other factors may lead to *deculturation* in the future. Deculturation (loss of traditional culture) occurs when people lose their culture or cannot use their culture because of changed circumstances (Cornish, 2004). Deculturation may be experienced by recent immigrants to Canada who speak neither English nor French. They may not be able to communicate in order to have their needs met, leading to a feeling of helplessness and culture shock.

According to Cornish (2004) in his book *Futuring: The Exploration of the Future*, another form of deculturation occurs when the accustomed culture changes rapidly due to population shifts by people who do not share the culture. Traditional ways of speaking, behaving, and doing things no longer fit the accustomed environment. In order to communicate effectively with new community members, individuals must learn a new language or change the way they behaved in the past. Deculturation can change a city or country in many ways—by forcing changes in political leaders, laws, and the way business is done. We can see this shift in multicultural Canada. As an example, Rona stores in Vancouver, British Columbia, which have a large Chinese customer base, have adapted to changing demographics by developing signs in English and Chinese in order to communicate more effectively with their customers.

DIMENSIONS OF CULTURAL DIFFERENCES

Although cultures can be very different, one researcher has identified four variables, or **cultural values**, that cultures share: masculine versus feminine perspectives; avoidance of uncertainty; distribution of power; and individualism versus collective achievement (Hofstede, 1980). A fifth value is the dimension of high context versus low context.

Masculine versus Feminine Perspectives

Some cultures emphasize traditional male values, while others emphasize more feminine perspectives. **Masculine cultures** value such things as material wealth, assertiveness, achievement, and heroism. **Feminine cultures** value relationships, caring for and nurturing others, particularly those less fortunate, and quality of life (Hofstede, 1980). The older, traditional cultures of much of Europe, Asia, the United States, Great Britain, and Canada are more masculine in nature. However, most of these cultures are changing as social and legal changes reflect more equality between the sexes.

Tolerance of Uncertainty versus Avoidance of Uncertainty

Some cultures are more tolerant of ambiguity and uncertainty than other cultures. Cultures that place value on avoiding uncertainty are more likely to have more rigid rules for behaviour and more likely to develop more elaborate codes of conduct. Cultures that are highly tolerant of uncertainty have more relaxed rules of conduct and are more permissive with the latitude of what is acceptable conduct. People from Portugal, Germany, Russia, and Japan seem to have a low tolerance for uncertainty. People from the Scandinavian countries are more tolerant of uncertainty (Hofstede, 1980, 1991).

Concentrated versus Decentralized Power

Some cultures accept the fact that power is hierarchical and that some people should have more power than others. These cultures have more bureaucracies based on power, with those higher on the ladder having more power than those lower on the ladder. Russia, France, and China put strong emphasis on the value of concentrated power (Hofstede, 1991). Studies continue to indicate that this notion is reflected in a wide range of institutions, including schools and businesses (Bolman and Deal, 1992; Schmidt and Yeh, 1992). The United States, Australia, and Israel value more decentralized power and tend to minimize power differences between people.

People who are not used to hierarchies may have difficulty adjusting to these differences in power. For example, young people in Canada who join the army or police services may have difficulty with the notion of following orders simply because they must.

Individualism versus Collectivism

Individualistic cultures emphasize the individual person and give priority to personal goals over the goals of the group. Western cultures, such as in the United States, Canada, and Great Britain, emphasize the importance of having individual goals and being responsible for yourself and your immediate family (Hofstede, 1980). Collectivistic cultures emphasize the importance of a larger social group, and individual identity is based on identity within a unit or group. Group goals are given priority over personal or individual goals (Hofstede, 1980).

To illustrate the difference between individualism and collectivism, in many Western (or individualistic) cultures, the answer to, Who are you? would likely be a set of personal attributes. In a more collectivist culture such as Japan, the response would likely include the identity of the father and mother and some information about descendants (Libra, 1976). Some research also indicates that African Americans tend to be more oriented towards collective interests like family than European North Americans (Gaines, 1995).

High-Context Cultures versus Low-Context Cultures

People from high-context cultures rely heavily on context and nonverbal cues in their interaction with others. Cultures that are characterized as more low-context rely on verbal language to communicate messages to others. Low-context cultures use fewer nonverbal cues to send and interpret messages (Hall, 1987). To more fully understand the difference between high- and low-context, think of eating at a familiar restaurant (context) that you and your friends enjoy every Friday night after work. You are well-known at this establishment by the servers. You simply have to catch the eye of a server and lift your hand and wave. At this signal, the server comes back with your favourite drink. This is a high-context situation. But suppose there is a new server. You wave your arm and he waves back with a smile. Suddenly, you are in a low-context situation and you will have to verbally indicate what you would like (or you may just get smiles and waves for awhile and be very thirsty).

Some cultures that are more high-context may use such nonverbal cues as dress, jewellery, hairstyles, and body marking to enhance messages for others within the culture. For example, young Amish men who are single do not have beards, but once married or at least betrothed, they grow beards to indicate their marital status.

THE GROUPS AND CULTURES OF CANADA

As a professional law enforcement worker, your contact with people may be wide and varied, depending on where in Canada you work. Large urban centres tend to be more culturally diverse than smaller rural communities; however, this only pertains to cultural diversity in terms of nationality and ethnic or racial origins. You also need to be aware of other cultural differences and their prevalence in Canada today. Before we begin to examine the barriers that affect our communication with other cultures, let's briefly look at other cultures, co-cultures, and diverse groups that make up Canada.

Visible Minorities and Other Cultural Groups

According to Statistics Canada (2001), visible minorities comprise 13 percent of the population. The number of Asian-born immigrants continues to increase, as does the number of people from the Caribbean.

Native Canadians

Native Canadians make up a significant portion of our population; approximately three percent of Canadians identify themselves with a least one Aboriginal group (Statistics Canada, 2001). In many areas such as education and employment, Native Canadians still face prejudice and discrimination. However, Native Canadian culture is a rich source of diversity, and many aspects of their culture, such as healing circles, medicines, and religious practices, are being adopted by non-Native Canadians.

LAW AND JUSTICE PERSPECTIVE

Culturally Responsive Policing Services in First Nations Communities

In June 1991, the federal government introduced the First Nations Policing Policy (FNPP) in order to provide First Nations across Canada with access to police services that are professional, effective, culturally appropriate, and accountable to the communities they serve. The portfolio of the Solicitor General [now Public Safety and Emergency Preparedness Canada (PSEPC)] was given responsibility for the First Nations Policing Policy on April 1, 1992. The FNPP operates on the principle of partnership to negotiate agreements for police services that are responsive to the particular needs of each community.

The purpose of the First Nations Policing Policy is to contribute to the improvement of social order, public security, and personal safety in First Nations communities. This is accomplished through cost-shared funding arrangements between the federal and provincial/territorial governments. First Nations communities may choose to develop and administer their own police service or they may choose a police service delivered by a contingent of First Nations officers working within an existing police force (e.g., the RCMP). The FNPP is implemented across Canada through tripartite agreements negotiated among the federal government, provincial or territorial governments, and First Nations. The Policy applies to all Indian reserves, to certain other Indian communities on Crown land, and to Inuit communities, and is designed to give First Nations communities greater control over the delivery and management of policing services in their communities.

The Aboriginal Policing Directorate is part of PSEPC and is responsible for the implementation and administration of the FNPP. Regional managers ensure that First Nations communities have easy access to the assistance provided by PSEPC, especially in the development of policing proposals. As well, the Aboriginal Policing Directorate, in partnership with First Nations, provinces, and territories, undertakes policy, research, and program development work, with the overall goal of ensuring

LAW AND JUSTICE PERSPECTIVE (*Continued*)

policing that is responsive to the needs of First Nations and other Aboriginal people living in rural and urban settings.

For more information on this policy or the Aboriginal Policing Directorate, visit the website below and others listed at the end of this chapter.

Source: Reprinted from Public Safety and Emergency Preparedness Canada, Archive, First Nations Policing Policy Overview (2002), ww2.psepc-sppcc.gc.ca/abor_policing/fir_nat_policing_e.asp.

Families Today

Families are very different today from years ago. Previously, the traditional family was made up of two parents—one of each sex—and their children. Recently, however, family makeup has been changing. For example, Statistics Canada has defined a census family as "a married couple (with or without never-married sons and/or daughters of either or both spouses); a couple (can be of opposite or same sex) living common-law (again with or without never-married sons and/or daughters); or a lone parent of any marital status with at least one never-married son or daughter living in the same dwelling" (Statistics Canada, 2001). Rather than emphasizing traditional roles and stereotypes, interpersonal relationships and interpersonal commitment are emphasized in the new definitions.

There is little doubt that families and how we choose to live are changing dramatically. Common-law families and lone-parent families are on the increase, and the vast majority of lone parents are women. In 1994, one in six children under the age of 12 lived in lone-mother families (Canadian Social Trends, 1997). Also, according to the National Foundation for Family Research and Education (NFFRE) Family Health Index, common-law unions are not as stable as marriages, and approximately 70 percent of such unions end within the first five years (NFFRE, 1998). Also, according to the Family Health Index, many of us are choosing to live alone and stay single. By 1996, the number of Canadians between the ages of 20 and 24 who had never been married rose to 89 percent. In 1971, this number was 56 percent (NFFRE Family Health Index, 1998).

Alternative Lifestyles

Many Canadians are adopting lifestyles that differ from the traditions of the past. Notice that in the definition of "family" the word "couple" is used and not "man and woman." The definition recognizes that a family can also be a same-sex couple that may or may not have children. While recognized in this official definition of family, many same-sex couples are still fighting for the rights afforded opposite-sex couples, such as survivors' pension benefits, and Canada Pension and Quebec Pension plans. In May 1996, the Canadian Human Rights Act was amended to prohibit sexual orientation as grounds for discrimination. At the federal level, family status still does not include families headed by a homosexual couple.

Other alternative lifestyles include communal living arrangements where a group chooses to live together in a variety of arrangements that are based on a common system of beliefs.

CANADIAN PERSPECTIVE

As a future police officer in Canada, it is important that you understand society and the communities you will serve. Part of that understanding comes from gaining knowledge on current and future societal trends. Below are the top trends for Canadian families from The Vanier Institute of the Family.

The Top Trends for Canadian Families:

1. Fewer couples are getting legally married.
2. More couples are breaking up.
3. Families are getting smaller.
4. Children experience more transitions as parents change their marital status.
5. Canadians are generally satisfied with life.
6. Family violence is under-reported.
7. Multiple-earner families are now the norm.
8. Woman still do most of the juggling involved in balancing work and home.
9. Inequality is worsening.
10. The future will have more aging families.

Source: Printed from The Vanier Institute of the Family's website at www.vifamily.ca 2006. To obtain more detail on these trends and issues relying on information collected by Statistics Canada 2001 Census, refer to The Vanier Institute of the Family, *Profiling Canada's Families III*.

As these groups continue to assert their rights through public awareness marches or protests, police officers may find that contact between these groups and those who disagree with them may rise. Even opponents and supporters of abortion have increasingly come into contact with law enforcement personnel.

Disabilities

People with disabilities and other physical challenges form another co-culture separate from the dominant culture. Agencies have been formed to help these groups gain rights and access to many services or jobs that had previously been denied them. These co-cultures also offer their members support, increased knowledge, and sharing of problems, concerns, and solutions. One such co-culture is the deaf culture.

The Growing Senior Population

Demographic trends show that the Canadian population is rapidly aging (Statistics Canada, 2001). The elderly will become a growing consumer of police services (Plotkin, 1996), as they tend to be more vulnerable to crimes such as abuse, fraud, and the misuse of their financial assets (McKenna, 1998). They may also call on the police for help in emergencies that may not be related to crime.

Mental Illness

The reorganization and restructuring of health care facilities has had an impact on many individuals with mental illness, especially in large urban areas. There are many support groups for the mentally ill, and these groups continue to lobby for the rights of people who may be incapable of lobbying for themselves. Law enforcement personnel should be aware that many people suffer from mental illnesses at one time or another.

Depression is Canada's most common mental illness. The Canadian Mental Health Association has estimated that nearly three million Canadians will experience depression at some point in their lives. Depression most often affects people in their working years (CMHA, 2006). Dealing with mentally ill people can be challenging for police officers, since many may not understand the symptoms of various mental illnesses.

Other Co-cultures

There is not enough room in this book to mention all the groups, movements, and societies that make up this nation. Regardless of their group, culture, reform movement, or lifestyle, all individuals deserve the protection of the law. There is no doubt that many influences have an impact on policing and on the delivery of policing services (McKenna, 1998). The challenge for officers is to be able to cope with these influences and to effectively deliver policing at an individual and force level. Since the focus of this chapter is to improve interpersonal effectiveness, let's examine the barriers to effective intercultural communication, and then look at the skills required to manage in a diverse society. While our focus will largely be on major cultures, keep in mind that these strategies can also be applied with co-cultures and other groups.

BARRIERS TO EFFECTIVE INTERCULTURAL COMMUNICATION

In a multicultural and multigroup society, problems are bound to occur as we attempt to communicate with people different from ourselves. However, the struggle is not what creates problems as we attempt to understand others' messages; rather it is the barriers that we consciously or even unconsciously erect. Let's examine some of these barriers in more detail.

KEY LEARNING POINTS

Barriers to Effective Intercultural Communication

- Stereotypes, prejudice, and discrimination
- Ethnocentrism
- Verbal and nonverbal communication barriers—different words, gestures, and symbols
- Different norms and codes of conduct

Stereotypes, Prejudice, and Discrimination

In Chapter 3 we discussed stereotypes, which are formed as part of the categorization process of perception. When we **stereotype**, we categorize people based on broad generalizations and assumptions that we hold about a particular group. The problem with stereotypes is that we lump large groups of people into the same category, often with a minimum of knowledge and experience about that particular category. For example, if you were to find out that someone wears glasses and had extremely high marks during high school and now writes textbooks, you might categorize that person as a "brain" or a "nerd"—an assessment based on very little knowledge about the other things that make up that person. Police officers, like all of us, use stereotypes also—and some of these stereotypes include criminals (Stansfield, 1996). Once you have stereotyped a person, you tend to treat them according to the stereotype, and your responses become biased and limited.

We also tend to seek information that fits with the stereotype and to ignore or dismiss information that does not fit (Philipchalk, 1995). For example, once a police officer has formed the stereotype that bikers belong to gangs, will he treat a young man on a motorcycle differently than he would an older woman on a motorcycle if he stopped either one for a speeding violation?

If we start to treat someone differently due to stereotyping, we have developed a prejudicial attitude and may discriminate against members of this group. **Prejudice** is an unjustifiable negative *attitude* towards a group and its members; **discrimination** is the resulting unjustifiable negative *behaviour* based on this attitude (Philipchalk, 1995). Our prejudicial behaviour may include verbal expressions of dislike, avoidance of group members, actual discriminatory practices such as excluding group members from certain activities or rights, and physical attacks. At the furthest extreme is the extermination of a group, such as Hitler attempted during World War II (Allport, 1958).

The problem with stereotyping, prejudice, and discrimination is that these processes deny the individuality of people. Once people are denied their individuality, they may actually begin to behave and react according to stereotypes. If a police officer believes that the typical criminal is a young, black, or Native urban male, then that officer no longer has to evaluate based upon individual characteristics and evidence (Stansfield, 1996). If police officers hold these stereotypes, the public may become aware of them. Therefore, the members themselves may become aware of how they are *perceived* by the police or by other members of society. For more information on perception and stereotyping in policing, revisit Chapter 3's Law and Justice Perspective box on racial profiling.

Let's look at a real example of the effect of stereotyping: An officer has spotted a car driving excessively slowly at around 3 a.m. on the outskirts of a city. She pulls the vehicle over. It is a dark night, there are no streetlights, the vehicle's windows are tinted, and from her vantage point behind the vehicle, she can make out only that there are two people in the car. When she approaches the vehicle, the window opens and a black Canadian starts to yell that the only reason she pulled the car over was because the occupants were black. In reality, however, what concerned her was the slow driving, which is sometimes indicative of impaired driving. Her suspicions are confirmed: the driver *is* impaired, and there is also a quantity of drugs, and a weapon. It is the manner in which the vehicle was being driven and not the race of the driver that alerted the officer; however, the driver believed that racial profiling was in play.

When we judge others based on stereotypes and then treat them in negative ways, or treat them based on our perception of the group, we are building barriers to honest and open communication. To treat someone like a "nerd" denies that they are a unique person, with many different qualities. When police officers use their powers of discretion, they must be aware of the dangers of stereotyping, prejudice, and discrimination.

Ethnocentrism

When you belong to a certain culture or group, you usually prefer to do things the way they are done in that group. For example, many people celebrate a holiday on December 25 that involves a figure called Santa Claus. They exchange presents, decorate a tree, share a meal with family and friends, and sing special songs. If you are part of this culture (or maybe even if you are not), you know that this holiday is called Christmas.

Other cultures also celebrate holidays at this time of year, holidays that do not involve giving gifts. Some people believe that the children of these cultures should also receive gifts, that it is not fair for these children to go without. But this type of thinking demonstrates **ethnocentrism**, which is a belief or conviction that your own cultural traditions, beliefs, and ideas are somehow superior to others'. When we believe that others' ideas and beliefs about how to celebrate a holiday are wrong, we assume that our way is better—or simply right. Voicing such ethnocentric views creates communication barriers.

Verbal and Nonverbal Communication Barriers—Different Words, Gestures and Symbols

In Chapter 5 we discussed a number of problems with words, which can have different meanings. This may be especially true when words are translated into another language. In Roger Axtell's book, *Do's and Taboos of Hosting International Visitors* (1989), the author presents a number of examples of advertising gone bad because of mistranslated advertisements. Here are just two examples:

- Pepsi's slogan "Come alive with Pepsi" translated to "Pepsi brings your ancestors back from the grave" in the Taiwanese market.
- Parker Pen's famous "Jotter" ballpoint pen needed a different name in some cultures, since "Jotter" translated into something like "jockstrap" in some languages.

Gestures also vary depending upon culture. In Chapter 4, we learned that what is an appropriate gesture in one culture may have an inappropriate meaning in another culture. Giving the thumbs-up sign in much of North America means "Way to go" or "great." In other cultures it translates to "Up yours." Just imagine a situation in which a tourist asks a police officer for directions in broken English. The officer signs the directions by pointing and using gestures. The tourist smiles and gives a nod of thanks and the officer feels good after helping someone. The tourist walks away in the right direction, but he turns around and the officer gives him the thumbs-up gesture. Imagine how the officer feels when the tourist screams back at him, returns the gesture (or another one that the officer doesn't understand) and storms down the street.

Sometimes one culture's important and cherished symbols may be misunderstood by another culture. Remember from Chapter 5 that symbols represent objects, concepts, and thoughts. Christians value the symbol of the cross and display or wear crosses as a symbol of their belief. The Star of David is an important religious symbol in Judaism. The turban and the kirpan (a kind of dagger) worn by Sikhs are important to their faith (Singh, 1990). In recent years the wearing of turbans by Sikh members of the Royal Canadian Mounted Police caused heated discussions in the Canadian government, in the RCMP, and among other interest groups.

Different Norms and Codes of Conduct

Norms are guidelines (usually unwritten) that govern the behaviour of members within a specific group. It should come as no surprise to you that different groups have norms that may be similar or different from those of other groups. Also, what is permissible conduct in one group may be frowned upon and even punished in another group. In the Canadian Perspective box that follows is information on business and social etiquette in China. For each rule, identify how your cultural group would handle this activity.

CANADIAN PERSPECTIVE

Learning about other cultures that are represented in Canadian communities can help us understand those cultures and communicate effectively with them. Good manners are part of respectful communications. The Chinese population in Canada now comprises the country's largest visible minority group (Statistics Canada, 2001), and below are some tips for business and social etiquette.

Business and Social Etiquette in China

Here are a few rules from China:

1. When greeting a Chinese person, use his or her family name only. The Chinese family name comes first. For example, a male named Ling Pan Fu would be addressed as Mr. Ling.
2. The Chinese way of greeting is a nod or slight bow.
3. At a dinner, always leave something on your plate.
4. Never wrap a gift in plain black and white paper, as these are the colours of mourning.
5. Deny a compliment graciously.

Source: Adapted from Sunun Setboonsarng, Greater China and SE Asia Trade Development Officer. *Business and Social Etiquette in China*. Oregon Economic Development Department, 1999.

At times we may also mistakenly believe that others are similar to us and then become confused when they act differently. We may unknowingly insult others from a different culture, or they may unknowingly insult us. If you are from a culture that greatly values punctuality, as Austrians, the Swiss, or the English do, you may feel angry when your new Italian acquaintance arrives 30 minutes late for a party. Since most Italians do not adhere to rigid time schedules for social events, you have just experienced a clash of different cultural norms.

IMPROVING INTERCULTURAL COMMUNICATION AND FOSTERING UNDERSTANDING

Depending upon where you choose to work, your contact with various cultures and groups will vary. If you work in a larger urban centre, cultural and ethnic diversity will be more pronounced than it is in more rural settings. However, all settings will have a large diversity of groups. It is in your best personal and professional interest, then, to learn skills that will help you in this nation of diversity.

Actively Seek Knowledge and Information

Often ignorance of different groups and their codes of conduct or other characteristics may be at the root of many communication problems and barriers. We all have our view of the world and how it works, but we must remember that this view was taught to us within the confines of our mother culture. In order to understand other groups, you need to prepare yourself by gaining knowledge and information.

When the controversy raged over Sikh RCMP officers wearing their turbans, many people had little idea about the significance of the turban. A little research might have explained the religious significance of the turban and why it was and is important for Sikh men to wear it. There are a number of sources available to find information— books about different countries, travel brochures, art, geography books and maps, and the internet. In fact, the information about Chinese etiquette in the Canadian Perspective box on p. 142 was found on the internet. Before launching into criticism or expressing our own ethnocentric views, we should take the time to research our differences. Such knowledge will often lead to better understanding.

Be Other-Oriented and Use Empathy

When you meet or deal with an individual from a different background, try to put yourself in her place. Listen and respond actively, using the skills from Chapters 4 and 5. She may have trouble with your language, and you may have trouble with hers. Nonverbal communication may be more important than words, and you may have to rely on gesturing and pointing. (Just be careful how you gesture!) The key is to try to understand the person and her point of view. Understanding and empathy do not necessarily mean agreement, but they will create the groundwork for mutual respect.

Don't Be Afraid to Ask Questions

Sometimes we are afraid to ask questions. We engage in negative self-talk, telling ourselves we might appear ignorant, or we'll be embarrassed, or we might offend. If you have travelled, you may have found yourself in the uncomfortable position of not knowing what to do next (like using chopsticks for the first time), so you watch and copy and maybe end up feeling foolish. But people are rarely offended by being asked questions. In fact, most people are pleased and complimented by your desire to learn their traditions or way of doing things.

Develop Tolerance

Tolerance does not mean that you stoically put up with something whether you like it or not. In the context of this discussion, **tolerance** means being aware of and acknowledging that cultural differences do exist. This kind of tolerance is based on empathy and knowledge that will allow you to cope with cultural and group differences. If your child comes home from a new friend's house and exclaims that Sam lives with two moms, you can use this opportunity to explain about same-sex couples (depending upon the age of your child) in a positive and enlightened manner. This kind of tolerance depends upon your flexibility and your willingness to understand how others are different.

Avoid Making Negative Judgments

"Here we go again—back to welfare alley for another domestic" is obviously a statement that is negative and prejudiced. First, the assumption is that because the call is in a low-income area, the call must be coming from someone on welfare. Second, this statement also indicates how the receiver feels about calls in this area. Could such an attitude lead to different treatment by the officer at the scene? It is possible—and probable.

There is evidence to suggest that attitudes can influence behaviour. For example, according to the **theory of reasoned action**, having strong feelings about how you are expected to behave, and strong beliefs that a certain outcome will occur, will influence your behaviour (Ajzen and Fishbein, 1980). In other words, your attitude about the behaviour and your norms about complying with the behaviour will lead *you* to behave in a specific way. For example, if you believe in the platform of the Conservative Party and all your friends know and expect that you will vote Conservative, chances are that your friends can predict your behaviour: you will most likely vote Conservative.

Refer to the Canadian Perspective box that follows for an example of negative attitudes and negative judgment followed by negative treatment.

CANADIAN PERSPECTIVE

Negative Attitudes and Negative Judgment Followed by Negative Treatment: A Case Study

Robert Stansfield's book *Issues in Policing: A Canadian Perspective* (1996) provides a case study that is a good example of negative attitudes and negative judgment followed by negative treatment. The case involved Kitty Nowdluk-Reynolds, an Inuk woman. She had been viciously raped and beaten. Based on her description, the attacker was arrested and charged with aggravated sexual assault. She continued with plans to move to Surrey, B. C., and a month later was served with a subpoena to testify at the trial. She was not informed of how to get travel assistance and therefore did not make it to the trial. In August 1990, she was arrested and was to be transported to testify at the trial. She was handcuffed, stripped, de-loused, fingerprinted, photographed, and put in a cell. She was imprisoned for five days, was denied her right to counsel, and was not even allowed basic personal hygiene. She was even transported to the court in the same van as her attacker. She was a poor, Native Canadian, and unaware of the intricacies of the law. Would she have received different treatment if she had been white and rich, and had a lawyer for a husband?

Having negative attitudes and making negative judgments influence how we think about and perhaps how we treat or mistreat others. Negative judgments create huge communication barriers, as evidenced in this case study. For instance, why did no one inform Kitty Nowdluk-Reynolds of her rights? Why was she not told that her expenses would be covered when she testified?

How can we avoid making negative judgments? First, remind yourself that you may be suffering from a bout of ethnocentrism. Your ways and ideas are not really better, just different. Second, ask yourself, Am I thinking about this person in a stereotypical way? As a police officer, you may have much in common with other officers, but you are also very different from other officers. Last, acknowledge differences as challenges, not barriers. A challenge is something that we can take on and accomplish, rather than a barrier that has to be overcome, broken, or made to disappear.

KEY LEARNING POINTS

Improving Intercultural Communication and Fostering Understanding

- Actively seek knowledge and information.
- Be other-oriented and use empathy.
- Do not be afraid to ask questions.
- Develop tolerance.
- Avoid making negative judgments.

DIVERSITY IN POLICING

Our look at diversity is not complete until we examine the makeup of the police force in Canada. As of June 15, 2005, there were 61,000 police officers, and of those, nearly 10,600 were female officers. Women accounted for 17 percent of the total, their highest proportion to date. Although this is an increase of 7 percent from 2004, it still does not represent the female population in Canada (Statistics Canada, 2005). While Canada is becoming more diverse, this trend does not appear in the ranks of police officers. According to the 2001 Census, 13 percent of the Canadian population was made up of visible minorities, and an additional three percent of the population is made up of people who identify themselves as belonging to at least one Aboriginal group. As stated earlier, the large urban centres have higher concentrations of some of these minority groups. When people and groups feel under-represented by professional service organizations such as police, the service organizations may find it more difficult to do their job effectively.

"During the past few years, relationships between the police and some groups representing visible minorities have been somewhat strained" (Linden, 1989). If Canadian immigration trends continue as they are and the Canadian birth rate does not significantly increase, there will be a definite need for the police to continue making efforts to improve relations with ethnic and cultural groups. These changes in the racial and ethnic population structure have five major implications for the police (Linden, 1989):

1. The effects of racism, when combined with social and economic deprivation, may lead some groups to increase their involvement in crime.

2. There will be an increasing number of immigrants who do not speak English or French and who will need police services.

3. Some immigrant groups bring their own crime patterns with them.

4. The growing presence of visible minorities may lead to an increase in racial tensions. Racism is still alive in Canada, as it is in other countries. Some minority groups already have longstanding conflicts that may spill over in areas where both groups are present.

5. In many parts of Canada, there is already tension between minority groups and the police. A great deal of work will be required to ease these already existing tensions.

In response, two major areas of change need to be implemented in police services. First, police officers require training in diversity. "Members must be familiar with the customs and values of various ethnic and visible minority groups within our society" (Working Group Response to Linden, 1989). This training should ideally include officers already working for services, as well as new recruits, and should include diversity training in police programs.

Second, recruitment practices must change. Police organizations have been making efforts across the country to ensure "that their policies, programs and practices bring forward a better cross-section of candidates for careers in policing" (McKenna, 1998). See the Law and Justice Perspective box that follows to find out how police services are actively recruiting officers to reflect Canada's multicultural mix.

LAW AND JUSTICE PERSPECTIVE

Diversity in Recruiting

According to a recent article from the *Toronto Star*, the Royal Canadian Mounted Police is becoming more active in its recruitment of visible minority officers. Like their provincial and municipal counterparts, the RCMP is "waking up" to Canada's increasing multiculturalism. The Toronto Police Service started actively recruiting visible minority officers in 1999. The RCMP is targeting Toronto, one of the most ethnically diverse cities in the world, to launch their major recruitment drive among visible minorities. The RCMP is a national police service and needs to represent Canada's changing communities and populations. According to the article, some cultures are suspicious of authorities. "If a police service can understand those issues they can work better with the communities. It makes good business sense." In Regina, 26 percent of the 90 new cadets now training come from visible minorities.

Source: Nicholas Keung. "Looking for Recruits: Mounties set sights on our multicultural mix." *Toronto Star*, March 18, 2006.

Not only police services will need to increase their diversity. The need extends to other agencies, businesses, and areas of public service as well. Agencies that equip their employees with the skills to communicate with diverse populations and that make concerted efforts to align the diversity of their service area with that of the population, will be ready for the next decade.

SUMMARY

In this chapter we have explored diversity in Canada, defining and looking at what a culture is and how culture is transmitted to others through acculturation and enculturation. We also discussed deculturation. Cultures differ along five dimensions: masculine versus feminine perspectives; tolerance of uncertainty; concentrated versus decentralized power; individualism versus collective achievement; and high-context versus low-context cultures. We also briefly examined some of the diverse groups in Canada, including visible minorities, non-traditional family styles, Aboriginal peoples, and various other groups.

A significant barrier to effective intercultural communication includes stereotyping, prejudice, and discrimination. Often stereotypes and prejudicial attitudes lead to discrimination that can take a number of forms, ranging in severity from negative feelings about a group to actual elimination of the group members. Other barriers include ethnocentrism, different verbal and nonverbal communication and use of symbols, and different norms and codes of conduct.

To improve your ability to span and conquer these barriers, there are a variety of strategies available to increase your intercultural competence. Actively seek knowledge and information about others different from you, use empathy and be other-oriented, don't be afraid to ask questions, and develop tolerance. The sixth important strategy is to avoid negative judgments, since they may lead to unfair treatment of the person you are judging.

Last, we looked at diversity in policing. Two strategies are important for police services and police personnel today. First, police officers need to be trained in understanding and managing diversity. Second, police services need to mirror the diversity of the population that they serve.

WEBSITES

ww2.psepc-sppcc.gc.ca/abor_policing/rel_links_e.asp
The Public Safety and Emergency Preparedness Canada site has extensive links to Aboriginal information and First Nations police services in Canada.

www.opp.ca/fnations/english/default.htm
This is the Ontario Provincial Police site for First Nations programs.

www.rcmp.ca/ccaps/aborig_e.htm
This is the site for the Royal Canadian Mounted Police, Aboriginal Policing Branch.

www.colorado.edu/conflict/peace/problem/cultrbar.htm
This is the site of an article on cultural barriers to effective communication.

www.culture-canada.ca
This is a multicultural website with cultural profiles.

www.culturecanada.gc.ca/index_e.cfm
This is the Government of Canada's Culture, Heritage and Recreation site.

www.narcc.ca/index.html
This site is for the National Anti-Racism Council of Canada.

www.culture.ca
Explore, find, and share the creativity and diversity of Canadian culture online.

www.statscan.ca
This is the Statistics Canada website.

www.fhi.org/en/index.htm
This is the Family Health International site.

www.vifamily.ca
The Vanier Institute of the Family Journal site has articles and other resources.

www.cmha.ca
This is the site for the Canadian Mental Health Association. From this site, you can access information on mental health and mental illnesses.

JOURNAL AND DISCUSSION QUESTIONS

1. What do you see as the main reasons for intolerance and prejudice?

2. Have you been a victim of prejudice or discrimination? How did it feel? What was your reaction?

3. Some people are against the active recruitment of visible minorities and women in many professions, including policing. Should hiring be based solely on group membership or should the best person be hired regardless of race, ethnic origin, or gender? Support your opinion.

SKILLS PRACTICE 7-1
A Plan for Learning

Identify a culture, race, or group that you have very little experience with and limited knowledge about. Develop a plan that will help you learn more about their customs and traditions and cultural expectations. Using library resources, travel agencies, personal interviews, cultural associations, or the internet, answer the following questions and add three of your own. You may be surprised by what you learn—and you will have developed at least one skill (knowledge) to help you with diversity.

Cultural Group _____

1. How do they greet friends and strangers?

2. What are some of their special holidays and celebrations?

3. What is their traditional family structure?

4. What foods do they typically eat and how do they organize their meals?

5. Are there significant religious practices or rites of passage in this culture?

6.

7.

8.

Part 2

The Dynamics of Groups and Teams

Chapter 8   Work Groups and Teams   152

Chapter 9   Community Relationships and Leadership Skills   185

Chapter 10   Adapting to Change   211

Chapter 8

Work Groups and Teams

LEARNING OUTCOMES

After studying this chapter you should be able to:

- Define groups and teams and note differences between them.
- Explain how groups and teams meet members' personal and professional needs. Explain why we are attracted to some people.
- Explain the stages of group development according to Tuckman's model.
- List the common characteristics of groups and teams and outline the advantages and disadvantages of working in groups and teams.
- Discuss conformity, compliance, and obedience as related to groups and behaviour within teams.
- Identify the characteristics of an effective group, differentiate between an effective group and an ineffective group, and identify barriers to effective teamwork.
- Identify the skills required for effective performance in teams and groups.
- Explain several factors that influence team success and outline the steps that must be considered when designing and building a team.
- Use a variety of skills to enhance personal performance on a team.

INTRODUCTION

Throughout your life, you will belong to a number of groups. Some, such as your college class or your ethnic or cultural group, are very large. Others, such as your immediate family, a small circle of friends, or a study or work group, are smaller. An understanding of groups and teams is critical to your future success in law enforcement. Community policing, and trends towards things like private policing, require candidates to be able to work well with others in teams that can perform at a high capacity.

Like other businesses and agencies, policing has undergone and will continue to undergo many transformations. At the heart of team and group work are people. It is not enough to know the types of teams and groups, the goals the group is striving to reach, and the tasks required to attain the goal. Being part of a group is an intricate balance of personalities that makes or breaks the team, and skills are required to be part of an effective team.

In this chapter we will define teams and groups and why we want and need to be part of them. We will examine interpersonal attraction, which is an important part of understanding why we get along with others and become close and intimate with still others, and why we do not like some people. Being attracted to team and group members can help establish positive relations within the group. Then we'll discuss the advantages and disadvantages of working in groups, and the barriers to effective team and group work. Next we will examine the factors and characteristics that make up an effective team. As well, we'll discuss how people assume behaviours and roles on teams, some of which enhance the group effort while others diminish group performance.

And finally, strategies to improve your ability and skill to work on teams and groups will be provided.

Before moving on, try Skills Practice 8-1 on p. 180 to assess your current level of skills, knowledge, and abilities in relation to groups and teams.

A canine unit is a specialized team.
Donald Fleming, OPP Canine Unit. / © Lindsey Maier Inc., www.lindseymaier.com

WHAT ARE GROUPS AND TEAMS?

People often use the words "group" and "team" interchangeably, as if they were one and the same. One day you may talk about the *group* that you have to work with and say that the group has no *team* spirit. The next day you may refer to the same *group* as your work *team*. You should realize that the two terms are different.

Groups

A **group** consists of "two or more people who are aware of each other, who both influence and are influenced by one another, who are engaged in an ongoing and relatively stable relationship, who share common goals and who view themselves as belonging to the group" (Alcock, Carment, and Sadava, 2005).

Let's examine each component of the definition to be clear what a group really is. First, a group consists of at least two people. Some researchers actually define a small group as comprising three or more people (Engleberg and Wynn, 1997).

Being aware of each other and being influenced by each other means that group members have interdependence. The members depend upon each other and therefore must communicate and interact. As you are well aware, this interaction involves both verbal and nonverbal communication. Through communication, meanings and relationships are developed that establish a group context. For example, some groups develop special language or codes that only group members understand. In the group, members establish what they consider appropriate and inappropriate behaviours. For instance, a group of friends may get together regularly for a meal. Is being late for the meal OK, or is it met with frowns of disapproval and a few sarcastic remarks?

Groups also share common goals. A **goal** is the purpose, circumstance, event, condition, or object that the group strives for in its interaction. Some goals may be informal, such as friendship. Others may be more formal, such as raising a certain amount of money for a specific charity.

Finally, people consider themselves to be part of the group. Group membership is deemed as important and necessary for the individual. If the group loses its importance for a member, the individual may opt out of the group or engage in other behaviours that may go against group rules or norms. You may have belonged to a group of friends in high school, but physical distance and new interests may diminish the importance of this group for you. On the other hand, some of the group members may still live in your hometown and membership in the group may continue to be an important part of their lives.

You likely belong to several groups—your family, the friends you do things with, study groups, sports groups, volunteer groups. You may belong to a group at work. As mentioned in the introduction, some groups can be very large, such as ethnic and cultural groups, while other groups are small and may consist of you and one other person. In Chapter 2 we discussed self-concept. Part of who you are and how you feel about who you are (your self-esteem) may be strongly attached to the groups that you identify with over time. Groups are an important part of our lives both on and off the job.

Teams

So how do workplace groups differ from teams? A team starts out as a group but reaches a new level of quality. Special feelings are created among members, and teams create their own processes and take leadership for their own development and performance (Kinlaw, 1991). A **team** is a special kind of group that is usually brought together for a special task and has some special characteristics (Lumsden and Lumsden, 1997):

- **A team is a diverse group of people.** In order to achieve its goal(s), a team is made up of people with specific abilities and resources. A group is often made up of a more casual alliance. For instance, a professional sports team usually draws from a wide arena of players with very different talents required for diverse positions on the team.

- **Members share leadership responsibility.** Because of the diversity of talents and abilities, each member must assume leadership as required for the task. For example, on a murder investigation team, one person may be more knowledgeable about one area of the crime scene than the others. At this point, this member gives direction to the other less knowledgeable members.

- **A team creates an identity.** More than an ordinary group, teams develop specific self-images. This image creates cohesiveness and helps to motivate the team. Hockey players may begin to identify themselves, for example, as a *Canadien*.

- **Team efforts are interconnected.** A team continuously weaves and interconnects the efforts of individual team members to develop a tighter energy and higher focus than most groups have. Each team member's efforts become an integral part of the team effort.

- **Members work to achieve a mutually defined goal.** Like groups, teams also have goals. However, team goals involve more intensive communication to develop a consensus as to what the goals are and how they should be achieved.

- **The team works within the context of other groups and systems.** "A team affects, and is affected by, the context, situation, the environment and the system within which it works" (Lumsden and Lumsden, 1997) While groups are affected the same way, relationships are more critical to team functioning.

When these factors are put together, a team can be defined as "a diverse group of people who share leadership responsibility for creating a group identity in an interconnected effort to achieve a mutually defined goal within the context of other groups and systems" (Lumsden and Lumsden, 1997).

In general then, teams are often more tightly knit and cohesive, are more focused on mutually defined goals, have more diverse members' backgrounds, and are usually formed for a specific purpose. In police work, there are many highly specialized and trained teams, such as special weapons and tactical teams, body recovery teams, forensic teams, and so on. These teams are usually made up of highly trained people who may have complementary and diverse talents, and have specialized goals.

WHY DO WE BELONG TO GROUPS AND TEAMS?

If you examine all the groups to which you currently belong, you can probably list several reasons *why* you belong. Being with others socially and professionally meets a number of needs. Using Skills Practice 8-2 on p. 181, list some of the groups you belong to and identify why you belong to these groups.

Several theories address the reasons we interact with others, and why we interact with others in groups. While it is impossible to cover all the theories here, we will concentrate on two of them: Maslow's theory, which we covered in Chapter 2, and the work of David I. McClelland.

According to Maslow's theory, interacting and communicating with others helps us meet basic physiological needs as well as higher-order needs of self-esteem. Maslow called this need "belongingness" and "self-actualization." We need people and we need to join groups to help satisfy basic needs, but we also join groups to help us reach our full potential. Many of you may want to join the police service to satisfy basic needs, but you may feel-higher order needs as well, such as the need to help others and to protect those who cannot protect themselves.

David I. McClelland and his associates have done considerable research on what is now termed *McClelland's acquired needs theory* (Schermerhorn, Hunt, and Osborn, 1994). This theory defines three needs that are acquired or learned over time through life experiences. The *need for achievement* (nAch) is the need and desire to do something very well, to do something better or more efficiently, to solve problems, and to master complex skills or tasks. The *need for affiliation* (nAff) is the desire to have and maintain warm and friendly relations with others. The *need for power* (nPower) is the desire to control and have influence over others and over their behaviour; the desire to be responsible for others. People vary in the strength and magnitude of these needs. Some people may have a low need for affiliation and are content with just a few close friends; they enjoy personal solitude and happily work in jobs where there is little contact with others. Others have a high need for affiliation and are continually surrounded by others; they like to work in large groups. Most of us fall somewhere between the extremes of each of the three needs. When you review the list you made of the groups you belong to, you will probably notice that your answers reflect some of these needs. For example, if you have a group of friends that you study with, this group may meet both affiliation and achievement needs (if the group actually studies). Groups and teams in the workplace may help fulfill all of these needs. As a group leader, your need for power may be met as you guide the group towards goal completion. Warm and friendly relations within the group may satisfy your need for affiliation. A group that strives for excellence may meet needs for achievement.

However, a word of caution: as we will see later, groups in which members have diverse needs or very different needs can come into conflict. For example, a group of low achievers or people who are content doing just the minimum required to get by can become a source of frustration for the group member with a high need for achievement. Two group members with a high need for power may jostle with each other as they both try to assume group leadership. A group with members who all have a high need for affiliation may accomplish little if social needs get in the way of business goals.

INTERPERSONAL ATTRACTION

Choosing policing as a profession means that you will spend a great deal of your professional life dealing with others. Unlike computer technicians, you will deal with human beings, not machines. You will communicate with fellow officers, representatives from numerous agencies, lawyers, judges, and the public. You will see people at their very best and worst, and out of all these people, you will like some and dislike others.

Chances are you will meet people who become your closest and most intimate friends, and many of these people will be fellow officers.

An understanding of why we interact with others and of interpersonal attraction will help you recognize some of the complexities of interpersonal communication and interpersonal relationships.

Several researchers have noted that managers spend as much as 80 percent of their time interacting with others (Klemmer and Snyder, 1972; Penley et al., 1991). Adults in general spend 71 percent of their time interacting with others (Csikszentmihalyi and Figurski, 1982). Obviously, interaction and **social affiliation** are important parts of work and personal life. Team- and group-based work has its foundation in interpersonal interaction. Let's examine the factors that determine **interpersonal attraction**. How much we like others on a team or group may have an impact on its performance.

Determinants of Interpersonal Attraction

While many of the theories and factors of interpersonal attraction refer to romantic relationships, they can also be applied to friendships and our initial platonic attraction to coworkers. These theories and factors are usually concerned with attraction to strangers and the beginnings of a relationship. Not all the factors will be discussed here. For further research and information, you may want to consult a social psychology text.

Proximity

We are more likely to interact with others with whom we can have contact. **Proximity**, or continued physical closeness, increases the likelihood of repeated exposures. This repeated exposure appears to facilitate attraction (Alcock, Carment, and Sadava, 2005). Increased exposure leads to more opportunities to learn about the other person, and it appears that this continued interaction leads to the comfort of familiarity. The officers that you work with regularly in a group or team thus become your friends due to this proximity.

Physical Attractiveness

While we may dislike seeming shallow, we tend to be attracted to people we find physically attractive. However, since we cannot all attract the most beautiful as friends, it appears that we tend to attract those who are roughly similar to us in physical attractiveness. This tendency to choose others who are similar to our own physical attractiveness is called the **matching hypothesis**. Matching occurs among romantic partners and female friends most often. It is less common among male friends (Feingold, 1988).

Similarity

We are also more attracted to those who have attitudes, interests, and values similar to our own (Alcock, Carment, and Sadava, 2005). It may make sense that you are attracted to others in the field of law enforcement since you have made a similar career choice. This foundation may lead to discovering further shared interests.

Reinforcement

In our dealings with others, we also like people who reward us and who do nice things for us. Some theorists believe that the principle of reinforcement is at the heart of all interpersonal attraction (Alcock, Carment, and Sadava, 2005). The **reinforcement-affect model** states that we are attracted to people whom we associate with events or stimuli that arouse positive feelings. Not only do we like those who reward us; we also like people we have met or have been in contact with during events or situations that we found pleasing. For example, you may be more attracted to someone at a party or social event if you are actually enjoying yourself and having fun.

However, one limitation to this model concerns how much we give or get. If we get too much or give more than the other person, an imbalance occurs. We like *equity* or fairness in a relationship. We may feel guilty or angry if we perceive that the relationship is not equitable.

SOCIAL EXCHANGE THEORY

According to **social exchange theory**, human relationships are largely based on self-interest. Research indicates that we measure our social, physical, and other assets against those of potential partners. Close matches tend to lead to long-term relationships. As with reinforcement, however, a lack of fairness in the exchange can lead to hurt feelings if one partner feels taken advantage of or feels that she is taking advantage (DuBrin and Geerinck, 2004).

How does all of this relate to working in groups and teams? Attraction is important to the formation of teams. Workers are often simply placed on teams or in work groups with little or no thought given to team or group makeup. Once a team is formed, it develops through the stages of group formation that were discussed earlier. Team members who are attracted to each other may be able to develop more quickly into a cohesive and fully functioning team than a team whose members do not feel any attraction towards each other. Can you recall a team or group that you worked on where members did not like each other? The experience can be unpleasant, and accomplishing work can be difficult on a team that suffers such discord.

Second, attraction to other members leads to positive feelings about the group experience. Cohesive teams invariably report that they liked the other members, liked being together, and felt that what they were doing was important and meaningful. In essence, team makeup is an important factor when differentiating between effective teams and ineffective teams.

LAW AND JUSTICE PERSPECTIVE

Emergency Response Teams

When people are in crisis, the police are often first on the scene. It is important that whoever is first on the scene has the skills to calm and control the situation rather than unintentionally make the scene worse and potentially more dangerous. A natural disaster or a missing child can quickly become a tragic incident. In order to more effectively respond to such emergencies, the Ontario Provincial Police (OPP) have developed Emergency Response Teams (ERTs). Officers are trained in techniques that prepare them for search and rescue operations; searches for physical evidence; crowd management at civil disturbances, riots, strikes, and demonstrations; V.I.P. security and containment of situations; hostage taking; barricaded persons; possible suicides; and the execution of high risk warrants.

There are several advantages of this type of team training. First, it is cost-effective because it is cheaper to train a select group than an entire service. Also ERT training prevents the occurrence of tragic incidents and reduces the number and severity of injuries to officers and citizens. Third, ERT training means that trained officers can respond to emergencies efficiently and effectively, therefore saving time. ERTs are a valuable resource to the OPP and the community.

Source: Ontario Provincial Police Field Support Bureau, www.opp.ca/specresteams/opp_001262.html. Retrieved from website on February 28, 2006.

THE STAGES OF TEAM AND GROUP FORMATION AND DEVELOPMENT

Teams and groups do not just happen. Teams, in particular, go through a series of identifiable developmental stages. There are several theories of group development, including those by Tuckman (1965) and the four phases of decision-making groups by Fisher (1970). For our purposes, we will examine the four stages of the Tuckman model, which are *forming*, *storming*, *norming*, and *performing*. A fifth stage, *adjourning*, has been added to these four stages (Laiken, 1994).

The *forming stage* usually occurs when the group or team is new or there are a number of new members. Members are cautious and uncomfortable as they attempt to determine personal relationships and define their tasks. Little work is accomplished. Groups members are finding out about each other and may be testing each other.

Once the group or team has some idea about goals and responsibilities, the *storming stage* begins. During this stage, members may argue and become more emotional, and conflicts and differences of opinion emerge during team meetings. Important issues and ideas are tabled, and emotions may run high. In this stage, group members deal with issues of power, control, and influence, and the team has to decide how to operate.

In the *norming stage*, group members are aware of and follow certain social rules and standards that guide their behaviour in the group. These norms allow for more comfort in the group. The *norming stage* can be clearly identified because conflicts are resolved and the group develops approaches for goal completion (norms are discussed further in this chapter).

The *performing stage* begins when the group begins to focus its energy on tasks to attain goals. Decisions are reached, problems solved, and the group is now a fully functioning team. Some characteristics of this mature stage are enjoyment, positive energy, increased motivation to accomplish goals, shared values, constructive conflict, trust, respect, and openness.

A final stage, the *stage of adjourning*, can be added to this model. Some teams, such as task forces and ad hoc committees, may be disbanded once the task has been completed or the goal has been reached. During adjournment, group members may experience several different and mixed emotions. They may be sad that the group is about to be disbanded and may actually experience emotions similar to the grieving process. There may also be relief that the work is now completed and members can focus their energy elsewhere. Members may also feel proud of their accomplishments (Laiken, 1994).

KEY LEARNING POINTS

The Stages of Team and Group Development

Stage 1: Forming

Stage 2: Storming

Stage 3: Norming

Stage 4: Performing

Stage 5: Adjourning

INFLUENCES WITHIN GROUPS AND TEAMS: CONFORMITY, COMPLIANCE, AND OBEDIENCE

Conformity, compliance, and obedience are rarely discussed in texts about team and group work, but the nature of policing and its relation to society require that they be discussed here. In groups and in society, others influence us to behave or not behave in certain ways. *Conformity*, *compliance*, and *obedience* are three different levels of social influence. Often we use the terms interchangeably, but their meanings are actually very different, with conformity at one end of the continuum and obedience at the other end (Philipchalk, 1995).

Entire books have been written on how to socially influence others, win friends, get your own way, or even attract the perfect mate. Within teams and groups, members influence each other through a variety of overt and covert techniques. How can you get others to agree with your ideas? How do you get group members to adhere to the group's rules or norms? We will briefly explore the second question.

Conformity

Conformity means adhering to the norms of the group and going along with or yielding to perceived group pressures. Subtle techniques can be used to pressure individuals in a group or on a team to conform. Earlier, we discussed nonverbal communication and nonverbal behaviour. A pursed lip or withdrawal of eye contact may be all that is needed to control a group member who is going against the norms of a group. Have you ever walked into a class or meeting late? Perhaps no one said anything to you, but you immediately knew that the rest of the group was displeased with your behaviour. Were you on time for the next meeting or did you continue to break the rule or norm of punctuality?

Social approval and fear of social disapproval may be major reasons why we adhere to group norms (Alcock, Carment, and Sadava, 2005), especially in highly cohesive groups where membership is highly valued. When the situation is unclear to us, we also conform to the group. As a new officer, you may look to other officers and model some of your behaviour after their behaviour in various situations. You may also conform to group influence if you truly believe that the group is correct in its position. This leads to

private acceptance, where you change your ideas or behaviour because you believe the group is right. This is very different from **public compliance**, where you go along with the group even when you do not believe it is right—you feel pressure to conform to the norms of the group. You may feel that being five or ten minutes late to a meeting is perfectly acceptable. Though you may change your behaviour, you may still ask yourself, What's the big deal?

Compliance

Compliance is yielding to a direct request from another person. As police officers, you will be in situations daily where citizens are expected to comply with your requests to move vehicles, stop loitering, pull over, or answer questions. You may comply with the request of a fellow officer who has more experience or expertise than you.

Obedience

As an officer within an organization of ranks, you will also be expected to comply with the requests of your superior officers. This type of compliance is actually obedience. **Obedience** is at the highest end of social influence and means complying with a direct request from someone whom you perceive to have higher authority. Lack of compliance may result in official sanctions and even expulsion from the group. Police officers also have the power and authority to demand obedience from the public when circumstances and the law make such obedience necessary. Ordering an individual to put down a weapon is done differently from requesting to see a driver's licence. The first is a direct request for obedience; the latter is a request for compliance. It is important that officers differentiate between conformity, compliance, and obedience so that communication can be adjusted accordingly. When obedience is an issue, tactical communication and the tactical use of force may be justified.

Do groups and teams expect obedience from members? That depends upon the type of group or team and what the team's tasks are at any given moment. In some youth gangs and other types of gangs, obedience to the leader is expected. In jobs that are based on rank, such as those in the army and policing, obedience to superior officers is part of the job. In other groups and teams, expecting and demanding obedience would probably result in the expulsion of the member who is attempting to get others to obey. Can you imagine how you would react if your best friend started to expect your unquestioning assent to his every request?

THE ADVANTAGES AND DISADVANTAGES OF GROUP OR TEAM WORK

Students are often unhappy to learn that part of a course grade will rely on team or group work. Why? (Try Skills Practice 8-3 on p. 182 to assess your best and worst groups.) Let's examine some of the advantages and disadvantages of working in teams and groups.

Advantages of Group or Team Work

If there were not significant advantages to working in teams and groups, such work would not be growing in popularity. As we saw in Chapter 1, effective teamwork is listed as an essential skill for today's workers. Let's briefly review some of the advantages that occur in a team or group that is working effectively.

- **Group Performance** The old saying that two heads are better than one may be true when it comes to work groups or teams. Team or group members can bring to the task a wide array of talents, abilities, and knowledge that can enhance performance. This is particularly true when the task is complex and when the answers are unclear. With more perspectives and expertise, groups perform better and make better decisions (McClernon, 1991). Also, jobs can be delegated within a group according to member preference or expertise. By delegating, the group may finish a task sooner, and individuals can choose to do the tasks they prefer to do to meet the goal. Teams and groups should be used for appropriate goals that are better completed by a group than by an individual.

- **Cohesiveness** Members of highly cohesive groups tend to like and have a positive regard for each other, although this kind of **cohesiveness** is more likely to occur on teams. Cohesiveness refers to the desire for the group or team to stay together and is demonstrated by feelings of harmony and solidarity (Alcock, Carment, and Sadava, 2005). In a highly cohesive group, members are attracted to and want to be part of the group or team. Thus, effective groups and teams may also meet our social needs even within a professional setting.

- **Learning** In effective groups and teams, a great amount of learning can be accomplished in a short amount of time. "By sharing knowledge, stimulating critical thinking, challenging assumptions and even raising standards of achievement," learning can be enhanced for group members (Engleberg and Wynn, 1997). In a group, people can learn from each other and can learn effective team skills.

Disadvantages of Team or Group Work

There are many pitfalls to team and group work. Have you ever sat in a meeting feeling that it was a waste of valuable time? Have you thought to yourself, I could have made that decision on my own in half the time? Like the saying that a camel was the invention of a group that was trying to invent a horse, most of these feelings result from having groups or teams working on the wrong goals or making a decision that is better made by an individual. Sometimes other group problems make it difficult for group or team members to interact (Engleberg and Wynn, 1997).

- **Time** Groups and teams take time to make complex decisions and to come up with answers to difficult questions. Without allowing for time, groups or teams that are hurried or have rigid time constraints may not be capable of making good decisions.

- **Energy and Other Resources** If organizations cannot provide the resources, including training, required for group and team efforts, the process will waste the time and energy of the participants. While team and group work is often fulfilling, it can also be draining, and company support is required for successful outcomes.

- **Conflict** When we work with others, the potential for conflict exists. Some people may not have effective conflict management skills or may cope with a conflict by using avoidance or becoming more aggressive. Experience with mismanaged conflict may be one reason why you now do not like being part of a team or group effort.

- **Personality Clashes and Personal Differences** When people come together from a diversity of backgrounds, interests, and viewpoints, they don't always share the same ideas and views on a topic. While differences may not lead to conflict, they can lead to dislike of other team members. Some people are not confident in their own abilities and may acquiesce rather than share their own thoughts. Other group members may be quiet. Later in this chapter, we will look at roles in the group and review some negative roles that group members may adopt.

EFFECTIVE AND INEFFECTIVE GROUPS AND TEAMS

Before we look at the skills you can develop to work effectively on teams and in groups, we need to determine what makes an effective team or group. Job requirements often include being a good team player or being able to thrive in a team-based environment. Police Foundations training in Ontario has several courses in communication, interpersonal skills, and group skills.

Think about some of these questions: What personal characteristics do you think are important for effective team and group work? Do you have to like fellow members or just be able to reach the goals of the group or team? What kinds of behaviours drive you crazy on a team or in a group? These are the questions researchers have been attempting to answer for years.

Effective Groups and Teams

According to Johnson and Johnson (2006), *effective groups* have three core activities: accomplishing goals; maintaining themselves internally; and developing and changing in ways to improve effectiveness. A fourth activity might be added: being able to respond and adapt to changing environmental conditions. Without using the entire model proposed by Johnson and Johnson in their book *Joining Together: Group Theory and Skills* (2006), we will examine and summarize their nine dimensions of group effectiveness. We will also add a tenth dimension.

1. *Group goals* are clearly understood, relevant to the needs of the members, evoke commitment, and promote positive interdependence among members.

2. *Group communication* is effective. Members freely express their ideas and feelings accurately to each other.

3. *Participation and leadership* are distributed among members. Everyone gets a chance to participate, to be listened to, and all members are "involved in the group's work, committed to implementing the group's decisions and satisfied with their membership."

4. Appropriate *decision-making* techniques are used based on the situation. The type of decision must be considered, and the available resources accounted for. How the decision is to be made is also relevant. *Consensus*—when all members unanimously support the decision—is the most effective way to make a decision.

5. *Power* and *influence* should be distributed equally in the group, based on knowledge, expertise, ability, and so on, rather than on authority or seniority.

6. *Conflict* should be encouraged, not discouraged, when it is focused on ideas and opinions.

7. *Group cohesion* should be high. When members like and respect each other, they desire to remain with the group.

8. *Problem-solving skills* and the ability to use those skills should be high.

9. Members' *interpersonal effectiveness* should be high. Effective interpersonal skills are essential for doing well in a group.

10. *Flexibility and adaptability* of the group are essential to continued success. The group must maintain an outward focus and adjust itself to outside changes that may have an impact on the success of the group in accomplishing its goals or tasks.

Team effectiveness is the extent to which a team can attain its objectives or goals, achieve and meet the needs of individual members, and sustain itself over time (McShane, 1995). This effectiveness results from a combination of the design and context of the team, the team characteristics, the interactive skills of its members, and the quality and action skills of the members (Wellins, Byham, and Wilson, 1991; McShane, 1995). An effective team is thus selected carefully, and the characteristics of the members are taken into account. As well, the type of skills and the quality of the work of the team members are also taken into consideration. Table 8-1 compares effective groups with ineffective groups on several of the dimensions above.

As you can probably ascertain by now, good teams and groups do not just happen. Training is at the heart of a functioning team. Training in team and group skills has also been the focus of research in policing and in recruit training. Several authors in policing (Robert Stansfield, 1996; Chacko and Nancoo, 1993) have demonstrated that recruits and officers need extensive training in team skills in order to manage community policing, the increasing diversity of this nation, and dealing with complex issues. This text can teach you the skills for effective team and group work. Briefly, the skills are listed here:

- **Interpersonal Skills** Later in this chapter we will cover the interpersonal skills for working effectively in a group. Some of these skills are a review of previous skills, but are based on small group interaction rather than person-to-person interaction. We will examine interpersonal attraction as it relates to groups.

- **Goal Setting, Decision Making and Problem Solving** There are several strategies that can help you help your group set goals, solve problems, and make decisions. Refer to Chapter 6 of this text.

- **Developing Leadership Skills** Effective teams share leadership. You need an understanding of power, leadership, and skills to be a team leader. Leadership will be covered in Chapter 9 of this text.

- **Skills for Adapting to Change** Groups and teams must be able to manage and adjust to change. Groups that remain static and do not change when the environment around them changes are doomed to eventual failure, or at the very least, a period of stress and upheaval. Understanding change and gaining knowledge of the changes in policing will be essential for your career. These skills will be

Table 8-1   Comparison of Effective and Ineffective Groups

Effective Groups	Ineffective Groups
Goals are clarified and modified so that the best possible match between individual goals and the group's goals is achieved; goals are co-operatively structured so that all members are committed to achieving them.	Members evaluate the effectiveness of the group and decide how to improve its functioning; goal accomplishment, internal maintenance, and development are all considered important.
Communication is two-way, and the open and accurate expression of both ideas and feelings is emphasized.	Interpersonal effectiveness, self-actualization, and innovation are encouraged.
Participation and leadership are distributed among all group members; goal accomplishment, internal maintenance, and developmental change are underscored.	Members accept imposed goals; goals are competitively structured so that each member strives to outperform the other.
Ability and information determine influence and power; contracts are built to make sure individuals' goals and needs are fulfilled; power is equalized and shared.	Communication is one-way and only ideas are expressed; feelings are suppressed or ignored.
Decision-making procedures are matched with the situation; different methods are used at different times; consensus is sought for important decisions; involvement and group discussions are encouraged.	Leadership is delegated and based on authority; membership participation is unequal, with high-power members dominating; only goal-accomplishment is emphasized.
Structured controversy in which members advocate their views and challenge each other's information and reasoning is seen as the key to high quality creative decision making and problem solving. Conflicts of interest are resolved through integrative negotiations and mediation so that agreements are reached that maximize joint outcomes and leave all members satisfied.	Position determines power; power is concentrated in the authority systems; obedience to authority is the rule.
	Decisions are always made by the highest authority; there is little group discussion; members' involvement is minimal.
	Disagreement among members is avoided, or suppressed. Quick compromises are sought to eliminate arguing, groupthink is lent. prevalent.
Interpersonal, group, and intergroup skills are stressed; cohesion is advanced through high levels of inclusion, affection, acceptance, support, and trust. Individuality is endorsed.	The functions of group members are stressed; cohesion is ignored and individuality is de-emphasized. Rigid conformity is promoted.
Problem-solving adequacy is high.	Conflicts of interest are resolved through distributive negotiations or avoidance; some members win and some members lose, or else conflict is ignored and everyone is unhappy.

Source: Johnson and Johnson (2006). *Joining Together: Group Theory & Group Skills*, 9th Edition. Allyn & Bacon, p. 26.

covered in Chapter 10. Armed with these skills, you will fulfill the requirements of a good team player and will have a solid idea as to what it really means to be part of a team.

Ineffective Teams and Groups

In addition to the traits of ineffective groups and teams outlined in Table 8-1, these groups do not attain their objectives, maintain themselves, or meet the needs of members. They do not adapt or respond to a changing environment in order to improve or develop. They may "play games," or there may be barriers that stifle group productivity.

Barriers for Effective Teams

Let's examine 11 barriers to effective team development and performance. Some of these barriers may be imposed upon the group by outside forces that the group may not be able to control. Other barriers are internal and result from group interaction and processes.

1. *Time Constraints* When a work group or team does not have sufficient time to make a decision, complete goals or tasks, or solve a problem, the members may not put forth their best efforts. This type of pressure can create stress and work overload. Conflicts may erupt. As a result, the group or team may perform poorly.

2. *Physical Barriers* Not all groups and teams work in environments conducive to structure. For example, in a course you may have had to work in groups during class. A room that is too small, too hot, too cold, too noisy, or has other negative environmental barriers is a more difficult place to work. Teams that have members spread out geographically find it more difficult to get together. These types of barriers need to be dealt with before the team is formed so that they can be dealt with early in team development.

3. *Inappropriate Group Size* Groups that are too large or too small, depending upon the purpose of the group or team, can create a barrier to effective performance. In a group that is too large, members may feel that they do not get enough opportunities for input, there may be more interpersonal conflict, and individual resources may not be fully utilized. Groups that are too small may not be able to handle the heavy workload.

4. *Conflicting Goals of Group Members* When people join a team or group, they also bring different motives or goals with them. Some members may be there to sabotage any group efforts. Others may want to assume leadership or display power. Some people may want to put in as little effort as possible. Some team members may have hidden agendas that may ultimately interfere with team performance. Hidden agendas are personal goals that a member keeps to herself, that may or may not be harmful to group efforts. The problem with hidden agendas is that they go against open communication in the group and destroy trust within the group. Even members with positive goals and motives in mind may have differences in such things as how the group should proceed, which goals should be given top priority, and how various tasks should be divided up among members.

5. *Games and Dysfunctional Roles People Play That Interfere with Group Processes* Previously, we acknowledged that people may "play games" when interacting with each other. These games interfere with interpersonal communication and lead to defensive behaviour and interpersonal conflicts. Unfortunately, people in groups may also assume roles and play games that negatively affect the group. While "playing games" and assuming these roles may be labelled in different ways, depending upon what research you read, the outcome is the same. These roles hurt group members and group performance. Some of these roles are summarized here (Engleberg and Wynn, 1997; Lumsden and Lumsden, 1997):

   - **Dominator** This person demands attention, tries to control the discussion, interrupts, and tries to control others. She monopolizes the discussion and prevents the team from concentrating on its tasks.

   - **Aggressor** Like the dominator, this person wants control. He puts down other team members, uses sarcasm, name-calling, and other negative means to get what he wants. This aggression may come in the form of passive aggression.

- **The Know-It-All** This person knows everything (although she often doesn't, really) and tries to impose this knowledge on the group. She uses age, experience, education, or anything else in her background to validate her "rightness" and everyone else's "wrongness."

- **Distractor** While distraction can be useful when members are stressed, its over-use results in poor team performance. This person may clown around by teasing and joking, changing topics, getting the group off-task, and generally "acting up." This person may also act aggressively, distracting the group by picking fights and "watching the fur fly" just for fun.

- **Non-participator** This person can be a psychological deserter who may appear bored or above the pettiness of group interaction. He may doodle, daydream, or nonverbally signal in other ways his lack of interest in the group work. He can also desert by leaving early, arriving late or not at all, or arriving completely unprepared.

- **Recognition Seeker** This person gets the group off-task by boasting about accomplishments and seeking to be the centre of the group's attention. If she is not the centre of attention, she pouts or becomes disruptive. She may try to hold side conversations or get recognition in other ways.

- **Mean and Unethical Player** This person can be unethical, dishonest, conniving, prejudicial, and nasty, and behaves this way consistently. He may lie, cheat, take credit for others' efforts, belittle others, and engage in other unacceptable behaviours that harm team members, hurt team spirit, and discourage group efforts. For example, he may repeatedly make sexist comments after a woman finishes speaking, belittling not only her, but her gender as well. His goal may be to get her to stop participating, since her participation may be getting in the way of his hidden agenda.

- **Special Interest Pleader** This person has outside interests and wants support from the group for these other interests. For example, as part of a task force, you set up the meetings over the dinner hour, and part of your responsibility is to provide supper. The special interest pleader may attempt to get you to use her family member or friend to do the catering.

- **The "Yes, but" Player** This person is basically irresponsible and usually does not have things done, is late, misses meetings, obtains the wrong data—all accompanied by excuses. At first, the excuses may sound legitimate, but as time wears on, it becomes obvious he is an irresponsible team member who refuses to do his part. He blames traffic, a constantly ringing phone, or losing track of time for his behaviour.

- **Whiner/Complainer** This person undermines the entire spirit of the group with constant complaining and whining. She meets every idea from others with a list of reasons the idea would never work. She may complain about personal problems and other injustices that she is currently managing in her life.

- **Super-Agreeable Player** This person never takes a stand. Perhaps because he is afraid of hurting others' feelings or simply doesn't care, he agrees with everyone. During discussions, he will side with one person and then flip and side with someone else. He has few original ideas and waffles on group decisions.

6. *Competition Instead of Co-operation* In a society that values individualism, competitiveness, and "doing your own thing," co-operation is difficult for some people. A structure that fosters competition among group members instead of co-operation becomes a barrier that hinders team and group work.

   In a competitively structured situation, communication may be lacking, distorted, or misleading. Competition usually results in **defensive behaviour**. Defensive behaviour occurs when people feel threatened or when they anticipate being threatened (Johnson and Johnson, 2006). People will behave in ways to defend themselves against real or perceived attack. Energy is diverted from group tasks and is used to defend instead. Members start thinking about how they look to others, how they can keep from losing, how they can win or dominate others, and how they can protect themselves from attacks. The more intense the competition, the less constructive the communication becomes between group members. Information becomes inaccurate or missing as people try to win against their opponents. It can become next to impossible to move towards group goals.

7. *Disregarding Individual Differences, and Ethnocentrism* In Chapter 7, ethnocentrism was discussed as a barrier to effective intercultural communication. A group member who disregards individual differences and makes the assumption that her way of doing things is better than or superior to another member's will quickly promote disharmony within the group. In a heterogeneous group, there may be significant differences among group members based on knowledge, experiences, training, culture, values, and interests. Differences need to be acknowledged (even celebrated) if a group is going to be effective. As well, while some strategies may be quicker, more effective, more creative, and more innovative than others, one is not necessarily *better* than the others. In this group and at this time, one method may simply work better than other methods or ideas. Ideas or methods should not be dismissed simply because they are different or unusual. As we saw in Chapter 6, "weird" ideas may be at the core of a great idea.

8. *Lack of Training in Team Building* Many organizations use the team concept, but unfortunately, few employees are trained to work on teams; most have little or no idea what skills are required and are often haphazardly thrown into work groups with no forethought by their well-meaning managers. How do you build a team— or do teams just happen? What are the specific skills that employees need to work on teams? Sometimes, these questions are not answered before the move to a team-based organization. Before delving into teams, organizations need to train their personnel so that effective team building and teamwork can happen.

9. *Evaluation Apprehension* Evaluation apprehension is anxiety that results from feeling that one's actions are being judged, monitored, or evaluated in some way (Philipchalk, 1995). In some groups and on some teams, members may feel that they are continually being evaluated by other group members. Such anxiety can create stress and actually hinder performance in the group. In the face of such anxiety, some members may reduce their involvement for fear of looking stupid, not being correct, or experiencing other negative side effects of evaluation.

10. *Social Loafing* Have you ever been in a group or on a team where one or two members did very little work? These members were content to ride along for free and did very little to help the group obtain its goals. Social loafing is the tendency for people to perform at a lower level when working in groups than when working alone (Albanese and Van Fleet, 1985; George, 1992). Social loafers do not try as

hard in a group as they do when they are alone. Social loafing occurs more often when individual contributions are not monitored or identified in some way, and in larger teams where individual efforts are less noticeable (McShane, 1995; Philipchalk, 1995). Witnessing such loafing and lack of effort can demoralize other team members and reduce motivation.

11. *Deviance* We discussed conformity as pressure, real or perceived, that individuals experience in a group. The group pressures the individual to conform to group norms and group rules, and such conformity is more likely in highly cohesive groups. Deviance is a lack of conformity to others' expectations within the group or team (Lumsden and Lumsden, 1997). Depending upon the type of deviance, it can hinder or help the group.

Deviance may occur for a number of reasons and may have different results (Lumsden and Lumsden, 1997). For example, deviance may be a positive factor if it reduces groupthink. A member who comes up with a new or different way of doing things can also be classified as deviant, though the deviance may be positive if it leads the group to better or more efficient means of working.

However, deviance can also lead to negative outcomes. A group member who insists on going against the group may cause conflict and tension among members. Other group members may try to change the individual's behaviour or ideas, and increase the pressure for compliance. The person with the contrary views—the deviant—may begin to feel like an outsider and of no value to the group, leading to further negative behaviours or the adoption of a negative role by the deviant member.

DESIGNING EFFECTIVE TEAMS

To help avoid many of the barriers just discussed, you must develop an understanding of **team building** that will help you become an effective team member. Team building is a formal intervention process that is directed towards improving the development and functioning of a work team (McShane, 1995). An examination of some of these processes will give you invaluable insight into how effective teams can be built within an organization.

In future employment you may be responsible for leading a team, sharing the leadership in a team, or actually putting teams together. With the diverse skills required for today's policing environment, developing this ability is essential for police work (McKenna, 1998). According to McKenna (1998), police organizations, like other organizations, are feeling the need for high-performance-capacity work teams because of rapid and substantial change. Since empowered team development is a relatively new idea or concept within policing, we can look to business for the strategies they use to develop high-calibre and self-managed teams. This does not mean that high-performance teams do not exist in policing, only that little formal longitudinal research has been done on them. Let's look at how effective teams are built.

The Steps to Building an Effective Team

When an organization prepares to incorporate or design teams, the organization itself must undergo a transformation that includes developing a vision; determining what the new structure is going to look like; designing the new organizational systems (or re-modelling the old ones), including the teams; selecting and training members; and monitoring the effectiveness of the teams (Wellins, Byham, and Wilson, 1991). For example, police services need to develop a vision of community policing and how it can be best accomplished, now and in the future. Part of developing a vision is looking outwards at environmental and other changes that have an impact on the organization. For example, increasing diversity in Canada, the increase in visible minorities, more emphasis on human rights, changes in the management of young offenders, and Aboriginal policing—all are changes that must be considered in any future vision and planning.

Entire books have been written on the formal process of team building, so we have little room to discuss all of the required steps in any detail. What we are interested in here are some of the steps that occur when any kind of team is being formed. In other words, what are some common steps that a team needs to concern itself with before—and when—it begins its work?

- **Developing and understanding the purpose of the team** Why was the team formed? What does the team do? While these questions may seem simplistic, team members will need a clear idea of what the team is supposed to be doing. As well, members should be aware of how the team fits into the organizational structure. For example, the purpose of a crisis management team is to assist in managing crises that occur in the community. A clear vision and sense of purpose must be established. The team also needs to be flexible enough to change when outside conditions change (Wellins, Byham, and Wilson, 1991).

- **Setting team goal(s)** Goals are events, circumstances, objects, conditions, or targets for which a team or an individual strives. Goals are clearer than a purpose. A crisis management team may have several goals—perhaps to assist other officers who are managing a potential suicide, or to assist other officers who are dealing with an individual with mental illness. Another more specialized team may respond to a hostage-taking situation. Conflict can occur between team members and between teams if people are not clear about their team goals.

- **Establishing team roles** Different members may have different roles on a team. Teams may include people from different departments, different organizations, and other diverse areas. Part of team building is to establish who is responsible for what. Will certain roles, such as leader, be shared? Will specific roles be established? Ensuring that all team members are aware of their roles and responsibilities will help the team establish positive relations. Confusion around who is to do what often leads to blame and conflict when something goes wrong.

- **Establishing meeting times** Some groups work together all the time, while other groups and teams see each other infrequently. Regardless of the frequency with which members see each other, meetings are essential. Regular meetings to review how the group or team is functioning are essential to building and maintaining an effective team.

- **Establishing group norms** How will the group manage inter-member conflict and controversy? How much work is each member expected to accomplish? How can group members support each other and assist each other in reaching established goals? If someone takes on a negative role, how will the group manage this behaviour? These are just a few of the questions that a team or group may want to examine prior to beginning work. Some teams and groups actually post their "norms" in a clearly visible location. By establishing norms, members are clear about what is acceptable and what is not. See Skills Practice 8-4 on p. 183 for an example of how one group's norms were established for team meetings.

- **Developing a system to monitor individual and team progress** Part of building your team is to develop a system to monitor how people are doing on the team and how the team is doing compared to other teams (Wellins, Byham, and Wilson, 1991). Are people completing their tasks on time? What is the quality of the work? Is there any social loafing? Is anyone having difficulty? These are questions that can only be answered if you have some way of monitoring individual progress. The purpose of such a system is not to be punitive but to be supportive. If someone is having difficulties, assistance can be offered.

  Team progress also needs to be monitored for future evaluation. Have deadlines or goals been met? If there are several teams doing the same job, how does one team compare to another team? These monitoring systems do not have to take large and formal measurements; rather, the key is to have some way of seeing whether the group is working effectively.

- **Accommodating different rates of progress** Because people are different, they won't always be ready and able to keep up with the team. Teams need to establish ways to cope with members who forge ahead aggressively, as well as with those who lag behind (Wellins, Byham, and Wilson, 1991).

Skills for Effective Team Involvement

Once a team has been built, your work is still far from over. Effective teams need to be maintained over time. Some teams may be permanent work teams or self-managed teams, while others may only be set in place for a certain period of time, such as task forces or ad hoc committees. Regardless of how long the team is to be in place, skills are required to maintain team effectiveness. Team development is not a linear process (Wellins, Byham, and Wilson, 1991). Team effectiveness can slip as new members come aboard or external pressures come to bear on the team. We learned problem-solving and decision-making skills in Chapter 6, but those strategies will not work unless the team can maintain itself in a positive way.

Here are some skills that you can use to maintain your team's effectiveness, maintain a high level of involvement and support, and continue to build a positive team climate. You have already learned many of these skills in Chapters 4, 5, and 6 (you may want to review these chapters' skills). The difference is that, in a group, you use these skills in a larger setting—the entire group or team witnesses what you say and how you behave. The more people present, the greater the likelihood of misunderstandings, so it is very important that you be as accurate as possible with your communication.

Help Create a Positive Climate

As a team begins to meet, a **communication climate** develops. A communication climate "describes the conditions that people create and are, in turn, influenced by" (Lumsden and Lumsden, 1997). Climates are created through the communication of team members.

A *positive climate* is open and supportive. Members are attracted to each other and to the team. The climate is challenging. According to one researcher, such teams have members with strong feelings of inclusion, loyalty, pride, commitment, and trust for each other (Kinlaw, 1991).

Conversely, a *negative climate* is closed and non-supportive. On this type of team, people withdraw, become defensive, engage in negative roles, and play manipulative games (Lumsden and Lumsden, 1997). Team performance and outcomes are poor.

A negative communication climate is one of the barriers to effective teamwork. To avoid the problems of a negative climate, **supportive behaviour** should be encouraged. Team members can create positive climates or improve negative ones with their communication (Lumsden and Lumsden, 1997). Positive climates are characterized by openness, trust, empathy, and the willingness of members to take risks and to disclose their thoughts and ideas.

In their book on communicating within groups and teams, Lumsden and Lumsden (1997) offer the same suggestions that we explored in Chapter 5 on the differences between a supportive or positive climate and a non-supportive or defensive climate. Review these six dimensions: evaluation versus description; control versus problem orientation; strategy versus spontaneity; neutrality versus empathy; superiority versus equality; and certainty versus provisionalism. View these dimensions with a team or group focus instead of a strictly interpersonal focus between two people.

If you demonstrate the positive side of these dimensions, you will be modelling appropriate behaviours for others in the group or on the team. For example, if a member of your team offers a rather controversial suggestion that has already been dismissed earlier in the meeting, instead of immediately dismissing the idea again or evaluating it, respond using description and some empathy. You might say, "I'm not really clear about what you're trying to tell us. Perhaps, we should revisit this idea. Could you reword it for everybody?" As another example, suppose a group member is behaving as if she has more superiority or power than others. You can use this as an opportunity to voice the equality of all group members in a non-threatening way.

As you go over these dimensions, try to think of ways that you could use them in a group or team setting.

Develop Your Ability to Assume Positive Roles

While some people assume negative roles in a group, others assume positive roles that help establish a positive climate. If you can adopt some of these positive roles on a team, you will help establish that positive climate. These roles can be divided into *task roles*—roles that focus on behaviour that is required for the group to achieve its goals—and *maintenance roles*, or roles that affect how group members get along with each other while working on group goals (Engleberg and Wynn, 1997). You can and should play a variety of roles, although you may find that you tend to play some more than others. Task roles have been summarized below.

Task Roles

- **Initiator role** Initiators provide direction for the group, and have ideas and suggestions.
- **Information role** The *information seeker* asks for needed facts, figures, and other relevant knowledge, and points out gaps in information or data. The *information giver* has necessary information for the group. He will spend time researching and organizing necessary information.
- **Opinion role** As with information roles, there are two different opinion roles: *opinion seeker* and *opinion giver*.

- **Clarifier/Summarizer role** This person can sum up what the group has just been talking about and helps to clarify what the group is attempting to do.
- **Evaluator/Critic role** The person in this important role can objectively assess the group's ideas and progress.
- **Motivator role** This person can keep the group going by helping to maintain enthusiasm.
- **Technical support role** This role is vital for smooth group functioning. Technical support provides everything from keeping minutes to arranging meetings.

Maintenance Roles

- **Champion** Fulfilling a variety of tasks, this person supports and encourages others, draws out those who are reluctant to speak, praises others for their input, and listens with empathy. This is one role that every member on the team should learn how to fill.
- **Conflict Manager** This person has several tasks. He helps resolve conflicts and emphasizes the need for teamwork. He often comes up with solutions that are acceptable to everyone, and his strength lies in negotiation and mediation skills.
- **Tension Releaser** When tempers flare or tensions get high, the tension releaser may be the one with the friendly joke. Often she has a great sense of humour and knows when to use it.
- **Observer/Interpreter** The observer/interpreter can read nonverbal language well and tries to explain what others are trying to say in a positive way. This person expresses the group's feelings and paraphrases other members' contributions.
- **Follower** This person supports the group and accepts others' ideas, opinions, and solutions. He readily accepts the undertaking of assigned tasks.

Handling Others Who Have Assumed Negative Roles or Behaviour

What do you do when a group member starts to challenge or treat other members poorly, or to behave in ways that hurt the group's progress? Too often it is easy to sit quietly, perhaps feeling guilty, not knowing what to do. You may launch into your own attack, or even worse, help the person out by supporting the behaviour. Even if you say or do nothing, you have, by your lack of intervention, supported the inappropriate behaviour. What should you do when this happens or if you are the target of such behaviour? Here are some suggestions to handle the individual before a negative group climate becomes a reality (based on Johnson and Johnson, 2006; Lumsden and Lumsden, 1997; DuBrin and Geerinck, 2004).

1. **Accept the behaviour.** Sometimes your best strategy is to simply accept the behaviour. Some behaviours are not critical to either group climate or group functioning. For example, while you may find a co-worker's green hair distasteful, it probably does not affect the brain underneath.

2. **Use positive reinforcement.** All parents know this one. Sometimes you can ignore the unacceptable behaviour and reward the good behaviour. For example, a whiner can be ignored until she says something positive. Over time, the whining will disappear, and she may contribute a more positive spirit to the group.

3. **Confront the individual one-to-one.** There are two ways to confront someone. The team leader (or assigned person) can talk to the person one-to-one outside of team

meetings, or he can attempt to find a way to terminate the behaviour. For example, an aggressor who continually challenges one group member may be best approached alone. A responsible and assertive (and maybe brave) team member who is the victim of inappropriate comments or treatment may confront the aggressor outside of the team, by saying, "In meetings, you continually make reference to my big salary compared to yours. I fail to see the significance of this in relation to what we are doing. In the future, do not make such references." This type of confrontation may also work for members who are always late, who do poor quality work, or who do not participate. If the reason for the behaviour is lack of understanding, lack of ability, or personal problems, dealing with it will be less embarrassing in a one-to-one meeting than in front of a whole group that is looking on with eager interest.

4. **Confront the person as a team.** At times it may be appropriate for the team to deal with the individual. If team members have discovered that an individual has a hidden agenda or has been lying, cheating, or acting unethically, group confrontation may be necessary. This kind of confrontation may be especially important if the individual has been playing team members off against each other. A united front may be your only recourse. Usually, a spokesperson is selected to start, but others may have information to share as well. For example, "It has come to the team's attention that there are discrepancies between your progress reports and the actual progress of the project. As a team, we would like to discuss this with you and come up with an acceptable way to resolve this as quickly as possible so that we can all get back to work." Team confrontation may work best when it is the entire team that has been affected by the negative role or behaviour. If a member continually makes sexist remarks to all the female members, the entire team needs to present a united front that condemns the unacceptable conduct.

5. **Go to management.** When the first four suggestions have failed, you may need to seek the help of a higher authority. Team members who do not respond to other interventions may need more help to change their behaviour.

6. **Expulsion.** When all else fails, you may have to expel the group member. Your team may not have the authority to do this, and in some environments expulsion may be impossible. You do not want to resort to tricks like making her team life unbearable or taking on negative roles yourself. However, teams have often been weighed down by poor team members; you may be able to expel the person by other sanctioned organizational methods. For example, a member who refuses to stop verbally harassing another individual may be dealt with by using the harassment policy of your organization.

Send Messages Effectively

The following suggestions offer a brief review and adaptation of previous techniques on listening and responding. When sending a message to others in the group, make sure that what you said is congruent with what was received by the group. Solicit **feedback** to ensure that your message is properly received, particularly if the message is a complex one. Ask group members if what you have said is clear. You might say, "I think I may be rambling a bit. Does everyone understand my point?" It also doesn't hurt to repeat yourself. Sending a message twice or more, or using different channels and ensuring that your verbal and nonverbal behaviour are congruent, will help team members understand what you are saying (Johnson and Johnson, 2006).

Receive Messages Accurately and Check Out Your Perceptions

When you receive a message from another person, you really have two jobs to do. First, you should let the sender know that you are interested in what he is saying and that you are trying to understand the message. Everyone knows what it's like to talk to someone who stifles a yawn or shuffles papers. The message seems to be, "I am really not interested in what you have to say." In a group, receiving messages accurately may be more difficult. The sender may not be looking directly at you, what he's saying may not directly affect your tasks, or you may be distracted by the behaviour of other group members. But you have a responsibility to demonstrate interest.

Second, you need to understand and interpret the sender's message accurately. Here, you may need to use your skills of *active listening* and *paraphrasing*. For example, one member in the group may voice agreement with another member's idea, but you read from nonverbal cues that there perhaps is not as much agreement as the verbal message indicates. You can say something like, "You say that you agree, but I'm not so sure you do. You sounded a little hesitant there. What are you really thinking?" You need to use the skill of *perception checking* to ensure that you have heard the message correctly. Remember that perception checking means tentatively repeating back to the sender what *you* think she is saying and giving her the opportunity to reply to your perceptions. Continue to discuss the issue until you and she agree what the message means. The entire group needs to be clear about what members are saying.

Monitor Your Nonverbal Behaviour

When you are working with a group, do you look interested? Do you fidget, doodle, chew gum, or daydream? Do you lean towards the speaker, display enthusiasm in your tone of voice, and express interest in the group? Police officers on emergency teams sometimes receive criticism for their casual approach in emergency responses. They were nonverbally conveying to the victims, "I'm really not interested in your problems."

Take time to monitor your nonverbal behaviour, and make sure that your verbal and nonverbal behaviour are congruent. Other people *will* pick up the discrepancies. A good team member will ask you about the apparent difference. On open and honest teams, you can say what you feel and think without censure. When dealing with the public, you have a professional image that you are required to maintain to do the job effectively.

Come to Meetings Prepared and Ready to Work

It's a very basic idea, but how many times have you shown up to a group or team meeting and discovered that someone was unprepared? Teams cannot work effectively unless everyone is prepared—and prepared to work. The required focus can be difficult to achieve, as many organizations hold team meetings at the end of the day or in the evenings. However, to be an effective team member, you must be ready and motivated to do your part.

Learn to Appreciate Individual Differences

The importance of appreciating individual differences is not a new idea to you, but it is worth repeating. Different beliefs, values, and ways of doing things are part of our national diversity. Rather than fighting diversity within a group, learn to tolerate and even appreciate differences. Differences can be a source of strength in groups, especially when goals are varied, tasks are complex, and creativity is needed to solve problems or make decisions.

KEY LEARNING POINTS

Skills for Effective Team Involvement

- Help create a positive climate.
- Develop your ability to assume positive roles.
- Develop your ability to handle others who have assumed negative roles or behaviour.
- Send messages effectively.
- Receive messages accurately and check out your perceptions.
- Monitor your nonverbal behaviour.
- Come to meetings prepared and ready to work.
- Learn to appreciate individual differences.

SUMMARY

In this chapter we explored teams and groups. In our professional lives, it is important to understand what groups and teams are and what skills are required for effective performance on a team.

We started by defining groups and teams and discussing the major differences between them. Although the terms "group" and "team" are often used interchangeably, teams are characterized by stronger cohesion and a stronger sense of purpose, with more clearly defined goals. Teams tend to have members with more diversity and have a stronger sense of identity, and leadership is a shared responsibility.

We also examined why we join teams and groups—both personal and professional reasons. Interpersonal attraction is one basis for getting along with others in groups and teams. We also explored how teams and groups develop, as well as some of the common characteristics of groups and teams. There are advantages and disadvantages to group and team work. A special section on conformity, compliance, and obedience discussed the different levels of social influence that may exist within teams and groups. The stages of group development were explained and we looked at effective and ineffective groups and teams, and several barriers to effective team performance and functioning. These barriers include time constraints; physical barriers; inappropriate group size; conflicting goals of group members; members who play games; inappropriate roles within the team; competition among members; disregarding individual differences; lack of training in team building skills; evaluation apprehension; social loafing; and deviant behaviour.

Teams and groups can use many strategies to build their own teams. These strategies include developing a purpose or vision for the team; setting team goals; establishing clear team member roles; establishing meeting times; establishing team norms; developing a system to monitor individual and team progress; and accommodating different rates of progress. Once a team has been established, members need to use effective interpersonal skills to maintain the team's progress and effectiveness. The most important skill is the ability to establish and maintain a positive team climate. Other skills include learning and adopting positive group roles; developing the ability to handle others who have adopted negative roles or behave inappropriately; sending messages effectively; receiving messages effectively and checking out your perceptions; monitoring your nonverbal behaviour; coming to team meetings prepared and ready to work; and learning to appreciate individual differences. Learning team skills is essential for success in policing or any other career.

WEBSITES

www.2h.com/Tests/personality.phtml
Here you can take different personality tests and learn more about yourself.

www.strategis.ic.gc.ca
A Canadian site about business in Canada, this site has links to many organizations and businesses across the country.

www.opp.ca
This is the site for the Ontario Provincial Police. From this site you can access their *How Do We Do It* manual, which has a great deal of information on how teams work in the OPP.

www.business.com/directory/human_resources/workforce_management/ organizations/
This site features a link for information on managing people.

www.workteams.unt.edu
This is the site for the Center for Collaborative Organizations, from the University of North Texas.

www.theiacp.org
This is the site of the International Association of Chiefs of Police. There are several links of interest here, including a link to *Police Chief* magazine.

JOURNAL AND DISCUSSION QUESTIONS

1. Now that you have completed this chapter on groups and teams, think of some strategies that you could use to improve your performance on a team or in a group.

2. Norms can help a group meet its goals, but norms can also interfere with goal completion. What are some norms that could develop in a group that would make reaching goals more difficult?

3. "In policing, being able to work effectively in teams is a critical skill." Discuss this statement.

4. What do you see as the most important skills for being an effective team member? Are some skills more important than others? Why or why not?

SKILLS PRACTICE 8-1

Group and Team Skills Quiz

Some of the answers to this quiz can be found in this chapter and Chapters 9 and 10. For each of the following, answer True if your response is true or mostly true, and False if your response is false or mostly false.

_____ 1. "Team" is another word for group.

_____ 2. Teams always have one leader.

_____ 3. **Heterogeneous teams** have members with diverse backgrounds and characteristics.

_____ 4. Competition between team members fosters a supportive team climate.

_____ 5. One way to reduce social loafing is to evaluate individual member progress.

_____ 6. People who behave inappropriately on a team should be automatically expelled.

_____ 7. Creative thinking is also referred to as lateral thinking.

_____ 8. Groupthink tends to occur in highly cohesive groups.

_____ 9. Group polarization is the making of risky decisions by a group.

_____ 10. Leadership and management are not the same.

_____ 11. Some research supports the notion that leaders do have unique qualities.

_____ 12. Leaders are usually low self-monitors.

_____ 13. There is a natural tendency for people to want to keep things the same.

_____ 14. Coercion is a method for overcoming resistance to change in a police organization.

_____ 15. According to force-field analysis, transition is the easiest part of the change process.

Scoring: Give yourself one point if you answered True for questions 3, 5, 7, 8, 10, 11, and 13.

Give yourself one point if you answered False for questions 1, 2, 4, 6, 9, 12, 14, and 15. Results:

0–5: Your knowledge about skills and abilities of groups and teams will require some hard work.

6–10: You have a moderate level of skill and ability in group and team dynamics. Pay special attention to the areas that you answered incorrectly.

11–15: You are highly skilled in group and team dynamics. Practise your skills so that they match your knowledge level.

After you have finished this book, try the quiz again!

SKILLS PRACTICE 8-2
Awareness: My Group Memberships

In the chart below, identify any groups or teams that you currently belong to, as well as a group or team you would like to belong to in the future, such as a police tactical unit. Beside the name of the team or group, explain the purpose of this group, and list the reasons you belong to this group. What purpose does membership serve for you personally? Refer back to your answers as you read the research and theories of membership after this exercise.

	Purpose of Group	**Reasons You Belong**
Team or Group #1:	_____	_____
		_____
		_____
Team or Group #2	_____	_____
		_____
		_____
Team or Group #3	_____	_____
		_____
		_____
Team or Group #4	_____	_____
		_____
		_____

SKILLS PRACTICE 8-3
Best and Worst Group Assessment

Think about groups that you have belonged to in the past. In particular, think about groups that were formed in order to get something done, such as a school or work project. Think of the best group and then think of the worst group and fill in the information below. Try to use headings such as Member Relations or Getting Along. While blanks for only three reasons have been provided, feel free to write as many reasons as you can think of.

My Best Group:

The reasons I liked this group:

1. _____

2. _____

3. _____

My Worst Group:

The reasons I disliked this group:

1. _____

2. _____

3. _____

When you are finished, read the advantages and disadvantages of group/team work on pp. 161–163. Do they match the ones that you have chosen?

_____

_____

_____

_____

_____

_____

_____

_____

_____

_____

_____

_____

_____

_____

_____

SKILLS PRACTICE 8-4

Designing Appropriate Rules for Effective Group and Team Work

Here is an example of meeting rules that one team established to help guide its regular meetings. In addition to the rules listed below, no meeting could last more than 90 minutes, there was a formal agenda, and minutes were taken that recorded who would do what and when. These rules were posted on the wall in the meeting room.

1. Be punctual and prepared.
2. Treat all members with respect and dignity.
3. Allow members to finish talking before you have your say.
4. No swearing.
5. If you cannot attend a meeting, notify the team leader at least 24 hours in advance, and make sure that all your work is passed on to another member who will share what you have accomplished.

There are many ways to remind group members of agreed-upon rules. One work group posted their rules of conduct over the sink in the staff kitchen. Another team had their rules taped inside the note binders that they used on the job. However a team decides to conduct its business, it is important that all members have input into the rules and then abide by those rules.

It is important to remember that rules should not be carved in stone. Many groups change their rules over time by adopting new ones or discarding or rewriting old ones.

Select a group or team of which you are a member, or pick a team that you may one day join, and use the above example to create meaningful and appropriate meeting or interaction rules.

_____

_____

_____

_____

_____

_____

_____

_____

_____

_____

_____

_____

_____

Chapter 9

Community Relationships and Leadership Skills

After studying this chapter you should be able to:

- Describe how to build and maintain relationships with the community and other partners.
- List ways to effectively manage and express emotions in your communication.
- Define leadership and differentiate leadership from management.
- Explain three approaches to leadership.
- List and explain the sources of power.
- Explain various styles of leadership.
- Explain effective leadership skills and behaviours.
- Demonstrate effective skills for dealing with superiors.
- Discuss leadership from a policing perspective.

INTRODUCTION

This chapter will explore building and maintaining relationships, and **leadership**. Effective relationships with the community and other partners is essential in today's policing environment. Leadership is essential in groups, teams, and organizations, and many of us answer to more than one leader. In policing or public safety, you may have a team leader, a staff sergeant, a sergeant, and a captain, and some work teams have *more* than one leader. In this chapter we will examine what leadership is and how it differs from management. We have all had good managers and bad managers. They have inspired us to do great things or have diminished our motivation and left us feeling angry and frustrated.

We will also examine some theories and research on leadership and leadership styles. Power or the ability to influence others is part of leadership, so power and the sources of power in a group or organization will be discussed. Since this is a skills-based text, effective leadership skills and behaviours will be examined from various perspectives. Using police research and ideas from police experts, we will end the chapter by discussing leadership from a police perspective.

Police officers require leadership skills as well as skills to build relationships in a diverse society.
Barrie City Police Services / © Lindsey Maier Inc., www.lindseymaier.com

WHY BUILDING AND MAINTAINING RELATIONSHIPS IS ESSENTIAL IN POLICING

As discussed in Chapter 1, globalization has brought competition in every sector. This competition—along with changing immigration patterns, technological advances, increased accountability to the public and other stakeholders, government cutbacks, and amalgamation—make it essential for police services to operate more as a business would in order to adapt and respond to a rapidly changing world. In addition to operating efficiently and effectively, a business model of policing incorporates some form of reputation management, as well as relationship building and maintaining. For example, it is important for police services to build and maintain a positive relationship with the media. We live in an information age, and the public has access and rights to information they never had before. Getting the information they need from the police service builds the public's trust in the belief that the police service will protect public safety. Building an effective relationship with the media helps the police reach the public, who obtain their information and then form perceptions based on what they read or hear in the media. If good relationships are established and maintained, the police and the media can effectively inform the public on safety issues.

Research on relationships demonstrates that building and maintaining effective relationships both internally and externally is good for business. In Canada, police services are publicly funded institutions, and as such, community and public support is critical. An effective relationship between the public and media help build positive community relations, which build public support. The importance of building and maintaining relationships is reflected in organizational philosophy and mission statements; for example, the Ontario Provincial Police's "Policing excellence through our

---

The Vision and Mission of the Ontario Provincial Police

Safe Communities . . . A Secure Ontario

The commitment to safe communities reflects our responsibilities to general policing in contract, non-contract and First Nations communities throughout the province, as well as to traffic management and enforcement.

The responsibility for maintaining a secure Ontario is what differentiates us as Ontario's provincial police force. Whether it's international border enforcement and intelligence units, provincial emergency response, joint force operations or specialized services in support of municipal police services across the province, our role is specific and the responsibility clear.

We carry this vision forward by delivering policing excellence through our people, our work and our relationships.

Figure 9-1   Police Service Mission Statements Reflect the Importance of Building Relationships

people, our work and our relationships" (OPP, 2006), as seen in Figure 9-1. Police officers interface with the community, and in doing so, have many diverse relationships.

As a police officer you will have internal relationships with your superiors, colleagues, and other departments, as well as external relationships with the public, the media, and community service agencies, to name a few. Your ability to effectively build and maintain these relationships will assist you in your career as a police officer.

HOW TO BUILD AND MAINTAIN EFFECTIVE RELATIONSHIPS

Relationship building includes four sub-competencies: establishing credibility, developing interpersonal awareness, demonstrating integrity, and building on diversity.

"Through trust, honesty, and integrity, the leader gains the respect of others, fosters mutual understanding and creates productive relationships" (Canadian Police College, 1998). All staff in an organization have a role in building and maintaining relationships because the behaviour of a staff member impacts the organization. Meaningful relationships are built on mutual trust, mutual respect, and shared vision or purpose. Each party in a relationship must perceive that their needs are being met (see social exchange theory in Chapter 8). Fundamentally, we build and maintain relationships through our communication with others. Trust is necessary for open communication. We build mutual trust and respect by the way we consistently conduct ourselves.

Trust is hard to build and easy to destroy; it is continually changing and will increase or decrease with each action we take. The key to building and maintaining trust is to be trustworthy. To build trust we must believe the other party will fulfill promises and behave in a co-operative way. Using the media–police relationship as an example, if the police promise the media that they will send additional information on a topic by a certain time, they must do so in order to build trust—or explain why they can't.

A key indicator of trust is disclosure, and it can work both ways. An organization's willingness to disclose pertinent information is essential to building and maintaining trust. In policing this means giving the public information they have a right to know or that will affect their public safety. Alternatively, will the public or other stakeholders have enough trust in the police to disclose information, or will they go to the media or a government regulatory body with complaints?

Mutual respect is demonstrated through listening, understanding, and showing empathy for others (DuBrin and Geerinck, 2004). When people feel heard and understood they also feel valued and respected. Using police–media relations as an example, both reporters and police officers have a job to do, and a good working relationship is based on mutual respect for each other's ability and professionalism.

Shared vision and purpose is another part of developing relationships. The police and the media have a shared purpose to inform the public, so by acknowledging and working towards this shared purpose, the police and the media can build an effective relationship.

It is not enough to simply build relationships. They must also be cultivated and maintained. Although conflict is inevitable in any relationship, the way in which we deal with and resolve the conflict determines the quality and future of the relationship. (Refer back to Chapter 6 for additional conflict management skills.) For instance, if a complaint from the media is responded to with care, concern, and respect, and the media's needs as a partner and client are met, then the relationship becomes stronger and the level of trust, respect, and loyalty increases.

Maintaining relationships involves ensuring that each party in the relationship is having its needs met. We can do this through open communication. For example, the police may request that the media urgently cover a story, such as in the case of an Amber Alert.

KEY LEARNING POINTS

Tips for Building and Maintaining Relationships with the Media

- Build on diversity. A good working relationship with the media is based on mutual respect for each other's ability and professionalism.
- Realize that the media is a community partner with the police.
- Demonstrate integrity and always be truthful.
- Never say "No comment."
- Establish credibility. Be reliable and accessible.
- Communicate effectively.
- Develop interpersonal awareness. Good manners play a key role when dealing with the media and all public relations.
- Acknowledge that the police and the media have a common goal to inform the public.

LEADERSHIP AND MANAGEMENT

There are many definitions of a **leader**, depending on what book or area of research you examine. It appears that **leadership** is the ability to influence people, or the process of influencing them. Leaders have the qualities, characteristics, abilities, or capabilities to influence people towards attaining the goals of their organization or team (Hollander, 1985; McShane, 1995; Bergner, 1998). Other researchers identify leadership as a process that empowers followers and provides an environment where goals can be achieved (McShane, 1995; De Paris, 1998). Leadership can occur anywhere in an organization and is not necessarily an assigned position (Portnoy, 1999).On the other hand, **management** refers to the tasks and the more technical aspects of managing—such as budgets, time management, and other activities (Bergner, 1998). Managers have the authority to manage and organize certain activities (Portnoy, 1999). To train people in these technical tasks is not difficult—and often it is police organizations and leaders that confuse management with leadership (Bergner, 1998). According to Laurie Bergner (1998), a law enforcement trainer and consultant, leadership cannot be measured with a paper and pencil test, as the skills of the manager can. McKenna (1998) succinctly states that "a leader is someone who is equipped to move people and events toward some goal or objective." Part of effective police leadership is management and the ability to manage information in a number of ways (McKenna, 1998). Therefore, leadership is essentially a process undertaken by an individual with specific characteristics and abilities that *include* the ability to perform management functions. Ideally, what organizations may really be reaching for is an individual who can also lead. The real question may not be how can we train effective leaders, but rather how can we train people from a variety of positions to demonstrate leadership and then have them assigned to positions in an organization where they can use their leadership skills?

THEORIES OF LEADERSHIP

The great leaders in history—Pierre Trudeau, Martin Luther King, Jr., Genghis Khan, Joan of Arc, Winston Churchill—are people very different from most of us. Social psychologists and other researchers have long been trying to determine how a person becomes a leader. Does a leader in one situation maintain that leadership in a different situation? Would Genghis Khan make a good president at your learning institution, or chief of your local police service? Likely not. Before we look at leadership today, we have much to learn from past and present theories, which have provided much of what we know about effective leadership.

The Trait or "Born Leader" Approach

The "Great Person Theory" or **trait approach** suggests that leaders have unique traits or characteristics that qualify them to lead. In the early 1940s and 1950s, a number of studies were done and a bewildering number of leadership characteristics were discovered. Improved computer technology eventually allowed for faster and more efficient analysis of results. Three areas of trait research have been of recent interest: charisma, self-monitoring, and gender (Philipchalk, 1995).

Charisma, or the unique leadership quality that inspires followers, has been studied intensely by one pair of researchers, Conger and Kanungo (1987, 1988, 1992). Several common behaviours were identified as making up charisma, including sensitivity to follower needs, striving to change the status quo, taking personal risks, and engaging in self-sacrificing behaviour. A very important feature of the charismatic leader is the ability to articulate a vision of radical change.

Self-monitoring is the degree to which people change their behaviour according to their perceptions of the social demands of a situation, and is really a continuum from low to high. Low self-monitors are relatively unaffected by social demands and continue to act according to their inner dispositions and tendencies. On the other hand, high self-monitors strive to adapt to social demands and change their behaviour accordingly. High self-monitors are very conscious of how other people are reacting to them and have a high ability to adjust their behaviour based on these reactions (Philipchalk, 1995). In studies of groups and leadership emergence (for example, Cronshaw and Ellis, 1991), high self-monitors, or those who could be classified as high self-monitors, have emerged as leaders—so apparently, leaders tend to be high self-monitors. It should be noted that this was research done with male subjects and the results may not hold true for female leaders. More research needs to be done with female subjects.

The third area of trait research is *gender*. For many years, leadership was considered a masculine trait (Philipchalk, 1995). But do women lead differently from men? If so, which is the best leadership style—the male or the female style? Several research studies have tried to answer these questions (Eagly and Johnson, 1990; Eagly, Makijani, and Klonsky, 1992; Rosener, 1990).

According to this research, there appear to be a couple of differences between how men and women lead. Women tend to be "transformational" leaders who motivate their subordinates to transform self-interest into interest for the welfare of the larger group. Men are more inclined to be "transactional" leaders and see leadership as a series of job transactions with subordinates. Women also tend to be more democratic or participatory in their leadership style and use a less autocratic or directive approach than men. The answer to which style is the best leads to further questions, since women are still under-represented in positions of leadership. Obviously, environment and situation also have much to do with leadership.

The Behavioural Approaches to Leadership

Some results of the research into charisma and gender had to do with the behaviours of the leader. A person may have specific characteristics or traits, but he or she can be identified only through the actual behaviour. What behaviours make a leader effective?

Several different groups of studies examined two specific behaviours of leaders: the degree to which a leader was concerned with people (variously called "employee-centred," "people orientation," "consideration," or "concern for people"), and the degree to which a leader is concerned with production (variously called "production-centred," "task orientation," "initiating structure," or "concern for production"). (For a brief summary of these studies, examine organizational behaviour texts such as Schermerhorn, Hunt, and Osborn, 1994.)

A people-centred leader is concerned with employees' feelings and welfare. A production-centred leader is concerned with getting the work done. The leadership grid developed by Robert Blake and Jane Mouton (1978) uses both of these styles and plots them on a graph. Thus a leader can be high on both, low on both, in the middle on both or at the extreme of each behavioural style. For example, a leader who is highly concerned with both people and production has a team-management approach. A leader who is concerned with neither has adopted an impoverished style.

The Situational Approaches to Leadership

The major problem of the behavioural approach to leadership is that it does not really address the environment in which leadership takes place, especially what type of subordinates or followers are involved. Several theories were developed that examine the situation where leadership occurs. The results indicate that no one leadership style is the best, and in order to be effective, a leader must pay attention to the external environment, including the capabilities and motivation of employees. Successful leaders adapt their behaviour (high self-monitoring) to meet the needs of followers and the demands of the situation. Leadership effectiveness depends on the leader, the followers, and all the elements of the situation (Blanchard and Hersey, 1996). The popular theory of Paul Hersey and Kenneth Blanchard (1988, 1996) has become the basis for much training in both Canada and United States.

Hersey and Blanchard's Situational Leadership Theory

Without going into great detail about this theory, some of its important components can be reviewed to increase your understanding of the complexity of leadership. The emphasis in this theory is that the leader changes his or her leadership style based on the level of maturity or "readiness" of employees. According to Hersey and Blanchard (1988), maturity or readiness is based on the ability and willingness of an employee to accomplish a specific task. Figure 9-2 provides a visual guide to enhance understanding. Followers fall into four categories of readiness, from low to high, or R1 to R4. The leader adjusts his or her style to manage followers and chooses from four different styles of leadership: *telling*, *selling*, *participating*, and *delegating*. Let's review each one using the level of readiness from low to high.

- **Telling or directing style for R1 followers** The leader has a high-task orientation and provides specific instructions and closely monitors performance. This might be the type of behaviour most appropriate when a person is first hired on a job with little or no experience. In policing, a field training officer with a new rookie would be a good example.

- **Selling style or coaching for R2 followers** The leader maintains a high task orientation while increasing support behaviour. Here the follower is more willing to perform the duties but may still lack many skills. There is still a lot of explaining and directing, but the leader also reinforces the willingness of the follower. The field training officer, although still very directive, can praise the rookie for properly handling an incident.

- **Participating or supporting for R3 followers** The leader increases support behaviour and decreases the amount of guidance and instruction. The employee is now able to do the task, but is still unwilling or insecure. The field training officer continues to offer encouragement to the rookie and allows the rookie to do more tasks independently.

- **Delegating for R4 followers** The leader decreases both supportive and task behaviour as the follower is now both willing and able or confident enough to do the tasks. At this stage, the field training officer may make her final assessment of the rookie, and the rookie may now be able to go out on his own.

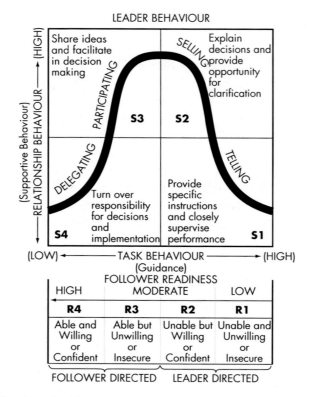

Figure 9-2 Situational Leadership

These two researchers have changed the model somewhat since their original ideas (Blanchard and Hersey, 1996). However, the premise is the same: leaders need to determine where their followers are "at" and adjust their behaviour accordingly.

This theory also points the way to several key ideas in training people to be effective leaders (discussed in the section on developing leadership skills). The most important idea from this situational approach is that an effective leader can assess the needs of subordinates and can vary her leadership style accordingly.

POWER

If leaders (or managers or captains) are going to influence followers towards achieving organizational goals, they have to have some sort of power. **Power** is the ability to get someone to do something that you want him to do; in organizations, having power influences subordinates to achieve the goals that the leader has defined. In other words, if someone has power over you, she can get you to do the things that she wants done in the way she wants them done. Leaders use power to accomplish organizational goals. Organizational leaders and managers derive power from five different bases that come from two different sources. The sources are *position power* and *personal power* (French and Raven, 1959; Raven, 1993). Not all of these sources are strictly controlled by those in managerial positions. Group and team members and other employees may also have power. Police officers have power to influence a large number of people in their daily duties granted by law. Here, however, we want to examine power as it occurs within organizations or within police services.

Position Power Sources

- **Reward power** Reward power is based on the ability of the leader or manager to control rewards. Rewards can include money, promotions, compliments, time off, vacation schedules, and work assignments.

- **Coercive power** Punishment, as well as rewards, can be used to influence others. Coercive power is the extent to which a leader or manager can deny rewards or use punishment. Withholding a pay raise, threatening a transfer, demoting, threatening to fire, personnel file letters, and threatening to stop a promotion are all examples of punishments. The manager who relies solely on coercive power is often not well liked by subordinates.

- **Legitimate power** Legitimate power is the perceived right of a manager or leader to influence others through the use of formal authority. The chain of command consists of a formal authority structure in police services and other organizations. However, even legitimate power is subject to rules, such as the policy and procedures of an organization, and other codes of conduct, such as laws against harassment.

Personal Power Sources

- **Expert Power** Expert power is the ability to influence another person's behaviour through special talents, knowledge, or abilities that the other person does not have but needs. In a group performing a specific task, the person that has the most knowledge in that area may lead and direct the group through the task. Access or control over specific information is important in building and maintaining this power base. If the knowledge that this person possesses is out of date, then he will no longer have this base for power. In any organization, both leaders and employees may have this source of power.

- **Referent power** Referent power is the leader's ability to influence another person's behaviour by being liked, respected, or having the person identify with the leader. Referent power is related to our earlier discussion on charisma. Those who have referent power have good interpersonal skills (Yukl, 1989). Again, both leaders and employees in an organization may have this type of power. For example, an employee who is well liked by her manager may receive better job assignments than co-workers who are not as well liked.

KEY LEARNING POINTS

Types of Power

Position Power Sources
- Reward power
- Coercive power
- Legitimate power

Personal Power Sources
- Expert power
- Referent power

Note that any person can have more than one source of power. A manager may have legitimate power, be well liked and respected by employees (referent power), and have the knowledge needed to orchestrate a major organizational restructuring project (expert power). Also, power can change in organizations in response to personnel changes, organizational restructuring, responses to external and internal changes, and any other factors that change the environment where the power is based. However, effective leaders have the ability to influence others, as well as an understanding of how to use their power in ways that empower subordinates to continue to meet organizational goals and challenges.

LEADERSHIP STYLES

Let's briefly review some of the styles that leaders and managers adopt. There is no one best style of leadership, but nevertheless, many managers tend to favour one style over the others. This is certainly not a complete list, and other styles are included in the previous theories. This list will give you a notion of the radically different ways leaders lead.

The Authoritarian Leader

This style is exactly what it sounds like. This leader keeps tight control over his staff and their functions and may use reward and coercive power to influence subordinates (Lumsden and Lumsden, 1997). This leader or manager is "by-the-book" and sticks to policies and procedures. He believes that employees should do exactly what they are told; the goal is success and perpetuation of the organization.

The Laissez-Faire Leader

This leader lets things happen and allows employees to do what they please. Although this type of leadership works for teams of experts who do not require leader involvement, it is rarely effective in the long run (Lumsden and Lumsden, 1997). If jobs get done, their completion has little to do with input from the leader. The jobs get done because the team is competent enough to work without leadership (at least for a while).

The Person-Centred Leader (Coach)

This leader is concerned with people and issues about people. Sometimes referred to as the human relations style manager (Dantzker and Mitchell, 1998), this leader recognizes the importance of the human element in the workings of the organization. This leader wants to have input from others when making decisions and solving problems. This type of leader also recognizes the importance of coaching and mentoring as leadership practices.

The Transactional Leader

The transactional leader (Bass, 1990) uses negotiation and rewards to influence followers. As stated previously, this type of leader views leadership as a series of jobs or transactions. Followers participate in decision making, but in contrast to working with the tranformational leader, there is not as much inspiration from this style for followers.

The Charismatic Leader

This type of leadership is characterized by an intensely personal relationship between the leader and followers. Charismatic leaders provide followers with visions of transformation; they are innovative and creative and try to change the status quo (Conger and Kanungo, 1992).

The Transformational Leader

The transformational leader is one of the most contemporary styles of leadership, and has some of the characteristics of the charismatic leader. This type of leader motivates, inspires, and develops the team, just as the charismatic leader does. The difference is that the transformational leader does this within the team and organization. This leader helps members to achieve their own goals while also fulfilling the vision and goals of the team and organization (Lumsden and Lumsden, 1997).

Transformational leaders have charisma, have the ability to inspire others with high expectations, stimulate team members intellectually, and treat people as individuals by giving personal attention (Bass, 1990). The focus of a transformational leader is two-fold: a high concern for people and a high concern for achieving goals.

KEY LEARNING POINTS

Leadership Styles

- The authoritarian leader
- The laissez-faire leader
- The person-centred leader (coach)
- The transactional leader
- The charismatic leader
- The transformational leader

DEVELOPING LEADERSHIP SKILLS

Now that we have some ideas about leadership styles, what leadership is, what leaders do (according to theory), and where their influence comes from, two questions remain: what are effective leadership skills and behaviours, and how are they developed? Despite what the earlier-mentioned Great Person Theory suggests, great leaders are not born but develop their skills over time. Leadership is a process that enables people to achieve goals—but what is this process? In reality, leadership is a "series of behaviours that enable a group or organization to accomplish commonly desired goals . . . to enable organizational members to choose to move in a common direction and to accomplish their organizational tasks" (Ray, 1999).

Leadership is the process of choosing and using specific behaviours to influence others. There is an incredible amount of research in this area and a great deal of controversy, but there appears to be one solid conclusion: the need for good leaders is great, including leaders in policing. As well, the characteristics of the transformational leader appear to be those characteristics most often credited to effective leaders, and may be the ones that potential leaders need to learn in the current environment of change. Most law enforcement writers agree that the times are chaotic and change is fast-paced. According to one pair of researchers, a leadership void is occurring (Bennis, 1989). Many law enforcement writers are echoing these same sentiments (Nancoo, 1993; Bergner, 1998; De Paris, 1998).

Because of the team and group approach in organizations, leadership does not occur just at the top. Leadership occurs at all levels in an organization, and leadership behaviour (including verbal and nonverbal communication) "facilitates a team's transactional and task processes in achieving members' and the team's needs and goals" (Lumsden and Lumsden, 1997). Leadership addresses both how the group functions (transactions) and what the group does (tasks). It is this approach that the rest of this chapter will reflect. All of us can be leaders in organizations even though we may not all be managers or leaders in the hierarchical sense of the words.

Leadership Skills, Behaviours, and Abilities

There are several skills, behaviours, and abilities that leaders have and know how to use. Many of these skills can be used by anyone within any team or organization. A few depend on the individual holding a formal position of authority. Each of the following 13 skills was found in at least two sources. For most of these skills, at least one reference is from law enforcement sources.

1. **Leaders have vision and can clearly articulate that vision.** It is difficult to lead if you have no idea where you are going. A vision is a clear idea of where the organization is headed, as well as of the set of actions required to get there (De Paris, 1998; Ray, 1999). In a climate of organizational change, the change processes need to come from the top down (De Paris, 1998). Leaders who have positions of management and authority need to develop their abilities in that particular area. Not only must the leader have a vision, but she also needs to break down this vision into doable components so that all employees can take their lead and do their part. For example, when the vision of community policing was born, people wondered what it really meant and how it is really done. For many police services, community policing meant a complete restructuring of how they did business. Effective leaders, by articulating the vision, can excite other group members and provide the impetus, and can move the organization forward. Martin Luther King, Jr., gave a clear image of what the social order should be—with all people being equal.

2. **Leaders communicate effectively.** For future police leaders, communication skills "will be paramount" (Lunney, 1989). Leaders can communicate effectively both verbally and nonverbally (Sewell, 1996; McKenna, 1998; Portnoy, 1999; Ray, 1999). Using strategies for listening and responding (see earlier chapters), leaders work hard at both understanding others and assisting others in understanding them. This also includes sharply honed writing skills (Sewell, 1996).

3. **Leaders manage and know themselves.** James Sewell, in his article about the four Rs for police executives, assigns one of the Rs to "Roots." Roots are grounded in who you are: your professional and personal philosophies, values, and experiences. These roots form the basis for your decisions, actions, and other visible displays of leadership (Sewell, 1996). Leaders take time to develop their own philosophies, to understand who they are, and to identify what it is that they stand for and support (Lunney, 1989; Sewell, 1996). Go to Skills Practice 9-1 on p. 208 to build your own personal philosophy and values statement.

4. **Leaders know how to get attention.** Effective leaders also draw others to them (Bennis, 1989). These leaders attract people who want to work with them and can gain the commitment of other group members. According to Lunney (1989), future police leaders will have a hands-on style and be action-oriented. They will be adept at being highly visible within their organizations and will therefore need to develop such skills as effective public speaking, effective listening, and the capacity to talk to a broad spectrum of people.

5. **Leaders recognize and encourage others in skill development.** Effective leaders help to develop people (Ray, 1999). While the leader models effective behaviours and skills, he also teaches these skills to anyone who wishes to learn them. He demonstrates and teaches the skills using learning methods suitable for members and then gives feedback when others practise these skills. Feedback must be clear, must describe the behaviour, and must not evaluate the person (Ray, 1999). Being able to give feedback is an essential leadership skill. Try Skills Practice 9-2 on p. 209 to improve your skill at giving feedback.

6. **Leaders work to establish positive climates.** Effective leaders use many techniques to create positive work and growth environments. With your knowledge of establishing supportive and positive climates, you will be able to use this knowledge in a leadership role. Good leaders create opportunities for group and team decision making, reward effective teamwork, discipline lack of teamwork, and know the skills needed to establish effective and competent teams (Bergner, 1998; Ray, 1999). Leaders openly suggest and encourage the development of positive group norms such as openness, mutual concern, mutual respect, co-operation, decision making by consensus, trust, and the involvement of all members (Lumsden and Lumsden, 1997).

7. **Leaders help manage conflicts among group members.** As we saw in earlier chapters, conflict is a normal process between people and between group members. Constructive conflict is welcome when it is managed with a focus on collaboration and win-win outcomes, and when the environment fosters negotiation. Leaders can help members who are experiencing a conflict and can act as facilitator and establish common ground for the conflicting parties (Ray, 1999). Part of conflict management is also the ability to develop alternative solutions (problem solving) that satisfy the differing opinions of the group. The leader assists in managing the conflict while still ensuring that the group and its members continue to work and advance towards their goals and objectives (McKenna, 1998).

8. **Leaders inspire others.** Effective leaders do more than influence followers; they inspire them to new levels of achievement and growth, or *encourage the heart* (Kouzes and Posner, 1987). These leaders do so by recognizing accomplishments and contributions in such a way that members are encouraged to continue their efforts. Perhaps you have had this kind of experience: during a team meeting (for any activity), you come up with an idea. Your team leader, or manager, welcomes your idea and enthusiastically applauds your continued efforts. You leave the meeting eager and ready to try your idea, with the knowledge that it has been supported.

9. **Leaders change their style to meet the needs of others.** Earlier we discussed the situational model of leadership and the finding that leaders tend to be high self-monitors. With the ability to read the social situation and to adapt leadership style, leaders can change their styles to meet the needs of followers. For example, a training officer notices some reluctance on the part of a rookie to do something. The training officer, reading the cues from the situation, adopts more of a telling or coaching approach to assist the rookie. According to Hersey and Blanchard (1988), good leaders are flexible in how they supervise and manage subordinates.

10. **Leaders engage in coaching and mentoring. Coaching** is encouraging someone toward a level of competency or proficiency in an area of development (McKenna, 1998). Usually the coach has superior skills in the area of competency. *Mentoring* is similar to coaching and involves learning a variety of skills or approaches from a

senior staff member. Programs that pair rookie officers with senior officers are good examples of mentoring in the police service. The rookie officer may learn a variety of skills from the senior officer. Effective leaders can also be effective coaches and mentors.

11. **Leaders stay current.** If leaders are going to inspire followers and assist in organizational change and restructuring, it is essential that they stay up to date by reading, examining, and questioning not only in their area of leadership but also elsewhere in the nation and the world. For police leaders this means reading trade and professional journals, journals outside traditional law enforcement literature, local and wider perspective newspapers, and books on management (Sewell, 1996). The police leader of the twenty-first century also needs to review writings that have a futurist perspective, and explore ideas about where the future is heading (Lunney, 1989).

12. **Leaders are ethical.** A leader in law enforcement is committed to ethics in law enforcement. "This includes the values of helping others and fighting 'bad guys' while staying within the boundaries of legal and ethical standards in his attempts to succeed" (Bergner, 1998). Leaders are models for others and must therefore model or demonstrate the behaviour they wish to see in other organization and team members.

13. **Leaders fulfill their managerial responsibilities.** Many people do rise in the ranks of organizations and forces and take on managerial duties. While many of us would prefer to spend our time inspiring, leading, visioning, and creating, legitimate leaders still have to engage in the day-to-day processes of management. Leaders who also manage are faced with responsibilities that require not only the previously mentioned skills, but also some additional, albeit more mundane, ones.

   - **Time management skills** An effective manager manages time efficiently and competently (Bergner, 1998). This means coming to work on time, working independently, and turning in well-written reports in a timely manner. By demonstrating these skills, he can expect others to do the same.

   - **Effective meeting skills** While all group members need to come to meetings prepared and ready to work, the manager must provide the framework for the meetings. Whether the individual is a manager by formal authority or a designated team leader, he must plan, distribute, and modify the agenda (Lumsden and Lumsden, 1997). He must also establish the climate of the meeting. For example, if he does all of the talking or behaves defensively, meetings can quickly develop a negative climate.

   - **Planning and organization** The managerial or leader function involves the ability to design the anticipated future, to develop the goals and organization for the future, and to assist the team or organization in getting there (Lunney, 1989; McKenna, 1998). Organization may involve creating set meeting times, providing information in some way, goal-setting with timelines for completion, and so on. Planning is often tied to decision making in the organization.

   - **Goal and objective setting** Good leaders and managers know how to set effective goals and objectives.

The Canadian Police College and Leadership

According to a publication from the Canadian Police College (CPC), managing police services will become an increasingly challenging and demanding task. "Public demand for a greater variety of police services continue[s] as do the increases in resource restrictions." As a result of the many societal and political changes, the CPC advisory committee recommended that the Canadian Police College training programs be redesigned using key competencies. One area was to identify the competencies of effective leadership and to design training to teach these competencies. Utilizing expert input from inside and outside policing (including focus groups from across the country) led to the development of six competencies that make up a teachable model of leadership. Interestingly, leadership was also defined as being different from management (as we have already discussed in this chapter). Listed below are the six competencies of leadership, with their accompanying sub-competencies. The competencies have been ranked as they should be taught.

1. *Continuous Personal Growth* includes these six sub-competencies: learning continuously; developing self-awareness/self-discipline; projecting self-confidence; demonstrating flexibility; finding the right balance; and practising stress-management.

2. *Communication Skills* include the following sub-competencies: listening in order to understand, and communicating to be understood. A leader requires the ability to interact with others to promote and foster understanding, affect behaviours, and achieve desired results.

3. *Relationship Building* includes four sub-competencies: demonstrating integrity; establishing credibility; developing interpersonal awareness; and building on diversity. "Through trust, honesty, integrity, the leader gains the respect of others, fosters mutual understanding and creates productive relationships."

4. *Stewardship* "is the management of others" in such a way as to create an environment that guides others towards fulfilling personal, professional, and team goals. The five sub-competencies are: creating an environment for empowerment; building commitment; developing others; resolving conflicts; and directing others.

5. *Critical Thinking* includes these sub-competencies: recognizing patterns in multi-dependency systems, dealing with complexity, and challenging assumptions/analyzing present paradigms. The leader demonstrates the ability to evaluate, question, analyze, and challenge both the internal and external environment with the goal of organizational improvement.

6. *Organizational Awareness and Renewal* includes the leader's ability to focus the attention of employees towards a vision of the future. The five sub-competencies include developing and enunciating vision; inviting, accepting and promoting change; recognizing and promoting the concept of the learning organization; being client-centred; and demonstrating a commitment to quality.

The Canadian Police College is continually responding to the changes in society and in policing, and providing the training required in a changing country.

CANADIAN PERSPECTIVE *(Continued)*

Sources: Adapted from Program Development and Evaluation Branch, S/Sgt. J. M. Desrochers, Sgts. N. Duquette, and G. R. Gregoire in collaboration with the Andrakon Consulting Group.

Raymond Labonté (1999). Leadership Development Program: Research Findings and Analysis. Ottawa: Canadian Police College.

Sgt. G. R. Gregoire (March/April 1999). Leadership competencies: The Canadian Police College model. *The Mezzanine*. Ottawa: The Canadian Police College.

The Canadian Police College website at www.cpc.gc.ca/about_e.htm.

SKILLS FOR DEALING WITH SUPERIORS

Although it may seem an odd thing to discuss in a chapter devoted almost entirely to leadership, knowing how to act around those who are senior or more skilled than you is an important part of developing leadership skills. Sometimes we are so busy trying to lead and influence, we neglect the fact that there are others who have leadership skills and abilities greater than our own. Also, many of us have to work under and be supervised by others. Policing is still very much a bureaucratic structure with different levels of authority. To be an effective officer, you need to develop a constructive relationship with your superior officers. Here are some strategies to develop this type of relationship.

1. **Display loyalty to the organization.** According to Bergner (1998), loyalty means displaying a commitment to the ethics and effectiveness of the law enforcement profession. Loyalty also involves a commitment to the department and to one's superiors that supersedes personalities. If an officer sees a problem or disagrees with something, he speaks up because of a commitment to achieve the best outcome. Even if the final decision is not what the officer would like to see, he will support the outcome and work hard towards it (as long as it is not something illegal or unethical).

2. **Appreciate the strengths of your superiors.** Rather than focusing on the things that your manager or superior does wrong (at least in your eyes), appreciate what your superior can do well and learn from it. Ask yourself, "What can I learn from this person that will help me advance my career?" (DuBrin and Geerinck, 2004).

3. **Be dependable and honest.** Many workers become thorns in the sides of their managers because they are not dependable. Workers who are not dependable are not trusted by managers or co-workers, since they cannot be counted on to do their share of work. Dependable workers are punctual, miss work only for legitimate reasons, complete their assigned duties with minimal complaint, prepare for and attend court dates, and turn in their reports on time (Bergner, 1998).

4. **Know your job responsibilities.** Managers and superiors appreciate workers who know their jobs. A good officer knows the law, works hard, and demonstrates good judgment (Bergner, 1998).

5. **Respect authority.** A common complaint about our society is that respect for authority is diminishing (DuBrin and Geerinck, 2004). While you may not always like your superior officers, they are due the respect that comes with their position.

6. **Minimize complaints.** While openness and honesty are seen as virtues, constantly complaining about work conditions, co-workers, the laws, and so on will not endear

you to your supervisor. You may end up with the reputation of a complainer, which is not conducive to developing relationships with co-workers.

7. **Take initiative in problem solving.** Too often, subordinates ask to see their superiors, who are already dealing with a multitude of tasks, when they are having problems (DuBrin and Geerinck, 2004). This only adds pressure to an already heavy workload. Try coming forward with not only the problem but also with some solutions in order to demonstrate your ability and willingness to help solve organizational problems.

8. **Demonstrate that you are a team player.** Participating actively with other team members, helping team members, and working co-operatively with your supervisor and fellow officers all demonstrate your ability to be an effective team member (Bergner, 1998). Too often officers are rewarded for individual acts and rarely for effective teamwork. As the focus in policing changes, supervisors will more often recognize the importance of being a team player.

9. **Engage in professional development activities.** Interested employees continue to develop skills that will enhance their performance in the workplace. These activities are not just the ones offered through the police force itself; professional development includes a broad range of activities including courses, reading, and even participating in sporting activities. Courses in language, psychology, sociology, and diversity may help you deal with the public. Many sporting activities provide opportunities to develop team and leadership skills. The key is to continue in personal growth efforts.

POLICING AND LEADERSHIP IN A CHANGING ENVIRONMENT

With the changes that are occurring in policing in Canada, there is a strong need for effective leadership. These changes and issues will be discussed in more detail in the next chapter, but they include the growing demand for Aboriginal policing, increasing population diversity, community-oriented approaches in policing, new partnerships, amalgamation, and changes to various federal and provincial acts that impact on policing. All of these changes are occurring within other significant social changes, such as the impact of new technology, changing national and international political scenes, unity issues, and so on. All organizations, including police organizations, need strong leaders so that these changes can be managed effectively.

One problem facing policing today is the "machine bureaucracy" (De Paris, 1998). Machine bureaucracies are characterized by a rigid organizational structure with a tall hierarchy. These systems are closed, have relatively narrow jobs with distinct specialization, and use one-way communication from the top down to get information to the ranks. Machine bureaucracies also have an elaborate system of rules, regulations, policies, and procedures. If you examine the current structure of many police services in Canada, you will see several services that have a large machine bureaucracy, such as the Ottawa-Carleton Regional Police Service and the Toronto Police Service (these organizational charts can be found in McKenna, 1998, pp.100–102). There is little lateral or horizontal communication in these structures, and several layers of organization. While such structures were once useful, "in today's dynamic policing environment, situations are too complex and varied for a machine bureaucracy to respond effectively" (De Paris, 1998).

Community oriented policing emerged in response to the many environmental changes that vary from community to community. As the police mission has expanded, as the public has sought input into the policing process, and as service demands continue to increase, a new structure is needed (De Paris, 1998). Machine bureaucracies were designed for stability and do not react well to change. De Paris (1998) has proposed a more organic structure that encourages flexibility and innovation. This structure—what he terms a "professional police bureaucracy"—is more decentralized; more open; has a flatter structure (fewer levels); less role definition; encourages and supports two-way communication; allows more decision making at lower levels; and has an environment that fosters collaboration. Police work, by its very nature, cannot permit an organizational structure without some sort of bureaucracy, but the organization can be restructured to include all of the previous characteristics—hence the term "professional police bureaucracy."

While we will not discuss the entirety of how police structures need to change and how many forces *are* currently changing, there are two fundamental differences in this new structure. First, the machine bureaucracy uses a hierarchy of authority whereby people go up the ranks, often based on some sort of testing system. The professional police bureaucracy relies instead on authority based on expert power or authority of a professional nature.

Second, rather than relying on pre-programmed rules and so on to carry out the work, the professional police bureaucracy focuses more on facilitating and supporting the work of skilled professionals. In other words, the authority is placed in the hands of the professionals, such as police officers, rather than the administrators. In essence, the pyramid of authority is turned upside down in regard to decision making. This type of structure gives greater autonomy to its officers. Officers will have the "flexibility to be innovative in developing solutions to community problems" (De Paris, 1998).

This does not mean that policing becomes a free-for-all. Officers are guided by the traditional ethics and rules, but are also guided by goals determined by the organization. The organization determines the goals through developing an organizational vision, and officers determine the processes by which these goals can be achieved. The new structure will still be based on a bureaucratic model but will be a more flexible organization that can meet the changing demands of the environment. Each police organization may structure differently. Some services have already undergone major restructuring with specialized and cross-functional units. Also, many services have moved to flattened structures with fewer supervisors (McKenna, 1998).

As police services restructure to meet new demands, leadership training becomes essential. The average police manager today typically has little formal preparation for the variety of managerial and leadership tasks that she must undertake. Most of the management experience that police managers bring with them is the knowledge and experience gained from climbing ranks (several studies quoted in Dantzker and Mitchell, 1998). Current structures provide little opportunity to develop leadership skills (Dantzker and Mitchell, 1998). In the Law and Justice Perspective box that follows, you'll find one law-enforcement author's ideas on how to develop police leaders.

Developing Leaders

According to Laurie Bergner, a law enforcement trainer and consultant, developing the skills and qualities for effective police leaders should start at the outset of a career in policing. Officers with potential should be recognized early and should rise to the top before promotional testing occurs. Leadership is more than passing a promotional test (as we saw from our characteristics of the effective leader). Her ideas about how police organizations can develop leaders involve two areas: creating conditions that encourage leadership qualities, and providing opportunities to try out leadership roles.

Creating conditions that encourage and promote good leadership qualities:

- Respect officers who share ideas and initiate suggestions with their unit. Publicly recognizing good ideas promotes a culture in which leadership is encouraged.

- Create opportunities for participatory decision making. This will give officers practice in thinking about options, choosing the best option and practising trying to influence others.

- Reward teamwork; discipline lack of teamwork. Too often departments reward those who go it alone with individual acts of courage or a spectacular arrest. But what about the officers who help another officer on a call by sending information by radio about the suspect's car to the officer who then makes the arrest? In sports this is called an "assist," and it is rewarded. Breaches of teamwork should be handled in a serious way.

- Recognize and reward good ethics and values; deal seriously with ethical violations.

Providing opportunities to act in supervisory and leadership roles:

Officers who are seen as having leadership potential should receive both formal and informal on-the-job training. This gives the department an opportunity to evaluate in order to see if these officers are as good as they seem.

- Use the role of Field Training Officer. This role contains several skills of supervision—teaching, assessing performance, and giving feedback.

- Use temporary shift command as an important opportunity to practise a leadership role. This gives the officer a chance to practise his or her leadership abilities.

- Assign probationers to take charge of crime scenes when they are first responders on the scene.

- Create opportunities to do training, both inside and outside the department.

According to Bergner, hoping that good leaders will surface is not a strategy that will pay off. Instead, each department should have a planned strategy that develops leadership qualities in potential leaders from the first day on the job.

Source: Laurie Bergner. Developing good leaders begins at the beginning. *Police Chief*, November 1998, 17–23. Reprinted with the permission of the International Association of Chiefs of Police, Alexandria, VA.

Job-Centred Qualities
- resourceful
- accomplishment-oriented
- decisive
- quickly processes new information

Interpersonal Qualities
- develops and sustains strong relationships
- demonstrates compassion and sensitivity
- maintains personal composure
- deals directly with individuals and groups

Team-Centred Qualities
- leads peers and subordinates
- fosters environment that promotes growth
- deals with problems among team members
- attracts quality team members

Self-possessed Qualities
- balances personal life with work commitments
- demonstrates self-awareness
- makes people comfortable in a variety of settings
- demonstrates flexibility in changing situations

Figure 9-3   Leadership Grid
Source: Paul F. McKenna (1998). *Foundations of Policing in Canada.* Prentice-Hall Canada Inc., p. 98.

A final note on leadership comes from a Canadian author. In his book *Foundations of Policing in Canada* (1998), Paul McKenna divides the required elements of leadership into a leadership grid (Figure 9-3). Note that this grid contains many of the skills that were discussed earlier. This grid charts the various qualities in terms of their focus.

SUMMARY

In this chapter we explored building and maintaining effective relationships with the community and other partners, and covered the very large topic of leadership. First, we discussed the importance of building and maintaining relationships in today's policing environment, as well as how to build and maintain relationships. Relationship building includes four sub-competencies: demonstrating integrity; establishing credibility; developing interpersonal awareness; and building on diversity. We then defined leadership and compared leadership to management. Leadership is more about personal qualities and skills, whereas management is more about the actual tasks associated with a higher position in an organization.

We then explored various theories of leadership including the trait approach, the behavioural approaches, and the situational approaches. An important situational theory is Hersey and Blanchard's Situational Leadership Theory, which explores the situation, the style of leadership, and the ability and/or willingness of the followers. Power and the sources of power were discussed, as were bases and sources of power for both leaders and managers. Leaders differ in their style of leadership: authoritarian, laissez-faire, person-centred, transactional, charismatic, and transformational are all styles of leadership.

Effective leaders demonstrate skills that influence and help others in the organization to reach organizational goals. Effective leaders have vision; communicate effectively; manage and know themselves; know how to get and maintain attention; recognize and encourage others to develop skills; establish positive communication climates; help manage conflicts; inspire others; adapt their leadership style; engage in coaching and mentoring; stay current; are ethical; and fulfill their managerial responsibilities. We are not all leaders, but we do need to develop skills that help us get along with our managers and superior officers. To develop good relations with superiors, employees should display loyalty to the organization; appreciate the strengths of superiors; be dependable and honest; know their job responsibilities; respect authority; minimize complaints; take initiative in problem solving; demonstrate team player skills; and engage in professional development activities. The chapter ended by examining leadership in policing within a rapidly changing environment, a topic that will be explored more deeply in the next chapter.

WEBSITES

www.queendom.com
This site has self-tests on leadership.

www.theproperthing.com
You can find tips on social etiquette and business protocol at this site.

www.cpc.gc.ca/home_e.htm
This is the Canadian Police College website.

www.selfgrowth.com
This is a site devoted to personal growth and self-improvement. You can sign up for a free email newsletter.

www.iacp.org
This is the site for the International Association of Chiefs of Police. There are several links at this site, including one for *Police Chief* magazine.

www.fbi.gov/hq/td/academy/academy.htm
This is the site for the FBI Academy.

JOURNAL AND DISCUSSION QUESTIONS

1. Write down the characteristics and skills that you would want the next police chief hired in your community to possess. Identify which ones you feel are essential for effective leadership.

2. Select two or three leadership skills, abilities, and characteristics that you currently feel you do not possess. Write an action plan for each one that will help you attain these identified skills.

_____

_____

_____

_____

_____

_____

_____

_____

_____

3. This chapter stated that there is not as much respect for authority as there was in the past. What are your ideas about this lack of respect? Where does this new disrespect come from?

_____

_____

_____

_____

_____

_____

_____

_____

_____

_____

SKILLS PRACTICE 9-1

Knowing Thyself: Creating Personal Values and Philosophy

As we learned in this chapter, leaders manage and know themselves. James Sewell, in his article about the four Rs for police executives, refers to one of the Rs as "Roots." Roots are grounded in who you are: your professional and personal philosophies, values, and experiences. These roots form the basis for your decisions, actions, and other visible displays of leadership (Sewell, 1996). Leaders take time to develop their own philosophies, to understand who they are, and to identify what it is that they stand for and support (Lunney, 1989; Sewell, 1996). Finish the sentences below to build your own personal philosophy and values statement.

My professional philosophies are:

_____

_____

My personal philosophies include:

_____

_____

My values are:

_____

_____

My experiences include:

_____

_____

I stand for:

_____

_____

I support:

_____

_____

I believe in:

_____

_____

I have a commitment to:

_____

_____

SKILLS PRACTICE 9-2

Giving Feedback

Many managerial and other leadership positions involve giving feedback on performance to others. This may be done as a formal performance review or evaluation, or with a simple question like "How am I doing?" or "Do you think I'm getting the job done effectively?" Before attempting the exercise below, let's briefly review the skills for effective feedback.

1. Feedback focuses on the behaviour, not the person.

2. Feedback must be clear and descriptive.

3. Try to start your feedback with a positive statement or by listing the demonstrated strengths of the person.

4. Be aware of why the person is soliciting feedback. In formal performance evaluations, this is not an issue. However, in informal situations, there may be more than the goal of improvement on his mind. He may want a compliment or increased attention or may just need some reassurance that he is a valuable team member (if indeed he is). It is appropriate to ask what the goal or purpose of the feedback is. You might say, for example, "I'm curious why you would be asking me about your target shooting skills."

5. Feedback should occur in a timely fashion and in an appropriate place.

6. Use "I" statements if the feedback is about your impression of performance. It is your perception you are giving—you own it, not the receiver. For example, you might say, "I think your writing has improved considerably. There are still several grammar errors that I would like to go over with you, but I saw only a couple of spelling errors."

7. Feedback should include specific ideas or alternatives about how to improve or where to go to access information for improvement. For example, "Since it appears that grammar is the really big problem, may I suggest the online grammar course at the Learning Centre? You can do it when you have time, and work at your own pace."

8. For ongoing development such as field training or other evaluation, set a goal for improvement, a time for completion, and a specific time for further feedback. For example, "You still have three weeks before the paper is due. Why don't you amend the errors that I have underlined using the program, and come and see me at the same time next week?"

9. The feedback session should end on a positive note. For example, "Thanks for letting me help you with this. I think with a bit of work, you will be a very competent writer."

Complete the exercises, using your imagination:

1. You are a teacher. A student has asked you to quickly proofread a paper. There are many spelling and grammar errors. The topic and the development of ideas are good.

Your Feedback:

_____
_____
_____
_____
_____
_____

2. You are a field training officer. The rookie under your guidance just issued her first ticket without any help from you. You stood back and watched. While she politely issued the ticket, you noticed several nonverbal indicators of nervousness. You noticed nervous laughter, and she used lots of "ums."

Your Feedback:

_____
_____
_____
_____
_____
_____
_____

3. You are a member of a project team at school and your group is presenting next week. One of the group members comes to you to show you the half-completed work. This member is responsible for preparing a visual chart to be hung up while the group speaks. Although the letters are the right size, it is messy and the colours may not show up at the back of the room. This person says to you, "Is this OK or what?"

Your Feedback:

_____
_____
_____
_____
_____
_____
_____

Source: Based on material from Engleberg and Wynn (1997) and Lumsden and Lumsden (1997).

Chapter 10

Adapting to Change

After studying this chapter you should be able to:

- Define change and the various types of change.
- Explain how organizations react to change.
- List the ways people react to change and why people may resist change.
- Use force field analysis to explain the process of change.
- List the organizational and personal methods that can be used to overcome resistance to change.
- Discuss changes occurring in Canada that impact policing.
- List ways of managing stress in policing.
- Identify ways to manage negative emotions.

INTRODUCTION

Person 1: *Look at this! Another meeting about reducing the number of staff sergeants and sergeants in the division and all the other restructuring.*

Person 2: *I know what you mean. Why don't they just do it and let us get on with our jobs?*

Person 3: *Well, I'm still not sure what it's all about. I could use a little more information about what is going on. Some of these changes are really baffling.*

Person 1: *Hey, just go with the flow. There's nothing you can do.*

Person 2: *And if you try, they just knock you down anyway. I gave up trying to understand what goes on in this department years ago.*

Person 3: *Well, I've only been here a few months. I thought they wanted our input and ideas.*

Canada—and policing in Canada—is in an era of change. Globalization has significantly impacted our social, economic, and political systems. Rapid advancements in technology are shaping the way we work. Diverse immigration patterns, legislative changes, and increased accountability to the public and other stakeholders make it essential for police services to operate more like a business in order to adapt and respond to a rapidly changing world. As policing organizations try to adapt, change continues. In this chapter we will explore the nature of change: what it is and how it affects us. We will look at one model of change and how the change process occurs in organizations. Then we'll examine some of the changes in policing and attempt to see what changes will affect policing organizations. Next, we will look at the skills you can use—some that you have already examined—when you are confronted with change. Finally, we will address managing stress in response to change.

WHAT IS CHANGE?

First, let's look at the process of change, examine the types of change, change agents, and reactions to change.

Types of Change

Change occurs when something is not working the way it used to work. If a store that used to be very busy is no longer busy, then something has changed. If a relatively crime-free area is suddenly a crime hot spot, something has changed. When something no longer works or suddenly has negative consequences, we must look more closely at what is going on. Why is there more crime in this area? Why are profits diminishing? Why are there fewer shoppers?

Changes can be positive as well as negative. Usually it is the negative changes that we concentrate on, but we may also want to examine positive change to continue movement in that direction.

Two kinds of change occur in organizations. One type of change is **radical change** or **frame-breaking change** (Nadler and Tushman, 1988). This is change that results in a major makeover of the entire organization or parts of the organization and is often caused by some sort of radical event. For example, a merger or takeover produces radical organizational restructuring. Many Canadian colleges experienced a sudden loss of funding several years ago, which led many to restructure to a flatter bureaucracy and to impose tuition hikes and program cuts. The good news for many of us is that radical change does not occur frequently in the life cycle of an organization (Schermerhorn, Hunt, and Osborn, 1994).

A more common form of change is **incremental** or **frame-bending change**. This type of change is less traumatic for an organization and can often be viewed as part of its natural evolution. Incremental change includes introducing new technology, introducing new products, and developing new systems. The nature of the organization remains basically the same. Incremental change builds on the way things are currently done and usually seeks to enhance or extend them (Schermerhorn, Hunt, and Osborn, 1994). A good example of incremental change was the introduction of computer networking in organizations, including police departments. For the most part, the process was planned in advance. The changeover was messy for many of us as walls and floors were ripped apart for new wiring to be installed, professional development was arranged for the computer illiterate or computer fearful, and software selected and loaded. The internet quickly followed, and for policing, this meant training in a new area of crime and enforcement. Organizations must constantly and incrementally improve to stay in tune with today's continuing changes (Schermerhorn, Hunt, and Osborn, 1994).

Change can also be planned or unplanned (Schermerhorn, Hunt, and Osbsorn, 1994). **Unplanned change** occurs spontaneously or randomly without any initial input from the organization. Wildcat strikes, the unexpected closure of a major supplier, or other unforeseen events can suddenly rock an organization. When unplanned change occurs, the goal is to act immediately to minimize the negative effects of the change and to maximize any possible positive benefits. This response to unplanned change can be referred to as *crisis management*. For changes in security and law enforcement post-September 11, 2001, see the Canadian Perspective box on p. 218.

Planned change comes about as a result of an organization's specific efforts to change. Usually, planned change results from the perception of a **performance gap** by a person or group of people within the organization. A performance gap is a discrepancy between what is occurring and what the desired state is. In some ways a performance gap is similar to a problem; a deviation between what is and what you would like. For example, the chief of a small police department that receives several public complaints about how officers are communicating knows that this is not how the public should perceive interaction with officers.

Change Agents

Change does not magically occur in organizations. Organizations are made up of people; people, therefore, have to make the changes. **Change agents** are the individuals or groups responsible for managing change within an organization by changing the existing pattern of behaviour, the way of doing things, or current practices of a person or social system. Using the example in the previous paragraph, the chief and two officers might examine the current communication practices of officers in the department. They might also interview all of those who have made complaints. From this, new procedures and guidelines about communicating with the public are established. These three individuals were responsible for making a change; in essence, they were change agents.

Reactions to Change

In the dialogue at the beginning of this chapter people are reacting to changes going on in the department. Two people want to be left alone, but the third person wants more information about the proposed flattening of the organization. When changes are about to happen or are already underway, people react in different ways. Let's examine some of the ways that people react to change.

1. **Inertia** is a non-reaction to change and "refers to a person's attitude about change" (Portnoy, 1999). The person who reacts with **inertia** does nothing; he is unaware of the need for change and continues to behave in the usual or routine pattern of doing things. The behaviour of a salesperson who continues to use high-pressure sales techniques and is unaware of the negative impact of such techniques is an example of inertia. He does not see any reason to change or that the current methods need revision.

2. **Supportive** Much to the delight of many change agents, some people embrace change and welcome it. The supportive attitude agrees that, "It's about time that someone fixed that!" These individuals volunteer to help get the changes rolling, champion the changes at meetings or other gatherings, and work hard to ensure positive results.

3. **Reluctant** These individuals understand the need for change, and will go along if given sufficient information and incentive to change their behaviour. Their reluctance may stem from being unsure about how to behave or how to actively implement the changes. For example, if the number of supervisors is being reduced, the individual may be unsure to whom they now report.

4. **Resistance** Unfortunately, the avid supporters are few, and many organizational change efforts are resisted by employees, managers, clients, and others who have

vested interests in the organization (McShane, 1995). Resistance stems from a natural tendency or motivation to keep things the same or to maintain the status quo rather than to change behaviour (McShane, 1995). It is not so much the change that is resisted as it is the implications of the change (Conner, 1994). When people feel unwilling or unable to change, then change becomes difficult and is resisted (Conner, 1994).

Resistance can occur in many forms, such as passive non-compliance. For example, an individual may continue to do things the old way, even though she is continually reminded of the new system. Complaining about current or proposed changes is another form of resistance. As we saw in the dialogue that opens this chapter, two people were complaining about proposed change. These two individuals may have also been trying to actively promote a negative attitude in others—another form of resistance (Conner, 1994). Other types of resistance are absenteeism, turnover, sabotage, collective action, and other methods of active non-compliance.

Below are some of the main reasons people resist change (McShane, 1995; Nadler, 1987; Katz and Kahn, 1978):

- **Direct costs** People resist change when they perceive that the new way will have higher costs or fewer benefits. For example, some people did not want computer training because they saw it as overly time consuming and did not perceive the long-term benefits.

- **Fear of the unknown** People resist change because it involves uncertainty and risk. For example, restructuring may mean working with new people and leaving some old and familiar colleagues behind.

- **Saving face** People may resist change to "prove" that the decision is wrong. This kind of resistance is often a political manoeuvre whose purpose is to make decision-makers look wrong and make resisters look right.

- **Disruption and breaking of routines** While routine may be boring, it is also comfortable and safe. When change occurs, people often have to abandon these comfortable ways and learn new ways. They may not feel capable of addressing the change and may dig in their heels (Conner, 1994). It takes time and energy to learn new behaviours.

- **Incongruent organizational systems** When organizations began to change over to computer networks and expected all employees to use computers, some organizational systems were not ready for the increased use. Many companies did not have enough computers, and employees were stuck sharing computers. Without organizational control systems such as rewards and training, employees sometimes become discouraged (McShane, 1995). Why learn computer skills if you cannot access a computer?

- **Incongruent team dynamics** Characteristics of teams can also discourage people from accepting change. For example, norms that protect and ensure the status quo of the team may result in team resistance to change.

Different Cultural Approaches to Change

Be aware that different cultures view, respond, and adapt to change differently. For example, Japan underwent industrialization in an extremely short period of time, so continual, proactive change became part of modern Japanese culture. Continental Europeans on the other hand are traditionally reactive. The British, once conservative to change, were converted to proactive change by a national crisis. North Americans became somewhat more proactive toward change in the late 1990s because of the micro-electronics industry, and were forced to be extremely proactive toward change after the terrorist attacks of September 11, 2001.

THE CHANGE PROCESS

Knowing that organizations face resistance to change, how do they go about making changes? How do change agents make changes that will benefit an organization? To answer these questions, a model was developed by behavioural scientist Kurt Lewin in the 1950s. Though it has been adapted and changed, this model has stayed much the same over the last 50-plus years. The model is referred to as **force field analysis** and consists of three phases or steps. Force field analysis helps change agents examine and diagnose forces that drive and restrain proposed changes in an organization. *Driving forces* are forces that push or propel the changes. *Restraining forces* are forces that resist the changes and attempt to maintain the status quo. When both types of forces are relatively equal, there is stability or equilibrium. Change occurs when the driving forces are greater than the restraining forces. This occurs by either increasing the strength of the driving forces or decreasing the strength of the restraining forces (Lewin, 1951). As these forces change in strength, there is a period of transition (Conner, 1994).

Thus, there are three processes embedded in this model. First, effective change begins by **unfreezing** the status quo or current situation. During this period, Conner (1994) states that people go through a period of transition as they "unfreeze" and then begin to "refreeze." Unfreezing occurs as the change agent introduces disequilibrium to adjust the driving and resisting forces. **Refreezing** is the introduction of new systems, methods, and conditions that reinforce and maintain new roles and patterns. Let's examine unfreezing, transition, and refreezing in more detail.

Step 1: Unfreezing

After change agents have identified a need for change (and have developed an action plan for the change), the status quo must undergo unfreezing. Unfreezing is accomplished by strengthening the driving forces, weakening the restraining forces, or some combination of both. For example, management could hold meetings to gather input into the desired changes and to inform employees why change is necessary. Free training can also be offered. Using force field analysis, change agents can brainstorm to determine what are the current driving and restraining forces maintaining the present situation or state. The forces that can be changed (strengthened or weakened) can then be identified. Try Skills Practice 10-1 on p. 230 to see if you can identify some of the forces that are maintaining a current situation.

Often change agents work on strengthening driving forces only. This is usually ineffective because the restraining forces often increase to meet the challenge (McShane, 1995). For example, if employees are threatened with being fired for not taking new training, they may counter by launching union grievances or sitting resentfully and learning nothing during the forced training.

Step 2: Transition or Change

The second stage in Lewin's model is the change or transition. From the stage of unfreezing to refreezing, people are affected by what is happening in the organization. During a change process, whether organizational or personal, individuals go through a transition process where old ways are discarded and new ways adopted. This is rarely an easy process. According to William Bridges in his book *Managing Transitions: Making the Most of Change* (1991), the beginning of transition is not simply reaching towards the end or the goal, but rather letting go of and discarding old ways—in other words, we must have an end to have a beginning.

A major problem with organizational change is that change agents fail to think through what people will be letting go of when the change occurs. For example, learning new computer skills means leaving behind multi-coloured markers, and the fun of designing and drawing on overheads. Computer software packages can do all this now, but it takes time and effort to learn these new things.

According to Bridges (1991), the transition is the psychological process that people go through during change. He views transition as a three-part process of *endings* or *letting go* of old ways; *a neutral zone*, characterized by disorientation, confusion, and uncertainty; and *new beginnings*, where people establish new relationships, develop new skills and competencies, and make new plans. While the process is much more complex than what is described here, the real key is to understand that people must make a transition from a current state to a new state, and they will vary in how quickly or appropriately they make that transition. The role of change agents is not only to identify what changes are required and how they should be implemented, but also to assist those affected by the changes to adapt to the new order.

Step 3: Refreezing

Refreezing is the implementation of systems and conditions that maintain the new changes and prevent slippage back to the old way of doing things. For example, if a college diploma is the new minimum requirement for becoming a police officer after a specific year, then new hiring and recruiting policies will have to reflect that change. Colleges and universities will need to be informed, potential candidates will have to be informed, and other activities will have to be completed to assure that this policy is carried out. Internal changes that need to be implemented, such as offering similar opportunities for current officers or other training initiatives, will also likely occur. See Figure 10-1 below for an illustration of these three processes.

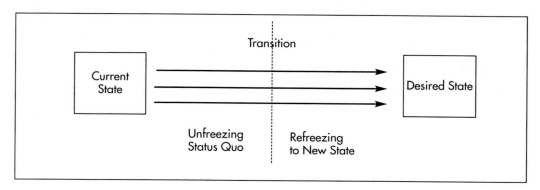

Figure 10-1   The Change Process

METHODS TO OVERCOME RESISTANCE TO CHANGE AND EASE TRANSITION

If you are going to become a change agent in the future (and you most likely will), or are going to experience change (you most definitely will), you will need to understand the methods you can use to help others and yourself cope with change and the transition process. We will discuss both organizational and personal methods. Organizational methods refer to the methods and strategies that change agents use to effect planned change in organizations. Personal methods refer to the skills and strategies that you can use to help *you* cope with organizational—and personal—changes.

Organizational Methods

Organizations may use one or several methods to go from unfreezing to refreezing. Below are some of these methods (adapted from McShane, 1995):

- **Communication** Communicating the change effort through all levels of an organization is an important strategy to reduce resistance. Organizational change requires a top-down approach (De Paris, 1998), and the ranks should be kept abreast of what is occurring, why it is occurring, and what the implications are for them personally. People who are well informed feel less fear of the unknown.

- **Employee involvement** When the individuals and teams that are going to be most affected by the change are given opportunities for decision making and planning around the change, they are more likely to support the change. Allowing input into the changes will likely mean more commitment to them (Pollock and Colwill, 1987). Teams and groups of employees can use problem-solving and decision-making strategies to develop goals and action plans to carry out proposed changes.

- **Training** One reason for resistance is the perceived costs of the change. One way to ease transition is to ensure that employees have the skills to handle the new ways. By increasing comfort levels and expertise levels, employees will experience the reduced cost of changing and are less likely to resist.

- **Plan change** Introduce changes slowly using a planned approach. Successful change is introduced slowly and incrementally (De Paris, 1998). Organizations need to develop action plans that introduce change in a logical sequence of steps until the new vision has been attained.

- **Negotiation** At times, organizations may need to negotiate other benefits for employees to offset some of the costs of a change.

- **Coercion** Although not highly recommended, coercion may be required to overcome resistance and to obtain the necessary compliance to implement the change. The major problem with coercion is that it produces adverse emotional effects. For example, a manager who is forced to follow new procedures may start complaining to others about how angry he is at the unfair treatment.

CANADIAN PERSPECTIVE

Changes in Security and Law Enforcement Post-September 11

An unforeseen tragedy can rock an organization, a country, or the world. In North America, the terrorist attacks of September 11, 2001, changed the face of security and law enforcement in Canada forever. Canadians, once comfortable with living in one of the safest countries in the world, realized they are vulnerable to terrorist attacks. We became aware that there are individuals and groups in Canada whose activities diminish our safety and threaten our security. We know that people guilty of war crimes hide out in Canada; computer hackers threaten our critical information systems; organized crime groups import and export illegal drugs, operate prostitution rings, steal credit cards, and smuggle people from other countries to Canada; and terrorist groups raise funds and plan operations here (Government of Canada, Privy Council Office, The Canadian Security and Intelligence Community, 2001). "No one really knows what form the next attack will take but most intelligence sources are agreed that it, or they, will come" (CSIS, Commentary No. 85, 2003, p. 5).

Since September 11, 2001, countries around the world, including Canada, have re-examined and restructured the way they manage intelligence, security, and law enforcement. The government of Canada announced wide-ranging measures to counter the threat of global terrorism (Foreign Affairs Canada, Issue 14, 2002). (For a list of these measures visit the websites below.) "Law enforcement agencies are placing increasing emphasis on developing non-traditional competencies and skill sets, and on building their capacity to deal with the new criminal and terrorist environment" (RCMP, 2006).

For more in-depth information on this topic visit these websites:

Foreign Affairs Canada, *Canada World View*, Issue 14, Winter 2002. www.dfait-maeci.gc.ca/canada-magazine/issue14/14t3-en.asp

Government of Canada Privy Council Office. The Canadian Security and Intelligence Community Cat. No. CP32-74/2001. www.pco-bcp.gc.ca.

Canadian Security Intelligence Service, Reid Morgan, Commentary No. 85, Fall 2003. www.csis-scrs.gc.ca/en/publications/commentary/com85.asp

Royal Canadian Mounted Police International Policing. www.rcmp.ca/intpolicing/intpolicing_e.htm

Personal Methods

Whether we are for it or against it, whether we like it or not, if we are not change agents, we will be on the receiving end of change many times in our lives. Sometimes we react unfavourably, even inappropriately (like throwing a temper tantrum), when change knocks on our own door. So rather than looking foolish or stressed out, or seething quietly (or perhaps not so quietly) with anger, consider ways to manage change. Below are just a few strategies:

- **Manage your stress.** Change can be very stressful, but two strategies may help you manage it. One strategy is to develop competence. *Competence* refers to both job skills and social skills, including being able to solve problems effectively, to manage conflict, and to control anger (Cowen, 1991). Many of the interpersonal skills discussed in this book will help you gain competence in these social skills. (Refer back to Chapter 6 to refresh your conflict management and problem-solving skills.) Being able to tell people how you feel; expressing your perceptions of a new situation using such skills as "I" language and perception checking; and using conflict and problem-solving strategies are just a few of the ways you can achieve the competency to manage change. A second strategy is to develop **resilience**—the ability to withstand pressure and stress and to emerge from the experience stronger than before (Cowen, 1991). Learning how to manage stress will help you develop resilience and to bounce back from a number of stressful events, including major organizational changes. Refer to Figure 10-3 on p. 226 for more tips to help manage the stress from change.

- **Manage your emotions and change your perceptions.** Changing your perceptions and managing your emotions are essential to helping you with personal change. The way you perceive a situation or a change and the meaning you give it determine your emotional reaction. If you remember back to the discussion on perception, you know that the brain does not know the difference between a real or imagined threat. If a change is perceived as negative (a threat), then your emotional reaction may be stress and anger. Refer to Figure 10-2 for short- and long-term solutions to dealing with anger.

  It is important to realize that you are responsible for managing your own emotional reactions. You can manage change by reviewing your current perceptions and modifying them. Although it may be difficult to see challenges as opportunities, this change in viewpoint may benefit you in the long run. You can ask yourself such strategic questions as, "What can this change do for me now and later?" or "What skills do I have that I can use at this time?" You can see the change as beneficial in the long term. For example, if yearly physical fitness testing becomes a reality, view it as a way to live longer rather than as some sort of gruelling torture test. If you are already in top shape, you can show your superiors that you take care of your health and ask if there is anything you can do to help out or coordinate the testing (an opportunity to practise and demonstrate your leadership ability). Modifying your perceptions and managing negative emotional reactions will help you cope with change.

- **Talk to others.** Talking to others can also help you cope with change. If you are a new employee, talking to veteran workers can be extremely helpful. Most long-term employees have probably experienced several changes in their careers and can help you gain some perspective. A veteran officer can tell you about the turmoil of the sixties and the number of legislative changes that have occurred as a result of acts such as the Human Rights Act.

  You can also ask questions to clarify the change. Ask your supervisors or others who are implementing the change. Co-workers may not always be the best source for some of your questions as they too may be unsure of the change. They also may be feeling negatively about the change and may not give you accurate information.

- **Realize that adjustment takes time.** Change takes time. According to De Paris (1998), successful strategic change in law enforcement agencies is a prolonged

Dealing with Your Anger

Feelings of anger are a normal reaction to some situations beyond your control. They can also indicate that you are simply under too much stress, and it can be hard to know if you should just let your anger pass or work at getting rid of it.

It is time to admit that anger is a problem and to look for ways of dealing with it if your anger is

- constantly on your mind for several weeks and is beginning to seriously harm your enjoyment of life,
- caused by something that happened a long time ago,
- causing you to do vengeful things,
- making you act violently to others or to yourself,
- interfering with your ability to do your job,
- hurting your relationships with your family and friends.

It is important to deal with your anger before it causes you discomfort or pain. Studies have shown that anger can cause serious health problems such as ulcers and heart disease. It can also make you behave in ways that cause you to lose your job or friends, or result in the break-up of your marriage. There are some things you can do to deal with your anger as it happens. Other things involve changing your way of approaching life by learning new attitudes and taking a number of practical actions.

Short-term solutions

- Admit that you are angry. If you bottle up your angry feelings, they will not go away, and they will keep coming out over and over again, painfully.
- Try not to overreact. Step back from the situation that is making you angry and ask yourself, "What would I think of someone else if I saw her getting angry in this situation?" or "Is this situation really as bad as I am making it out to be?"
- Try to make yourself think about something else. Turn your attention to some pleasant memory rather than the line-up, traffic jam, or whatever is irritating you.
- Identify the source of your anger. If the actions or words of another person are hurting you, try to deal with him directly in a peaceful and productive way.
- Listen carefully to what others are saying to you, and let them finish without interruption. Very often, you will not understand the real message if you jump in after a few words. Give people a chance to explain themselves.

Long-term solutions

- If your anger is caused by something beyond your control, such as a job lay-off, find out how others have dealt with the problem successfully, and try to follow their lead.
- Avoid blaming yourself, even if you are angry because of misfortune caused by your own mistake. It is best to try to learn from your experiences and avoid making the same mistakes again.
- Reduce tension by finding time for some physical activity. Go for a brisk walk, play a hard game of tennis with a friend, work in the garden, or clean the house.
- Reduce your stress level. Learn some stress management methods, such as relaxation and deep-breathing exercises. Try to find ways of doing more of the things you enjoy.
- Learn to meditate. When you are alone, practise withdrawing your thoughts from your day-to-day concerns. This may make you more able to do the same when you find yourself getting angry.
- Learn to laugh at yourself. If you can learn to see the silly side of things, you can laugh instead of lashing out.
- Learn to trust the abilities of others. Some of your anger may be coming from a lack of faith in the capabilities of other people.
- Look for professional help. If your problems are serious, you may need the help of a mental health professional, such as a psychiatrist, psychologist, or social worker. Your family doctor can help you find these professional people.
- Talk to someone you trust (a family member, a close friend, or a member of the clergy) who may be able to see things more clearly than you do.

For more information visit the website below or check your local bookstore and library for books on the subject. You can also contact a local community organization such as the Canadian Mental Health Association to find out about counselling services and other resources available in your community.

Figure 10-2   Dealing with Your Anger

Source: Canadian Mental Health Association, *Feeling Angry*, 2006, www.cmha.ca/bins/content_page.asp?cid=2-63-64&lang=1.

process. "Accordingly, an incremental approach—in which personnel are able to identify with the new vision and internalize the new vision and behaviours necessary for its attainment—is essential." Unfortunately, many organizational changes may not be as well planned as they should have been, leaving employees rushing to behave in new roles. When this happens, remember that it will take time for you to adjust, and do not be too hard on yourself if you cannot remember everything and do everything new all at once.

CHANGES IMPACTING POLICING IN CANADA

Change can come in many different forms and from many different directions. When change occurs in society it causes a ripple effect in organizations, including policing. The list below, though not complete, is a summary of some of the major changes in our society that are affecting current policing practices. As we saw earlier in this chapter and in previous chapters, police services undergo frequent changes to adapt and cope with these new challenges. Policing is more community-focused, more collaborative, and more sophisticated than ever before (Canadian Police College, 2006). The skills, abilities, strategies, and knowledge in this text will help you in many ways with a career in law enforcement. While you manage yourself on and off the job, these skills will also help you to cope with the challenges of changing police practices across the nation.

KEY LEARNING POINTS

Changes Impacting Policing in Canada

- Globalization
- Demographic and population changes
- Aboriginal policing
- Legislation
- Emphasis on community policing and building partnerships
- Changes in recruitment, selection and training
- An increased concern with ethics
- Technological advances
- Increasing stress

Globalization

Globalization has significantly impacted our social, economic, and political systems, which has in turn affected the direction of police services in Canada. Government funding downloads or decreases to police services are a result of globalization. Globalization and the social and economic principles it brings with it have impacted government policy directions and decisions. Citing the reality of global competition, government can rationalize a no-handouts, survival-of-the-fittest mindset in policy decisions. "The emergence of a global economy is shifting our attention away from a national economic strategy and towards a strategy geared towards increasing local and regional participation in world markets" (Knowles, 1995).

Globalization has brought with it competition and increased accountability in all sectors. For example, municipalities in Ontario must now pay for their policing. This has resulted in a flurry of restructuring, amalgamations, and even competition between provincial and local services to determine which would be the police organization in a given area. Police services found themselves in the unusual position of competing for a local market share.

We are living in a climate of fiscal restraint, competition, and increasing accountability. In response, there has been a shift in police services to operate in a more businesslike way. While the general public expects top-of-the-line service, such service has become more difficult to deliver, given the current financial situation of many areas. Restructuring and reorganization will continue as police services deal with a changing social, political, and economic climate.

Demographic and Population Changes

As discussed in previous chapters, the Canadian population is changing. There is more ethnic and cultural diversity; a continuing increase of visible minorities, especially in large urban areas; increased representation of women in the workforce; and an aging general population. These changes impact all organizations, including policing organizations. In response to these changes, police services are making efforts to increase minority representation to reflect demographic makeup and to provide services to some of these more crime-vulnerable groups (such as the elderly and women). In Chapter 7 we noted that, because of the rapidly changing face of Canada, both new immigrants and other Canadians might experience some form of culture shock. This culture shock, added to conflicting values and lack of tolerance for diversity, may contribute to increased violence and other criminal activity. Potential continues to grow for ethnic and racial violence that is transplanted from homelands to Canada (McKenna, 1998).

The threat of terrorism is very real in Canada post-September 11. Responding to violence and terrorism will require specialized forms of police intervention—not an easy task. "There will be a continuing need to ensure that the criminal justice system and, in particular, the front-line officer are in tune with the expectations and requirements of Canada's diverse population" (McKenna, 1998).

In this text, many of the skills you need in order to effectively deal with people from other cultures have been discussed.

Aboriginal Policing

As mentioned in Chapter 7 on diversity, in 1996 the federal government endorsed a new First Nations Policing Policy to support the ongoing development of law enforcement services that meet the different needs of aboriginal communities. The policy has led to negotiations of tripartite agreements involving the federal government, provincial or territorial governments, and band councils. The policy is directed towards self-policing for First Nations and Aboriginal peoples (Canada, Solicitor General, 1996).

As a result of this policy, changes will continue as agreements are entered into for new policing services for First Nations and Aboriginal peoples. For more information on the First Nations Policing Policy visit ww2.psepc-sppcc.gc.ca/abor_policing/fir_nat_policing_e.asp.

Changes Due to Legislation

In the last 20 years there have been significant legislative changes in Canada that have impacted policing. The North American Free Trade Act, the Human Rights Act and several other legislative changes have greatly influenced Canadian society. Revisions and amendments to the Police Services Act, the Regional Municipalities Act, and the District Municipality of Muskoka Act have had major impact in Ontario. As mentioned earlier, municipalities must now pay for their policing, resulting in restructuring, amalgamations, and even competition between provincial and local services to determine which police organization will serve a given area. Police services have found themselves competing for a local market share. While the general public expects first-rate service, such service has become more difficult given the current financial status of many areas.

It is too early to assess the effectiveness of many new amalgamations and the major restructuring of forces. Restructuring and reorganization will continue as police services deal with a changing political climate.

Emphasis on Meeting the Needs of the Community: Community Policing and Building Partnerships

Law enforcement continues to become more proactive as the twenty-first century begins. Community policing is necessary in our increasingly diverse society, and involves a two-strategy approach. The first is a community-service approach, which is proactive and based on persuasion instead of force, and on expanding the police mandate to include visibility. The second part of the strategy is a collaborative approach developed jointly by the police and the community. Collaboration seeks to establish communication networks between police officers and citizens, storekeepers, and community groups (Canadian Police College, 1998).

"In a relatively short time, community policing has replaced professional crime control policing as the dominant ideology and organizational model of progressive policing in Canada" (Murphy, 1993). The goal of this approach is to proactively identify and solve problems to maintain the peace, rather than to simply respond to calls after the peace has been broken (Stansfield, 1996). According to Stansfield (1996), the real key of community policing is the use of teams that are responsible for working in an identified zone or in team areas. These teams work with members of the community that may represent population diversity. Teams or zones can be identified based on the unique characteristics of the area or zone.

Police services are accountable to the community and must respond to their needs, including the need for information and to participate and have a say in their public safety. In response, police services are developing websites dedicated to building relationships by informing the community of the services they offer. The websites are a low cost public relations tool used to keep the community updated on activities such as crime statistics and crime prevention. Law enforcement will continue to find ways to have better relations with the citizens that are its clients. Police services realize that the public is entitled to have their say in the management of public safety (Canadian Police College, 1998). Police services will continue to build and expand new partnerships in the communities they serve.

Changes in Recruitment, Selection, and Training

Community policing is very different from traditional policing and therefore calls on its officers for a different and expanded skill set. Community policing programs require people capable of critical and independent thinking, the ability to respect and work with culturally diverse community members, and the ability to problem-solve and communicate effectively. A substantial amount of research has been undertaken in recent years to try to determine what precise knowledge, skills, and abilities are required for effective policing duties (McKenna, 1998).

In Ontario, the Ministry of the Solicitor General's Strategic Planning Committee on Police Training and Education has identified 20 areas of knowledge, skills, and abilities that more closely align policing to a profession with complex skills. These skills include analytical skills and problem-solving abilities, communication skills, knowledge of human behaviour, interpersonal and sensitivity skills, and the ability to serve victims (Ontario, Ministry of the Solicitor General, 1992). Skills in conflict resolution, interpersonal communication, problem solving, crisis management, managing diversity, and teamwork are essential for you to work effectively in this new type of policing environment.

Traditionally, once an individual has applied to a police service, she must undergo an assessment process that includes a physical skills test, and a background and reference check that usually takes place after the interview.

The most noticeable changes have occurred in assessment and training prior to police service application and assessments. This area has seen massive research and change as a result of the implementation of community policing and in response to changes in society. Let's examine this area a little more closely. With the emphasis on community policing, how can services attract the best candidates to fill this new role, and what are the skills and training required for this role? In other words, how can services attract recruits and then assess whether they are suitable for the responsibilities of being a community police officer?

Recruitment and selection include more than just attracting applicants. Police services want to attract people who are qualified, and will make selections based on criteria that determine an individual's ability to be a good officer. Most police agencies employ several criteria and methods to ensure as good a selection as possible (Dantzker and Mitchell, 1998). Many services use a variety of tests, including aptitude tests like the G.A.T.B. (see Law and Justice Perspective box below), personality tests such as the Minnesota Multiphasic Personality Inventory (MMPI-2), and physical skills and ability testing (McKenna, 1998). You may be using this text for one course in the Police Foundations Training. It is highly likely that questions on the tests you are required to take will reflect the learning outcomes of this course. Are you ready?

LAW AND JUSTICE PERSPECTIVE

Using the General Aptitude Test Battery (G.A.T.B.)

The Police Constable Selection Project in Ontario (Ontario Ministry of the Solicitor General, 1992) established a number of competencies that would be required at the entry level for officers. The General Aptitude Test Battery was researched as part of

LAW AND JUSTICE PERSPECTIVE (*Continued*)

this project and has been deemed as a reliable and valid testing tool that can be used in the process of selecting police constables. For use as a test in policing, three of the eight aptitudes are tested. These three aptitudes make up the "G score," or General Learning Ability. Each of the three sub-tests is timed, although individuals are not penalized for wrong answers. The questions get more difficult, and individuals are not expected to complete all the questions. A score that is above average for the "G score" has been identified for police recruits.

The three aptitudes used from the G.A.T.B. are:

- **Numerical aptitude** Some questions will test a person's ability to quickly perform arithmetic operations, including addition, subtraction, division, and multiplication.
- **Spatial aptitude** This part of the test measures an individual's ability to select what shape a flat object will take when it is folded in a specific way.
- **Verbal aptitude** This part of the test measures an individual's ability to understand the meaning of words and to use them effectively, as well as the individual's verbal comprehension.

An Increased Concern with Ethics

Police leaders are increasingly concerned about ethics in policing as a result of serious questions raised by the public. These questions centre on standards of police accountability, the excessive use of force, and the proper use of police discretion. As mentioned in a previous chapter, the actions of one person can impact an entire organization's credibility. As a result, many services are reviewing their current training programs on ethical standards of policing (McKenna, 1998). As part of new selection and training procedures, police organizations will be making increasing attempts to ensure that they are attracting people who will operate at high moral and ethical levels.

Ethics and morals can be tied into earlier chapters on perception and diversity. Raised in different families and cultures, we all have different morals and values. For example, some cultures have more of a close-knit family structure than others. While cultures have different values and display them in different ways, police services need to attract candidates from diverse cultures that place high moral and ethical value on protecting the weak and valuing human life.

Also, how we perceive an event or are influenced by others may change our behaviour. Therefore, it is important that police services hire only individuals with strong moral and ethical values and that current officers behave in ways that reflect these values and ethics on and off duty.

Technological Advancements

Technology is changing our lives and workplaces at a dizzying speed (McShane, 1995). Advanced information systems now allow citizens to have real-time information relating to crime. Information that once depended on access and transmission by dispatchers on antiquated computer systems is now instantly at officers' fingertips in their patrol cars (Sewell, 2002). According to the Canadian Police College (2004), the literature reveals an explosion of technologies available to police in telecommunications and forensic sciences. Mobile data computers, mobile cameras, thermal imaging, alcohol screening devices, global positioning systems, night vision systems, and laser and photo radar are just a few of the technologies used in policing.

Technologies are advancing irreversibly and quickly. These technologies help in prevention, identification, investigations, management, and the protection of police officers (Canadian Police College, 2004). "Because policing relies so heavily on the latest developments in technology, it is important that we have a good understanding of this area" (McKenna, 1998). Computer technology, weapons, identification techniques, and the internet are just a few of the areas of technological advancement.

Unfortunately, these advancements can also be misused. For example, use of the internet for fraud and other cybercrimes will continue to increase. One report also reveals the use of encryption technology and software that allows terrorists to send virtually unbreakable coded messages across the internet (United Press, 1999). Often these kinds of crimes continue until new statutes can be enacted.

Police officers are confronted with a wide array of new technology to master. New car equipment, newer and faster computers, and other new technology can be bewildering for anyone—even with professional development training.

Increased Stress

As mentioned earlier, policing in Canada is changing. The diverse needs of communities, rapid technological advancements, and the changing capabilities and structures of

---

- Eat healthily. Cut down on caffeine and eliminate any other maladaptive behaviours or substances.
- Exercise regularly.
- Get plenty of rest and sleep.
- Recognize your cues and symptoms of stress.
- Learn relaxation techniques such as breathing techniques and meditation.
- Develop time-management strategies.
- Decide what you can change in your life to manage stress more effectively.
- Develop a proactive attitude towards change.
- Choose to think positively about situations. Expect and envision positive outcomes.
- Talk to yourself in a kind way and build your confidence.
- Be grateful. Help others. Give and accept support.
- Use appropriate humour and smile more.
- Effectively communicate your needs. Talk to others you trust and seek support and professional assistance if necessary.
- Do not be too critical or competitive.
- Set realistic goals. Determine your mission and your priorities. Give yourself a sense of purpose and meaning.
- Get organized.
- Balance your life with time to reflect, enjoy hobbies, read a book, or listen to music. Treat yourself well.
- Moods can be contagious. Have fun and surround yourself with positive people you enjoy.
- Deal with emotions such as anger in healthy ways.

Figure 10-3 Tips for Managing the Stress Associated with Change

Source: Adapted in part from the Canadian Mental Health Association, *Tips for Dealing with Stress and Tension*, 2006, www.cmha.ca.

police services demand that those services continually examine and improve their ways of operation. All of these changes affect policing and compound the stress inherently associated with the profession (Sewell, 2002). Police leaders need to be aware of the stress that change can create among officers and develop long-term and ongoing strategies to introduce change at levels that can be managed. Figure 10-3 outlines some tips for managing the stress associated with change. In changing times, consciously implementing stress reduction programs can help organizations and employees manage the stress of change (Sewell, 2002).

SUMMARY

In this chapter we explored change by first defining what change is and the types of change that occur within organizations. Change agents are individuals or groups within organizations that can facilitate the change process. Organizations undergo restructuring; people undergo the changes. People's reactions to change are different and range from inertia, support, and reluctance, to various types of resistance. People resist change for several reasons, including direct costs of the change; fear of the unknown; saving face; disruption and breaking of familiar routines; incongruent organizational systems; and team dynamics that do not promote acceptance of the changes.

Change is a process that occurs in three stages, according to force field analysis: unfreezing, transition, and refreezing. The model of force field analysis can actually be used to assist change agents in managing organizational changes. There are several methods that can be used to overcome resistance to change. Organizations can use communication, employee involvement, and training opportunities, and can introduce change at an appropriate pace and use negotiation to move ahead. Although it should be avoided, coercion can also be used to facilitate change. Because change happens to people, we also need to use strategies to help us cope with change. Some strategies are managing stress, talking to others, realizing that adjustment to change takes time, and changing our perceptions.

The last part of the chapter concluded with exploring changes that are having significant impact on policing in Canada. Globalization; diverse immigration patterns in Canada; technological advancements; increased accountability to the public and other stakeholders; government cutbacks; and amalgamation—all these things make it essential for police services to operate more like a business in order to adapt and respond to a rapidly changing world. Changes in Canada affect policing and compound the stress inherently associated with the profession.

Police leaders need to be aware of the stress that change can create among officers and should develop long-term and ongoing strategies to introduce change at levels that can be managed. Equipped with the knowledge and skills from this text, you are well on your way to developing the skills and abilities that will help you become an effective police officer.

WEBSITES

www.ccohs.ca/oshanswers/occup_workplace/police.html
This is Canada's National Occupational Health and Safety Resource site. This site discusses health and safety issues for police and preventative measures.

www.canadian-health-network.com/servlet/
The Public Health Agency of Canada site has useful articles on change and information, with links to a variety of sites on change and stress.

www.suicideinfo.ca
This is the Centre for Suicide Prevention site.

www.HereToHelp.bc.ca
This British Columbia site provides information on stress.

www.safecanada.ca
This government of Canada site has a wide variety of information on safety issues.

www.cmha.ca/bins/content_page.asp?cid=2-28-30&lang=1
This site from the Canadian Mental Health Association has information on coping with stress. Rate your current level of stress.

www.mentalhealth.samhsa.gov/publications/allpubs/KEN-01-0097/default.asp
This site features the article "Care tips for survivors of a traumatic event: What to expect in your personal, family, work, and financial life."

www.psepc-sppcc.gc.ca
This is the site for Public Safety and Emergency Preparedness Canada. This site has links to recent agreements with First Nations and other information on changes in policing.

JOURNAL AND DISCUSSION QUESTIONS

1. What are some significant changes that have occurred in your life in the past two to three years? What was your reaction to these changes?

2. Organizations do not always manage change very well. Examine a company in your area that is managing change well and one that is not. How do these two organizations differ?

3. Change is constant in our society. What changes do you need to make in order to become more proactive and responsive to change?

SKILLS PRACTICE 10-1

Using Force Field Analysis to Implement Change

One practical use of force field analysis is to identify current forces that are maintaining a situation in its present state and then to develop a strategy to overcome these forces. Let's use a somewhat fictionalized example from policing. This may be a good exercise to conduct in teams, using a brainstorming approach.

The Current Situation: Because of several changes across the country, it is becoming apparent that recruits need more formal education and training before being accepted into services. If policing is to be viewed as a professional occupation, more formalized training and higher education is necessary to turn this traditional job into a profession.

Your Responsibilities: Your team is a provincial group of experts from a variety of fields including policing, higher educational institutions, and various ministries. You have been assigned to examine this issue and to come up with some strategies about how this training should be implemented.

1. As a team, first identify the existing forces that will help you implement formal officer training. Second, identify the forces that will hinder your implementation of higher education standards in officer training. These are the restraining forces. Place them on the areas identified below.

Driving Forces	C	S	Restraining Forces
	U	T	
	R	A	
	R	T	
	E	E	
	N		
	T		

2. Circle the forces that you (or your team) feel could be most easily used to change the current state or status quo. In other words, what driving forces could you increase to help implement the change? What restraining forces could you decrease to help you implement the change?

3. Select two of the forces that you have chosen and develop a plan that would increase or decrease that force. Ideally, choose one restraining and one driving force. You may want to use the models for goal setting, decision making, or problem solving for this process.

_____

_____

4. Identify potential problems with your action plan, solution, or decision.

_____

_____

SKILLS PRACTICE 10-2

Group Exercise: Change Success Stories

Individually, brainstorm to remember five major changes you have experienced in your lifetime.

1. _____

2. _____

3. _____

4. _____

5. _____

In your groups, discuss the following questions and record your conclusions.

1. What made the change difficult or stressful?

_____

_____

_____

_____

2. How did you feel during the stages of change (before, during, and after)?

_____

_____

_____

_____

3. What was the key to your success in dealing with the change?

_____

_____

_____

_____

4. What did you learn as a result of the change that you can pass on to others?

_____

_____

_____

_____

SKILLS PRACTICE 10-3
Managing the Stress of Change: My Self-Care Plan

Use the questions below to help you develop your own self-care plan. Refer back to Figure 10-3 for useful stress management tips.

What are the key interpersonal behaviours that are essential components of dealing effectively with change (e.g., communicating effectively, living a balanced life)?

_____

_____

_____

_____

_____

_____

_____

How can I implement these behaviours?

_____

_____

_____

_____

_____

_____

_____

What adaptive behaviours have helped me deal with stress in the past?

_____

_____

_____

What are my dreams, priorities, and goals?

What am I most grateful for?

What support systems do I have in place to help me through tough times in life? What can I do to build on or add to that list?

What do I have control over and what can I not change?

_____

_____

_____

_____

_____

_____

_____

Glossary

A

Abstract A representation of an object, thing, or concept; for example the word "chair," which represents a specific piece of furniture.

Acculturation The process whereby one culture is modified by contact with another culture.

Active listening An active process whereby the listener tries to understand exactly what the speaker is saying and feeling by reflecting both feelings and content back to the speaker.

Actor-versus-observer bias The tendency to view others' behaviour as being caused by internal factors, while viewing our own behaviour as being caused by situational factors.

Aggressive behaviour Behaviour whereby an individual gets what he wants without concern for others.

Ambiguous A thing that is not clear or well understood.

Artifacts Personal objects that announce who we are and that we use to personalize our environments.

Assertive behaviour Behaviour whereby an individual communicates in a straightforward and honest manner while still maintaining the rights of others.

B

Beliefs The things that you hold as true or false.

Body language The postures, movements, and gestures that nonverbally communicate information to others.

Brainstorming A process of encouraging creative thinking by generating "free-wheeling" ideas and alternatives.

C

Central traits Primary traits to which other traits are attached or grouped.

Change When a thing is different from what it used to be or in some other manner.

Change agents Individuals or groups that take responsibility for managing a change within an organization.

Charisma The quality in a leader that inspires followers to attain the goals of the leader.

Chronemics The study of how we perceive and use time.

Closure The process of filling in missing information.

Coaching Encouraging someone to a higher level of competency or skill in an area in which the coach already has greater skill.

Co-culture A culture that exists within a larger culture.

Cognitive complexity The level of ability to develop a sophisticated set of personal constructs.

Cohesiveness The extent to which members are attracted to and want to be part of a group or team.

Communication climate A condition or environment that is created within a team or group by the interaction of its members.

Communication continuum A range of communication that varies from not knowing a person exists to intimate communication with a person. We vary our communication with others along this continuum in order to manage relationships.

Community policing Delivery of police services based on a partnership with the community. The community and police jointly identify issues and work together to resolve these issues to mutual satisfaction.

Compliance Yielding to a direct request.

Confirming responses Responses that indicate that both the listener and the speaker are valued, and that also demonstrate respect for individuals.

Conflict A condition that occurs when two sets of demands, goals, or motives are incompatible.

Conformity Going along with the norms or rules of a group or team due to perceived pressure.

Connotative level of meaning The subjective and personal-level meaning of a word.

Consensus Agreement by all members of a group about a decision or solution.

Constructive controversy Conflict in which team or group members debate their different opinions about an issue without involving personal issues.

Constructs A set of opposing specific qualities that we use to categorize people and situations.

Covert conflicts Conflicts that are not expressed openly but are hidden and expressed indirectly.

Creative thinking The ability to process information that results in a product that is new, original, and meaningful.

Crisis An event that goes beyond an individual's ability to cope when the event is occurring.

Crisis prevention A set of strategies that can be used to avoid a crisis or to prevent a crisis from escalating.

Cultural Values A set of central and enduring goals in life and ways of life that are important to a specific culture.

Culture A learned and shared system of knowledge, beliefs, values, attitudes, and norms.

D

Decentring The ability to think about another person's thoughts and feelings.

Decision The selection of one option from a set of options or alternatives.

Decision making The process of developing and selecting from a set of options or alternatives.

Decoding The process whereby a receiver interprets a message into meaningful information.

Defensive behaviour Acting in a way to protect one's self when feeling threatened.

Denotative level of meaning A word's literal level of meaning that is shared by a large group or culture.

Disconfirming responses Responses that devalue another person and do not project respect towards that individual.

Discrimination Unjustifiable negative behaviour directed towards members of a group.

E

Empathizing The ability to put yourself in another person's "shoes," to feel what another person is feeling.

Encoding The process of organizing ideas or thoughts into a series of symbols to communicate with a receiver.

Enculturation The process whereby culture is transmitted from one generation to another.

Ethnocentrism A belief or conviction that the way that your culture does things is superior to another culture's ways.

Extroversion An attitude characterized by outgoing behaviour and ways of interacting and mingling with others.

F

Feedback Information that tells you how well you have performed.

Feminine cultures Cultures that stress more traditional feminine values such as valuing relationships, caring for others, and emphasizing the quality of life.

Force field analysis A model of change that consists of unfreezing, transition, and refreezing. The model consists of driving and restraining forces that influence proposed changes.

Fundamental attribution error Over- estimating and attributing another's behaviour to dispositional or internal factors.

G

Goal An event, circumstance, object, condition, or purpose for which an individual strives.

Group Two or more people who are aware of each other, who influence and are influenced by each other, who are engaged in an ongoing and relatively stable relationship, who share common goals, and who view themselves as belonging to the group.

Group polarization A situation in which a group's decision is more extreme—either more conservative or more risky—than the decision individual group members would have made by themselves.

Groupthink A process of faulty decision making by a cohesive group.

H

Halo effect Attributing a set of positive characteristics to someone we like.

Haptics The use of touch to communicate a message.

Hearing The physiological process of sound waves entering the ear and hitting the eardrums.

Heterogeneous team A team composed of people with a diversity of characteristics, interests, cultures, and values.

Hidden agenda Personal goals or motives that an individual hides from the rest of the group.

Hierarchy The structure of a group, based on power and status differences.

Homogeneous team A team composed of people who share things in common, such as expertise, characteristics, culture, and values.

Horn effect Attributing a set of negative characteristics to someone we dislike.

Human communication Sharing observations with others as we try to make sense of the world.

I

Impersonal communication A type of communication whereby we treat the other person as an object or respond only to his or her role.

Impression formation The process of forming an impression of someone based on a collection of perceptions.

Incremental change (frame-bending change) Change that occurs in series of steps over time.

Inertia A reaction to change whereby the individual does nothing.

Inferences Guesses, opinions, and ideas about a person, object, or event that are not necessarily true or factual.

Interference Noise that interferes with the transmission or reception of a message.

Internalize Taking external information and making this information part of who you are or part of your psychological makeup.

Interpersonal attraction The factors that bring people together at the early stages of a relationship.

Interpersonal communication A form of communication between two people that occurs simultaneously, where there is mutual influence, and where it is used for the purpose of managing the relationship.

Interpersonal perception The process of selecting, organizing, and interpreting others' actions and behaviour.

Intimacy The degree of closeness we feel with another.

Intimate distance A range of distance from touching to about 46 centimetres, which is reserved for intimate communication.

J

Jargon Abbreviations or short forms of a word or phrase that are shared by a specific group, and which may not be understood by others outside of the group.

K

Kinesics The use of body movement and gestures to communicate.

L

Lateral thinking Another term for creative thinking, or the ability to process information that results in a new idea or product.

Leader The person with the skill or ability to influence others towards obtaining organizational and personal goals.

Leadership The ability to influence or the process of influencing people towards attaining goals of the organization or team.

Listening The active process of trying to understand exactly what the speaker is saying in interpersonal communication.

M

Management The technical tasks of a presecibed position within an organization.

Masculine cultures Cultures that value more traditional masculine characteristics such as material wealth, assertiveness, achievement, and heroism.

Matching hypothesis The hypothesis that we are attracted to others who are similar to us in physical appearance.

Monopolizing An ineffective listening strategy where the speaker continually re-focuses the conversation on himself or herself.

Myers-Briggs type indicator (MBTI) A psychological instrument used to help identify personality preferences.

N

Nonassertive behaviour Behaviour in which an individual does not stand up for her rights or let her feelings be known.

Nonverbal communication Behaviour that communicates meaning to another person but that is not written or verbal language.

Norms Shared beliefs about what constitutes acceptable and unacceptable behaviours within a group or team.

O

Obedience Complying with a request made by someone perceived to be of higher authority.

Overt conflicts Conflicts that are expressed openly between individuals. Issues and differences are expressed and discussed between parties.

P

Paralanguage Vocal communication that does not include actual words, but rather sounds, voice volume, pitch, tone, and intensity.

Paraphrasing As part of active listening, repeating in different words the feeling or content of what a speaker has said.

Perception The process of selecting, organizing, and interpreting stimuli to make sense of the world.

Perception checking A process of soliciting feedback to confirm the accuracy of a perception.

Performance gap A discrepancy between what is currently occurring and what should be occurring.

Peripheral traits Traits that do not appear to be related to other traits.

Personal constructs Specific qualities that we use to categorize people.

Personal distance A distance between people, ranging from 46 centimetres to 1 metre, which is reserved for friendly relations.

Personality clash An antagonistic relationship between two people that results from differences in characteristics and attributes, preferences, interests, values, and personal styles.

Personality traits Enduring characteristics of an individual.

Physical noise External noise that interferes with the transmission or reception of communication, such as loud music or traffic noise.

Planned change Change that occurs as a result of specific efforts.

Polarization In language and communication, describing events, people, or objects in terms of extremes.

Positive reinforcement Rewarding behaviour to increase the likelihood that the behaviour will be repeated or maintained.

Power The ability to get someone to do what you want him or her to do.

Prejudice An unjustifiably negative attitude towards a group and its members.

Private acceptance Conformity as a result of changed beliefs.

Problem A gap between what currently exists and the desired state.

Problem solving A complex decision-making process that involves analysis of the problem and develops a plan to correct the problem or reduce its effects.

Prototypes Cognitive structures that represent the best or clearest example of a category.

Proxemics The study of spatial communication or how we use space to identify relationship intimacy.

Proximity Physical nearness to others.

Pseudo listening Pretending to listen to another person when in reality you are attending to other things or focused on internal thoughts.

Psychological noise Internal noise, such as hunger or distraction by other thoughts, that interferes with the transmission or reception of communication; any internal interference that reduces an individual's capacity to send or receive a message.

Public compliance Conforming to a behaviour publicly without truly believing the behaviour to be correct or appropriate.

Public distance A distance between people, ranging from 4 metres to 8 metres and beyond, which is maintained for very impersonal interpersonal contact.

R

Radical change (frame-breaking change) Change that results in the major make-over of an organization.

Reflected appraisal Your view of yourself based on the assessment of others.

Refreezing Re-establishing equilibrium after a change has been implemented.

Reinforcement affect model The idea that people are attracted to others who are associated with pleasurable events or stimuli.

Relational level of meaning The level of meaning that defines our identity and relationships with others on three levels: interest, responsiveness, and power.

Resilience The ability to withstand pressure and stress and emerge stronger from stressful or taxing experiences.

Restricted code A set of words or phrases that are developed and used by a small group, such as a family.

Role A position or place held in society; a set of attitudes and behaviours attributed to a position or place in society.

Role conflict Conflict that is caused by competing demands or expectations.

S

Scripts Series of actions or behaviours that serve as guides in various daily activities.

Selective attention The process of attending to a limited amount of stimuli.

Self-concept What you think of yourself and who you think you are.

Self-disclosure The process of revealing your inner self to another.

Self-esteem The positive or negative evaluation of your self-concept.

Self-handicapping strategy Setting up an external reason for possible failure.

Self-monitoring The degree to which people change their behaviour according to their perception of the demands of a situation.

Self-presentation The process of conveying who we are to others.

Self-sabotage Behaviours, including negative self-talk, that interfere with or stop change efforts.

Self-serving bias Attributing success to internal factors and blaming failure on external factors.

Semantic noise Interference that arises from differences in the perception of the meaning of a transmitted message, such as not knowing the meaning of a word.

Similarity Grouping stimuli together based on common characteristics.

Simplification Organizing stimuli in the easiest way possible.

Social affiliation Association with others; being with others in a group or team context—one of the reasons we join groups.

Social comparison Trying to present ourselves and see ourselves in a favourable light by observing others around us.

Social distance From 1 metre to 4 metres, this distance is used to conduct more impersonal interaction.

Social exchange theory The theory that, in relationships, people measure their social, physical, and other assets against those of a potential partner.

Social identification Defining ourselves in relation to those around us.

Static evaluation Maintaining the same evaluation of something without recognizing the changes that may have occurred.

Stereotypes Placing people or situations into separate and distinct categories based on broad generalizations and assumptions.

Strategic self-presentation The process of conveying a certain image to others to obtain specific goals.

Supportive behaviour Behaviour that encourages openness, trust, and self-disclosure.

Symbols Representations for concepts, thoughts, ideas, and objects.

Synergy Energy that results from the combined efforts and contributions of individual team members.

T

Tactical communication A standardized communication system used by law enforcement personnel.

Team A group of diverse people who share leadership responsibility for creating a group identity in an interconnected effort to achieve a mutually defined goal within the context of other groups and systems.

Team building A formal intervention process directed towards improving the functioning and development of a team.

Team effectiveness The extent to which a team achieves its objectives, meets the needs and objectives of members, and maintains itself over time.

Theory of reasoned action One theory that discusses the link between attitudes and behaviour.

Tolerance Being aware of and understanding that cultural differences do exist and being able to actively cope with these differences through understanding and empathy.

Trait approach The theories that suggest that leaders have unique qualities or traits qualifying them to lead.

Transmission The sending of a message through a chosen medium, such as verbal or written communication.

U

Ultimate attribution error Attributing internal causes for positive behaviour of people we like while attributing external causes for their negative behaviour. Also, attributing external causes for positive behaviour of people we dislike while attributing internal causes for their negative behaviour.

Unfreezing Changing the status quo or current state to prepare the organization for change.

Unplanned change Change that occurs spontaneously or randomly.

V

Values A set of central and enduring goals in life and ways of living that you feel are important, right, and true.

Vertical thinking A traditional thinking style that is logical, sequential, and analytical.

W

Win-lose The notion that in the outcome of a conflict there must be a winner and a loser.

Win-win The notion that in a conflict both sides can get what they want and both sides win.

References

J. L. Adams (1979). *Conceptual Blockbusting: A Guide to Better Ideas*, 2nd Edition. New York: Norton.

I. Ajzen and M. Fishbein (1980). *Understanding Attitudes and Predicting Social Behaviour.* Englewood Cliffs, NJ: Prentice-Hall.

R. Albanese and D. D. Van Fleet (1985). Rational behaviour in groups: The free-riding tendency. *Academy of Management Review, 10,* pp. 565–581.

J. E. Alcock, D. W. Carment, and S. W. Sadava (2005). *A Textbook of Social Psychology,* 6th Edition. Toronto: Pearson Education Canada.

Gordon W. Allport (1958). *The Nature of Prejudice.* New York: Doubleday.

Luigi Anolli and Rita Ciceri (1997). The voice of deception: Vocal strategies of naive and able liars. *Journal of Nonverbal Behaviour, 21* (4), pp. 259–284.

M. Argyle (1983). *The Psychology of Interpersonal Behavior.* London: Penguin.

E. Aries (1987). Gender and communication, in P. Shaver (Ed.), *Sex and Gender*, pp. 149–176. Newbury Park, CA: Sage.

William Arnold (1980). *Crisis Communication.* Dubuque, IA: Gorsuch Scarisbrick Publishers.

S. E. Asch (1946). Forming impressions of personality. *Journal of Abnormal and Social Psychology, 41*, pp. 258–290.

Roger E. Axtell (1989). *Do's and Taboos of Hosting International Visitors.* New York: John Wiley and Sons.

Robert A. Baron, Bruce Earhard, and Marcia Ozier (1995). *Psychology*, Canadian Edition. Scarborough, ON: Allyn & Bacon Canada.

Robert A. Baron, Bruce Earhard, and Marcia Ozier (1997). *Psychology*, 2nd Canadian Edition. Scarborough, ON: Allyn & Bacon Canada.

B. M. Bass (1990). From transactional to transformational leadership: Learning to share the vision. *Organizational Dynamics*, Winter, pp. 19–31.

Aaron Beck (1988). *Love Is Never Enough.* New York: Harper and Row.

Steven A. Beebe, Susan J. Beebe, and Mark V. Redmond (1999). *Interpersonal Communication: Relating to Others.* Needham Heights, MA: Allyn & Bacon.

Steven A. Beebe, Susan J. Beebe, Mark V. Redmond, and Terri M. Geerinck (2004). *Interpersonal Communication: Relating to Others,* 3rd Canadian Edition. Toronto: Pearson Education Canada.

Warren Bennis (1989). *Why Leaders Can't Lead.* San Francisco: Jossey-Bass.

Laurie L. Bergner (1998). Developing leaders begins at the beginning. *The Police Chief.* November, pp.17–23.

Eric Berne (1964). *Games People Play.* New York: Grove.

Robert R. Blake and Jane S. Mouton (1978). *The New Managerial Grid.* Houston: Gulf.

Kenneth H. Blanchard and Paul Hersey (1996). Great ideas revisited . . . *Training and Development, 50*, p. 42.

Lee. G. Bolman and Terrence E. Deal (1992). Leading and managing: Effects of context, culture and gender. *Educational Administration Quarterly, 28*, pp. 314–329.

William Bridges (1991). *Managing Transitions: Making the Most of Change.* Don Mills, ON: Addison-Wesley.

J. K. Burgoon, D. B. Buller, and W. G. Woodall (1989). *Nonverbal Communication: The Unspoken Dialogue*, p. 324. New York: Harper and Row.

Canadian Mental Health Association (2006). Depression in the workplace. Retrieved February 27, 2006, from www.cmha.ca/bins/content_page.asp?cid=3-86-87-91&lang=1.

Canadian Police College (1998). *Redefining Police-Community Relationships.* Marcel-Eugene LeBeuf: Ottawa.

Canadian Police College (2004). *Canadian Police Information Technologies: Current Overview.* Marcel-Eugene LeBeuf, Simon Pare, and Miguel Belzile: Ottawa.

Canadian Police College, Police Executive Centre (2006). www.cpc.gc.ca/execut_e.htm.

Canadian Social Trends (1997). Canadian children in the 1990s: Selected findings of the national longitudinal survey of children and youth. *Canadian Social Trends.* Spring.

J. M. Carroll and J. A. Russell (1996). Do facial expressions signal specific emotions? Judging emotions from the face in context. *Journal of Personality and Social Psychology, 70,* pp. 205–218.

James Chacko and Stephen E. Nancoo (Eds.) (1993). *Community Policing in Canada.* Toronto: Canadian Scholars' Press Inc.

Robert E. Coffee, Curtis W. Cook, and Phillip L. Hunsaker (1994). *Management and Organizational Behaviour,* pp. 197–120. Burr Ridge, IL: Irwin.

J. A. Conger and R. N. Kanungo (1987). Towards a behavioural theory of charismatic leadership in organizational setting. *Academy of Management Review, 12,* pp. 637–647.

J. A. Conger and R. N. Kanungo (1988). Behavioural dimensions of charismatic leadership. In J. A. Conger and R. N. Kanungo (Eds.). *Charismatic Leadership.* San Francisco: Jossey-Bass.

J. A. Conger and R. N. Kanungo (1992). Perceived behavioural attributes of charismatic leadership. *Canadian Journal of Behavioural Science, 24,* pp. 86–102.

Daryl R. Conner (1994). *Managing at the Speed of Change: How Resilient Managers Succeed and Prosper Where Others Fail.* New York: Villard Books.

Edward Cornish (2004). *Futuring: The Exploration of the Future.* Bethesda, Maryland: World Future Society, USA.

Emory L. Cowen (1991). In pursuit of wellness. *American Psychologist,* April, p. 406.

S. F. Cronshaw and R. J. Ellis (1991). A process of investigation of self-monitoring and leader emergence. *Small Group Research, 22,* pp. 403–420.

M. Csikszentmihalyi and T. J. Figurski (1982). Self-awareness and overside experience in everyday life. *Journal of Personality, 50,* pp. 15–28.

Mark L. Dantzker and Michael P. Mitchell (1998). *Understanding Today's Police.* Scarborough, ON: Prentice-Hall Canada.

Edward De Bono (1972). *Lateral Thinking: Creativity Step by Step.* New York: Harper and Row.

Richard J. De Paris (1998). Organizational leadership and change management: Removing systems barriers to community-oriented policing and problem solving. *The Police Chief,* December, pp. 68–76.

Joseph A. Devito (1995). *The Interpersonal Communication Book,* 7th Edition. United States: HarperCollins.

Joseph A. Devito (1996). *Messages: Building Interpersonal Skills,* 3rd Edition. New York: HarperCollins College Publishers.

Joseph A. Devito (2005). *Messages: Building Interpersonal Communication Skills,* 6th Edition. Boston: Pearson Education Canada.

Joseph A. DeVito, Rena Shimoni, and Dawne Clark (2005). *Messages: Building Interpersonal Communication Skills, 2nd Canadian Edition.* Toronto: Pearson Education Canada.

Mary K. Devitt, Charles R. Honts, and Lynelle Vondergreest (1997). Truth or just bias: The treatment of the psychophysiological detection of deception in introductory psychology textbooks, *The Journal of Credibility Assessment and Witness Psychology,* 1(1), pp. 9–32.

Andrew J. DuBrin and Terri Geerinck (2004). *Human Relations for Career and Personal Success, 3rd Canadian Edition.* Toronto: Pearson Education Canada.

A. H. Eagly and B. T. Johnson (1990). Gender and leadership style: A meta-analysis. *Psychological Bulletin, 108,* pp. 233–256.

A. H. Eagly, M. G. Makijani, and B. G. Klonsky (1992). Gender and the evaluation of leaders: A meta-analysis. *Psychological Bulletin, 111,* pp. 3–22.

P. Ekman (1992). Facial expression of emotion: New findings, new questions. *Psychological Science, 3,* pp. 34–38.

P. Ekman and W. V. Friesen (1978). Facial action coding system (FACS): A technique for the measurement of facial action. *Journal of Personality and Social Psychology, 39,* pp. 1125–1134.

Isa N. Engleberg and Dianna R. Wynn (1997). *Working in Groups: Communication Principles and Strategies.* Boston, MA: Houghton Mifflin Co.

A. Feingold (1988). Matching for attractiveness in romantic partners and same-sex friends: A meta-analysis and theoretical critique. *Psychological Bulletin, 104,* pp. 226–235.

Robert S. Feldman (1998). *Social Psychology,* 2nd Edition. Upper Saddle River, NJ: Prentice-Hall.

B. Aubrey Fisher (1970). The process of decision modification in small discussion groups. *The Journal of Communication, 20 (1),* pp. 51–64.

J. R. P. French and B. Raven (1959). The bases of social power. In D. Cartwright, *Studies in Social Power.* Ann Arbor, MI: University of Michigan Press.

S. Gaines Jr. (1995). Relationships among members of cultural minorities. In J. T. Wood and S. W. Duck (Eds.), *Understanding Relationship Processes, 6: Off the Beaten Track: Understudied Relationships.* Thousand Oaks, CA: Sage, pp. 51–88.

Jennifer George (1992). Extrinsic and intrinsic origins of perceived social loafing in organizations. *Academy of Management Journal, 35*, pp. 191–202.

J. R. Gibb (1961). Defensive communication. *Journal of Communication, Vol. 11, No. 3*, pp. 141–148.

Naomi Golan (1978). *Treatment in Crisis Situations.* New York: The Free Press.

J. Greenberg and R. A. Baron (1993). *Behavior in Organizations,* 5th Edition. Boston: Allyn & Bacon.

M. S. Greenberg and R. B. Ruback (1982*). Social Psychology of the Criminal Justice System.* Belmont, CA: Wadsworth Publishing.

E.T. Hall (1963). Proxemics: A study of man's spatial relationships, in *Man's Image in Medicine and Anthropology.* New York: International Universities Press.

J. A. Hall (1987). On explaining gender differences: The case of nonverbal communication, in P. Shaver and C. Hendricks (Eds.), *Sex and Gender,* pp. 177–200. Newbury Park, CA: Mayfield.

D. Hart and W. Damon (1986). Developmental trends in self-understanding. *Social Cognition, 4,* pp. 388–407.

Lynne Hendersen and Philip Zimbardo (1996). Shyness. *Encyclopedia of Mental Health.* www.shyness.com/encyclopedia.html.

N. M. Henley (1977). *Body Politics: Power, Sex and Nonverbal Communication.* Englewood Cliffs, NJ: Prentice-Hall.

Paul Hersey and Kenneth H. Blanchard (1988). *Management of Organizational Behavior: Utilizing Human Resources*, 5th Edition. Englewood Cliffs, NJ: Prentice-Hall.

Geert Hofstede (1980). *Culture's Consequences: International Differences in Work-Related Values.* Beverly Hills, CA: Sage.

Geert Hofstede (1991). *Cultures and Organizations.* London: McGraw Hill.

M. Hojat (1982). Loneliness as a function of selected personality variables. *Journal of Clinical Psychology, 38*, pp. 136–141.

E. P. Hollander (1985). Leadership and power. In G. Lindzey and E. Aronson (Eds.), *Handbook of Social Psychology, 3rd Edition, Vol. 2.* New York: Random House.

Dominic Infante (1988). *Arguing Constructively.* Prospect Heights, IL: Waveland Press.

I. L. Janis (1972). *Victims of Groupthink.* Boston: Houghton Mifflin.

I. L. Janis (1982). *Groupthink,* 2nd Edition. Boston: Houghton Mifflin.

David W. Johnson and Frank P. Johnson (2006). *Joining Together: Group Theory and Group Skills,* 9th Edition. Boston: Pearson Education Canada.

D. Katz and R. L. Kahn (1978). *The Social Psychology of Organizations,* 2nd Edition. New York: Wiley.

H. H. Kelley (1950). The warm-cold variable in first impressions of persons. *Journal of Personality, 18*, pp. 431–439.

H. H. Kelley (1972). Causal schemata and the attribution process, in E. E. Jones, D. E. Kanouse, H. H. Kelley, R. R. Nisbett, S. Valins, and B. Weiner (Eds.), *Attribution: Perceiving the Causes of Behavior.* Morristown, NJ: General Learning Press.

Dennis Kinlaw (1991*). Developing Superior Work Teams: Building Quality and the Competitive Edge.* Lexington, MA: Lexington Books.

C. L. Kleinke (1986). Gaze and eye contact: A research review. *Psychological Bulletin, 100,* pp. 78–100.

E. T. Klemmer and F. W. Snyder (1972). Measurement of time spent communicating. *Journal of Communication, 22*, June, pp. 142–158.

Gary T. Klugiewicz (1996). An introduction to defensive tactics, in Ed Nowicki (Ed.), *Total Survival,* pp. 203–207. Powers Lake, WI: Performance Dimensions Publishing.

M. Knapp (1978). *Nonverbal Communication in Human Interaction.* New York: Holt, Rinehart and Winston.

Knowles, J. (1995). A matter of survival: Emerging entrepreneurship in community colleges in Canada. *Challenge and Opportunity: Canada's Community Colleges at the Crossroads.* Vancouver: UBC Press.

James Kouzes and Barry Posner (1987). *The Leadership Challenge: How to Get Extraordinary Things Done in Organizations.* San Francisco: Jossey-Bass.

Patrick Lahey, Mary Trant, Rudolph F. Verderber, and Kathleen S. Verderber (2005). *Communicate! First Canadian Edition.* Toronto: Thompson Nelson.

Marilyn E. Laiken (1994). *The Anatomy of High Performing Teams: A Leader's Handbook.* Toronto: OISE Press.

Kurt Lewin (1951). *Field Theory in Social Science.* New York: Harper and Row.

T. S. Libra (1976). *Japanese Patterns of Behavior.* Honolulu: University of Hawaii Press.

Rick Linden (1989). Demographic change and the future of policing, in Donald J. Loree (Ed.), *Future Issues in Policing: Symposium Proceedings,* pp. 111–127. Ottawa, ON: The Canadian Police College.

Frances Litwin (1996). Careful: That mood is catching! *Better Health Magazine, Vol. 2, No. 2.*

Gay Lumsden and Donald Lumsden (1997). *Communicating in Groups and Teams: Sharing Leadership.* Belmont, CA: Wadsworth Publishing Co.

Robert Lunney (1989). The role of the police leader in the 21st century, in Donald J. Loree (Ed.), *Future Issues in Policing: Symposium Proceedings.* Ottawa, ON: Canadian Police College, pp. 197–213.

L. A. Malandro and L. L. Barker (1983). *Nonverbal Communication.* Reading, MA: Addison-Wesley.

D. N. Maltz and R. Barker (1982). A cultural approach to male-female miscommunication, in J. J. Gumpertz (Ed.), *Language and Social Identity*, pp. 196–216. Cambridge: Cambridge University Press.

Abraham Maslow (1954). *Motivation and Personality.* New York: Harper & Row.

Richard J. Mayer (1990). *Conflict Management: The Courage to Confront.* Columbus, OH: Batelle Press.

Ed McDaniel and Peter A. Andersen (1998). International patterns of tactile communication: A field study. *Journal of Nonverbal Behaviour, 22 (1)*, pp. 59–75.

Paul F. McKenna (1998). *Foundations of Policing in Canada.* Toronto: Prentice-Hall.

Murlene "Mac" McKinnon (1993). Looking glass cops. In Ed Nowicki (Ed.), *Total Survival*, pp. 239–248. Powers Lake, WI: Performance Dimensions Publishing.

David W. McRoberts (1993). Courtroom demeanor and testimony. In Ed Nowicki (Ed.), *Total Survival*, pp. 249–259. Powers Lake, WI: Performance Dimensions Publishing.

Steven L. McShane (1995). *Canadian Organizational Behaviour,* 2nd Edition. Toronto: Times Mirror Professional Publishing Ltd.

Albert Mehrabian (1972). *Nonverbal Communication*, p. 108. Chicago: Aldine-Atherton.

Albert Mehrabian (1981). *Silent Messages: Implicit Communication of Emotions and Attitudes*, 2nd Edition. Belmont, CA: Wadsworth.

B. M. Montgomery (1988). Quality communication in personal relationships, in S. W. Duck (Ed.), *Handbook of Personal Relationships*, pp. 343–366. New York: John Wiley.

H. W. More, Jr. (Ed.) (1985). *Critical Issues in Law Enforcement,* 4th Edition. Cincinnati: Anderson Publishing Company.

Chris Murphy (1993). The development, impact and implications of community policing in Canada. In James Chacko and Stephen E. Nancoo (Eds.), *Community Policing in Canada.* Toronto: Canadian Scholar's Press.

D. A. Nadler (1987). The effective management of organizational change. In J. W. Lorsch (Ed.), *Handbook of Organizational Behavior.* Englewood Cliffs, NJ: Prentice Hall, pp. 358–369.

David Nadler and Michael Tushman (1988). *Strategic Organizational Change.* Glenview, IL: Scott, Foresman.

Stephen E. Nancoo (1993). Epilogue, the future: Trends and issues. In J. Chacko and S. E. Nancoo (Eds.), *Community Policing in Canada.* Toronto: Canadian Scholar's Press.

The National Foundation for Family Research and Education. Family Health Index. November 1998.

William E. Nolen (1995). Reading people (nonverbal communication in internal auditing). *Internal Auditor, 52 (4)*, p. 48.

Ontario. Ministry of the Solicitor General (1992). Strategic planning committee on police training and education. *A Police Learning System for Ontario: Final Report and Recommendations.* Toronto: Ontario Solicitor General.

Ontario Provincial Police (May 1997). OPP Community Policing Development Centre, *How Do We Do It* manual. http://www.opp.ca/cpdc/english/how/output/how.html.

Roland Ouellette (1996). Management of aggressive behaviour, in Ed Nowicki (Ed.), *Total Survival*, pp. 289–297. Powers Lake, WI: Performance Dimensions Publishing.

L. E. Penley, E. R. Alexander, I. E. Jernigan, and C. L. Henwood (1991). Communication abilities of managers: The relationship to performance, *Journal of Management, 17*, pp. 57–76.

PFR Training Associates Ltd. *Guide Your Problem-Solving Group.* Vancouver, BC.

Ronald P. Philipchalk (1995). *Invitation to Social Psychology.* Orlando, FL: Harcourt Brace and Company.

Martha R. Plotkin (1996). Improving the police response to domestic elder abuse victims, *Aging*, 367, pp. 28–33.

M. Pollock and N. L. Colwill (1987). Participatory decision making in review. *Leadership and Organizational Development Journal, 8 (2)*, p. 710.

Robert A. Portnoy (1999). *Leadership: 4 Competencies for Success.* Upper Saddle River, NJ: Prentice-Hall.

Province of Ontario (1993). *Use of Force Model Training Manual.*

G. Puth (1994). *The Communicating Manager.* Pretoria: Van Schaik.

B. H. Raven (1993). The bases of power: Origins and recent developments. *Journal of Social Issues, 49*, pp. 227–251.

R. Glenn Ray (1999). *The Facilitative Leader.* Upper Saddle River, NJ: Prentice-Hall.

Wolf J. Rinke (1988). Maximizing management potential by building self-esteem. *Management Solutions*, March, p.11.

Joann Ellison Rodgers (1999). Flirting fascination. *Psychology Today,* Jan/Feb.

D. Roger and W. Nesshoever (1987). Individual differences in conversational strategies: A further study. *British Journal of Social Psychology, 26*, pp. 247–255.

J. B. Rosener (1990). Ways women lead. *Harvard Business Review, 68,* pp. 119–125.

John R. Schermerhorn, Jr., James G. Hunt, and Richard N. Osborn (1994). *Managing Organizational Behavior,* 5th Edition. New York: John Wiley and Sons, Inc.

Stuart Schmidt and Ryh-Song Yeh (1992). The structure of leader influence: A cross-national comparison. *Journal of Cross-Cultural Psychology, 23*, pp. 251–264.

James D. Sewell (1996). The four R's for police executives. *The FBI Law Enforcement Bulletin, 65.* July, pp. 9–14.

James D. Sewell (March 2002). Managing the stress of organizational change. *FBI Law Enforcement Bulletin, Vol. 71, No. 3*, pp. 14–20.

Kevin Shyne (1982). *Shyness: Breaking Through the Invisible Barrier to Achievement, Success,* July, pp. 14–16, 36–37, 51.

Pashaura Singh (1990). Sikh traditions in Ontario. *Polyphony, 12,* pp. 130–136.

Solicitor General Canada (1996). *Outlook.* Ottawa: Solicitor General of Canada.

Ronald T. Stansfield (1996). *Issues in Policing: A Canadian Perspective.* Toronto: Thompson Educational Publishing.

Statistics Canada (2005). Police personnel and expenditures 2004 and 2005. *The Daily.* December 15, 2005. Ottawa: Government of Canada.

Statstics Canada Census (2001). 2001 census data.

J. B. Stiff, G. R. Miller, C. Sleight, and P. Mongeau (1989). Explanations for visual cue primacy in judgments of honesty and deceit, *Journal of Personality and Social Psychology, 56*, pp. 555–564.

W. B. Swann Jr. (1992). Seeking "truth", finding despair: Some unhappy consequences of a negative self-concept. *Current Directions in Psychological Science, 1*, pp.15–18.

D. Tannen (1990). *You Just Don't Understand: Women and Men in Conversation.* New York: Morrow.

D. Tannen (1998). How to stop the war of words; How to turn debate into dialogue; Why it's so important to end Americans' war of words and start listening to one another. *USA Weekend.* March 1, 1998.

Kenneth Thomas (1976). Conflict and conflict management, in Marvin D. Dunnette (Ed.), *Handbook of Industrial and Organizational Psychology*, pp. 900–902. Chicago: Rand McNally College Publishing.

B. Tuckman (1965). Developmental sequence in small groups. *Psychological Bulletin, 63*, pp. 384–399.

United Press International (January 15, 1999). Report: Terrorists use latest cybertech. Ottawa: United Press International.

J. L. Walsh (1977). Career styles and police behaviour, in D. H. Bayley (Ed.), *Police and Society*, pp. 149–176. Beverly Hills, CA: Sage Publications.

B. Weiner (1974). *Achievement Motivation and Attribution Theory.* Morristown, NJ: General Learning Press.

B. Weiner (1980). A cognitive (attribution)-emotion-action model of motivated behavior: An analysis of judgments of help giving. *Journal of Personality and Social Psychology, 39*, pp. 186–200.

Richard S. Wellins, William C. Byham, and Jeanne M. Wilson (1991). *Empowered Teams: Creating Self-Directed Work Groups that Improve Quality, Productivity, and Participation.* San Francisco, CA: Jossey-Bass Publishers.

D. E. Williams and M. M. Page (1989). A multi-dimensional measure of Maslow's hierarchy of needs. *Journal of Research in Personality, 23*, pp. 763–768.

Julia T. Wood (1997). *Communication in Our Lives.* Belmont, CA: Wadsworth Publishing.

Julia Wood and Angela Henry (2002). *Everyday Encounters: An Introduction to Interpersonal Communication,* 2nd Canadian Edition. Scarborough, ON: ITP Nelson.

Working Group Response to Rick Linden's paper. Demographic and economic disparity: The community challenge (1989). In Donald J. Loree (Ed.), *Future Issues in Policing: Symposium Proceedings*, pp. 129–136. Ottawa, ON: The Canadian Police College.

G. A. Yukl (1989). *Leadership in Organizations.* Englewood Cliffs, NJ: Prentice-Hall.

R. B. Zajonc and D. N. McIntosh (1992). Emotions research: Some promising questions and some questionable promises. *Psychological Science, 3*, pp. 70–74.

Philip Zimbardo (1977). *Shyness: What It Is, What to Do About It.* Reading, MA: Addison Wesley.

M. Zuckerman, R. F. Simons, and P. Como (1981). Verbal and nonverbal communication of deception. In L. Berkowitz (Ed.), *Advances in Experimental Psychology, Vol. 14*, pp. 1–59. New York: Academic Press.

Index

A

aboriginal policing, 136–137, 222
aboriginal Policing Directorate, 136–137
accommodation, 106–107
acculturation, 133
active listening, 72–89
actor-versus-observer-bias, 47
adjourning stage of group development, 159
aggression, 111
aging population of Canada, 138
alternate lifestyles of Canada, 138
anger management, 220
artefacts, 66
assertiveness, 91–92
   in conflict management, 111–112
attribution errors and biases
   actor-versus-observer-bias, 47
   categorization, 39–40, 45
   fundamental attribution error, 46
   halo effect, 43
   horn effect, 43
   over-simplification, 45
   in perceptual process, 44–46
   prototypes, 40, 45
   scripts, 41
   self-handicapping strategy, 48
   self-serving bias, 47–48
   stereotypes, 40, 45, 139–140
   ultimate attribution error, 48
attribution theory, 43–44
authoritarian leader, 194
Automobile Association Driver Education Foundation
   (AADEF), 46
avoidance, in conflict management, 107
avoidance of uncertainty, 134
Axtell, Roger, 141

B

behavioural approaches to leadership, 190–191
belonging needs, 27
Bergner, Laurie, 189, 200, 203
Berne, Eric, 104, 106
biases. *See* attribution errors and biases
Blake, Robert, 190
Blanchard, Kenneth, 191, 197
body language, 65
body position, 124
brainstorming, 121–122
Bridges, William, 216
building stone walls, 106

C

Canada
   changes impacting policing, 221–223
   changes post-September 11, 218
   Chinese population in, 142
   diversity of, 131, 132–133, 222
   workplace violence in, 108
Canadian culture(s)

aging population, 138
alternate lifestyles, 138
disabled people, 138
family trends, 137–138
mentally ill people, 138–139
native Canadians, 136
visible minorities, 131, 132, 136, 145–146
Canadian Mental Health Association, 139
Canadian Police College (CPC)
   six competencies of leadership, 199
CAPRA Conflict Management System, 115
categorization, 39–40, 45
central traits, 43
change
   defined, 212
   different cultural approaches to, 214
   group adaptation to, 164
   incremental, 212
   organizational methods, 217
   overcoming resistance to, 217–221
   personal methods, 218–221
   planned versus unplanned, 212–213
   radical, 212
   reactions to, 213–214
change agents, 213
change process, 215–216
charisma, 190
charismatic leader, 194
Chinese business and social etiquette, 142
chronemics, 66
coaching, 197–198
coercive power, 193
cognitive complexity, 41
cohesiveness, of groups, 162
collaboration, 107
collectivism, 135
communication
   see also intercultural communication; interpersonal
     communication; listening; nonverbal communi-
     cation; verbal communication
   and change process, 217
   effective, 19, 22
   within groups, 174–175
   hierarchy of needs, 26–28
   impersonal, 7
   and leadership, 196, 199
   misconceptions, 8
   tactical, 2, 62
   and technology, 28–29
communication climate
   creating a supportive, 86–88
   in groups and teams, 171–172
   influence of leaders on, 197
   supportive versus defensive, 86
communication competence
   defined, 10
   strategies for achieving, 9, 10–12
communication continuum, 7–8
communication process
   components of, 5, 6, 79

interference, 5–6
community policing, 21–22, 202, 223
competition
     in conflict management, 106
     in groups, 168
compliance, within groups, 161
compromise, 107
concentrated power, 134–135
Conference Board of Canada
     Employability Skills Profile, 11
confirming responses, 86
conflict
     see also goals
     causes of, 104–106
     covert, 104
     defined, 103–104
     in groups, 162–163, 166
     personality clash, 105, 163
     in policing, 102–103, 104
     role conflict, 105–106
conflict management
     assertiveness, 111–112
     effective responding and listening, 112–113
     emotional control, 109–110
     empathy, 110
     leadership and, 197
     openness and honesty, 110
     problem-solving approach to, 113–114
     strategies, 108–115
     styles, 106–108, 109
conformity, within groups, 160
constructive controversy, 121
constructs, 41
context, in communication, 69
Cornish, Edward, 134
court presentation, 90–91
covert conflict, 104
creative thinking, 121–122
crisis
     defined, 122
     indicators of, 122–123
     intervention strategies, 124–125
     prevention, 123–124
     stages of, 122–123
crisis prevention, 123–124
cultural diversity in Canada, 131, 132–133, 136
     see also diversity
culture(s)
     see also Canadian culture(s); intercultural
          communication
     approaches to change, 214
     communication among different, 84, 93
     defined, 132–134
     different norms, 141–142
     dimensions of, 134–135
     impact on perception, 49

D

De Bono, Edward, 121
De Paris, Richard, J., 201–202
decentralized power, 134–135
decision, 116
decision making, 116
     see also goals; group decision making
decoding of message, 5
deculturation, 133–134
defensive behaviour, 168
depression, 139

deviance, in groups, 169
Devito, Joseph A., 110
disabled people, 138
disconfirming responses, 86
discrimination, 139–140
diversity
     adapting to, 28
     importance of understanding, 4
     in policing, 145–146, 222
     in recruitment, 146
Do's and Taboos of Hosting International Visitors
     (Axtell), 141
dysfunctional group roles, 166–167

E

effective groups
     barriers to, 165, 166–169
     characteristics of, 163–164, 165
     communication climate, 171–172
     communication in, 174–175
     designing, 169–171
     handling negative behaviour, 173–174
     roles in, 170, 172–173
     skills for maintaining, 171–175
Emergency Response Teams (ERTs), 158–159
emotions
     coping with change, 219–220
     control of, 109–110
     and perception, 48–49
empathy, 12, 72, 87, 90
     see also other-oriented attitude
Employability Skills Profile, 11
encoding of message, 5
enculturation, 133
equality, 87
ERTs. *See* Emergency Response Teams (ERTs)
ethics
     in leadership, 198
     in policing, 225
ethnocentrism, 141–168
evaluation apprehension, 168
expert power, 193
eye contact, 63, 124

F

facial expressions, 62–63
Family Health Index, 138
family trends of Canada, 137–138
feedback
     in effective listening, 71
     influence on self-concept, 23
feminine cultures, 134
First Nations Policing Policy (FNPP), 136–137, 222
Fisher, B. Aubrey, 159
force field analysis, 215–216
forming stage of group development, 159
Foundations of Policing in Canada (McKenna), 204
four interpersonal distances, 66–68
four R's for police executives, 196, 208
frame-bending change, 212
frame-breaking change, 212
fundamental attribution error, 46
Futuring: The Exploration of the Future
     (Cornish), 134

G

Games People Play (Berne), 104, 106
G.A.T.B.. *See* General Aptitude Test Battery (G.A.T.B.)

gender differences
   and leadership, 190
   in listening skills, 72
   in nonverbal communication, 60–61
   in perception, 49
General Aptitude Test Battery (G.A.T.B.), 224–225
gestures, 65, 141
Gibb, J. R., 87
globalization, 221–222
goals
   for changing self, 29–30
   effective, 117–118
   of groups and teams, 154, 163, 170
   importance of, 117
Great Person Theory, 189–190
Greenberg, M. S., 105
group decision making
   barriers to effective, 118–120
   constructive controversy, 121
   creative thinking, 121–122
   external expertise, 122
   group polarization, 118–119
   groupthink, 119–120
   organizational and external pressures, 119–120
   overcoming barriers to, 120–122, 163
   power differences, 120
group dynamics, value of studying 3–4
group performance, 162
group polarization, 118–119
groups
   see also effective groups; teams
   advantages of, 161–162
   defined, 154
   disadvantages of, 162–163
   dysfunctional roles in, 166–167
   importance to policing, 152
   influences within, 160–161
   reasons for belonging to, 155–156
   stages of development, 159–160
groupthink, 119–120

H

Hall, Edward T., 66
halo effect, 43
haptics (touch), 65
Hersey and Blanchard's Situational Leadership Theory, 191
Hersey, Paul, 191, 197
high-context cultures, 135
horn effect, 43

I

"I" language, 69–86, 88–89, 112, 113
impersonal communication, 7
implicit personality theory, 43
impression formation, 43
incremental change, 212
individualism, 135
inferences, 85
Ingham, Harry, 23
intercultural communication
   barriers to effective, 84, 139–142
   communication differences, 141
   ethnocentrism, 141
   improving, 93, 142–145
   nonverbal communication, 59
   stereotypes and discrimination, 139–140
interference, 5–6

International Labour Organization (ILO)
   workplace violence, 108
interpersonal attraction
   defined, 156–157
   determinants of, 157–158
interpersonal communication
   see also communication climate; communication competence
   assertiveness, 91–92
   defined, 7–8
   empathy, 87, 90
   "I" language, 86, 88–89
   mutual influence, 8
   other-oriented attitude, 89–90
   principles of, 9
   relationship management and, 8
   respectfulness, 90–91
   self-disclosure, 7, 92
   strategies for improvement, 9–12, 88–93
   value of studying, 3–4
interpersonal perception, 39
   see also perception
interpretation in perceptual process, 42
   errors in, 46
intimate distance, 67
Issues in Policing: A Canadian Perspective (Stansfield), 144

J

Janis, Irving, 119
jargon, 83
Johari Window, 23–2001
Johnson, David W., 163
Johnson, Frank P., 163
judgements, 143–144

K

Kelley's attribution theory, 44
kinesics (body language), 65

L

laissez-faire leader, 194
lateral thinking, 121
leadership
   see also power
   in a changing environment, 201–203
   characteristics of, 196–200
   dealing with superiors, 200–201
   defined, 189, 195–196
   development of, in policing, 203
   in effective groups, 163, 164
   and gender, 190
   and management, 189, 198
   six competencies of, 199
   styles, 194–195
leadership grid, 204
leadership theories
   behavioural approaches, 190–191
   situational approaches, 191–192
   trait approach, 189–190
learning, in groups, 162
legitimate power, 193
Lewin, Kurt, 215
lie detection, 64–65
listening
   active, 72–89
   barriers to effective, 70–71
   defined, 70

skills for effective, 71–73, 113
low-context cultures, 135
Luft, Joe, 23
Lumsden, Donald, 172
Lumsden, Gay, 172

M

machine bureaucracies, 201–202
maintenance roles of groups, 173
management, and leadership, 189, 198
Managing Transitions: Making the Most of Change
    (Bridges), 216
Martin Luther King, 196
masculine cultures, 134
Maslow, Abraham, 26, 156
Maslow's Hierarchy of Needs, 26–28, 156
matching hypothesis, 157
Mayer, Richard J., 106
McClelland, David I., 156
McClelland's acquired needs theory, 156
McKenna, Paul, 204
Mehrabian, Albert, 61
mentally ill people, 138–139
mentoring, 197–198
message composition, 62
Mouton, Jane, 190
mutual influence, 8

N

National Foundation for Family Research and
    Education (NFFRE), 138
native Canadians, 136
    see also aboriginal policing
nonverbal communication, 57–69
    among cultures, 59
    conflict management and, 113
    in crisis management, 124–125
    described, 57–59, 73
    gender differences in, 60–61
    in groups, 175
    relational-level meanings, 60
    six functions of, 58–60, 61
    skills for interpreting, 68–69
    types of, 61–68
    versus verbal communication, 59
norming stage of group development, 159
norms, 141–142
Nowdluk-Reynolds, Kitty, 144

O

obedience, within groups, 161
OC Transpo, 108
Ontario Human Rights Commission
    racial profiling, 42
Ontario Provincial Police (OPP)
    Emergency Response teams (ERTs), 158–159
    mission statements of, 187
    PARE Analysis Problem-Solving Model,
        115–116
organization in perceptual process, 40–41
    errors and biases in, 45
other-oriented attitude
    communication and, 11–12, 89–90
    conflict management and, 110
    with diverse cultures, 143
    perception and, 50
Ottawa-Carleton Regional Police Service, 201
over-simplification, 45

P

paralangue, 62
paraphrasing, 72, 125
PARE Analysis Problem-Solving Model, 115–116
perception, 39–50
    see also attribution errors and biases
    attribution theory, 43–44
    described, 38–39
    implicit personality theory, 43
    impression formation, 43
    influential factors on, 48–49
    interpretation, 42, 46
    organization, 40–41, 45
    road rage and, 46–47
    selection, 39–40, 45
    stages of, 39
    strategies to improve, 49–50
perception checking, 68–69
    guidelines, 85
performing stage of group development, 159
peripheral traits, 43
person-centred leader, 194
personal change
    importance of, 10
    strategies for, 29–30
personal constructs, 41
personal distance, 67
personal power sources, 193
personality clash, 105
    in groups, 163
physical needs, 26–27
physical noise, 6
polarization, 84
Police Constable Selection Project, 224–225
police organizational structure
    community policing, 21–22, 202, 223–224
    machine bureaucracies, 201–202
    professional police bureaucracy, 202
policing
    see also community policing; Ontario Provincial
        Police (OPP); Royal Canadian Mounted Police
        (RCMP)
    aboriginal, 136–137, 222
    changes impacting, 211, 221–223
    conflict in, 102–103
    leadership in, 201–204
    diversity in, 145–146
    ethics in, 225
    importance of relationships to, 186–187
    importance of teams and groups to, 152
    recruitment, selection and training, 224–225
    relationships with media, 188
    roles of, 20–22
    stress management, 226
    styles, 105
polygraphs, 64
position power sources, 193
positive reinforcement, 89–90
power
    centralized versus decentralized, 134–135
    defined, 192
    influence of, in group decision making, 120
    types of, 193–194
problem, 116
problem solving, 116
    see also goals; group decision making
problem-solving approach to conflict manage-
    ment, 113–115

problem-solving models
 CAPRA Conflict Management System, 115
 PARE Analysis Problem-Solving Model, 115–116
professional police bureaucracy, 202
prototypes, 40, 45
proxemics, 66–68
psychological noise, 6
public distance, 67
Public Safety and Emergency Preparedness Canada
 (PSEPC), 136–137

R

racial profiling, 42
racism, 145
radical change, 212
RCMP. *See* Royal Canadian Mounted Police (RCMP)
referent power, 193
reflected appraisal, 23
reinforcement affect model, 157–158
relational-level meanings, 60
relationships
 between media and police, 188
 building and maintaining, 187–188, 199
 importance to policing, 186–187
respect, demonstrating, 90–91
restricted code, 84
reward power, 193
road rage, 46–47
role conflict, 105–106
roles of police officers, 20–22
Royal Canadian Mounted Police (RCMP)
 CAPRA Conflict Management System, 115
 core values of, 21–22
 diversity in recruitment, 141, 146
Ruback, R. B., 105

S

safety needs, 27
scripts, 41
security, post-September 11, 218
selection in perceptual process, 39–40
 errors and biases in, 45
self
 see also self-concept; self-esteem
 components of, 22, 26
 self-presentation, 25
self-actualization needs, 28
self-concept
 defined, 22–23
 development of, 23
 impact on perception, 49
 improving, 29–30
 Johari Window and, 23–24
self-disclosure, 7, 92
self-esteem
 defined, 25
 increasing, 29–30
self-esteem needs, 27–28
self-handicapping strategy, 48
self-monitoring, 190
self-presentation, 25
self-serving bias, 47–48
semantic noise, 6
September 11, 218
Sewell, James, 196, 208
simplification, 40, 45
situational approaches to leadership, 191–192

social affiliation, 157
social comparison, 23, 119
social distance, 67
social exchange theory, 158
social identification, 119–122
social loafing in groups, 168–169
Stansfield, Robert, 144
static evaluation, 84–85
stereotypes, 40, 45, 139–140
storming stage of group development, 159
Strategic Planning Committee on Police Training and
 Education, 224
stress management, 217–226
superiors, dealing with, 200–201
symbols, 141

T

tactical communication, 2, 62
Tannen, Deborah, 111
task roles of groups, 172–173
team building process, 168, 170–171
team effectiveness, 164
teams, 154–155
 see also groups
teamwork
 advantages of, 161–162
 disadvantages of, 162–163
technology and policing, 28–29, 225–226
theory of reasoned action, 143–144
tolerance of uncertainty, 134
Toronto Police Service, 201
trait approach, 189–190
transactional leader, 194
transformational leader, 195
transmission of message, 5
Tuckman model of group development, 159–160

U

ultimate attribution error, 48

V

Vanier Institute of the Family, 137
verbal communication
 see also communication; words
 barriers to effective, 83–85
 biased and loaded language, 84
 in crisis management, 125
 generalizations, 84
 inferences versus facts, 85
 static evaluation, 84–85
vertical thinking, 121
visible minorities, 131, 132, 136, 145–146
vision, 196

W

Weiner's theory of achievement attributions, 44
Wood, Julia, 28
words
 abstract versus concrete, 82
 characteristics of, 80–82, 94
 connotative versus denotative, 82
 jargon, 83
 occupational labels, 81
 power of, 82–83
 restricted code, 84
workplace violence, 108